Pathways to Freedom
Political and Economic Lessons
From Democratic Transitions

COUNCIL *on*
FOREIGN
RELATIONS

John Campbell, Isobel Coleman,
Grzegorz Ekiert, Joshua Kurlantzick,
Terra Lawson-Remer, Shannon K. O'Neil,
Carlos Pio, George Soroka,
Jan Teorell, and Andrew Wilson

Edited by Isobel Coleman
and Terra Lawson-Remer
with Charles Landow

Pathways to Freedom
Political and Economic Lessons
From Democratic Transitions

The Council on Foreign Relations (CFR) is an independent, nonpartisan membership organization, think tank, and publisher dedicated to being a resource for its members, government officials, business executives, journalists, educators and students, civic and religious leaders, and other interested citizens in order to help them better understand the world and the foreign policy choices facing the United States and other countries. Founded in 1921, CFR carries out its mission by maintaining a diverse membership, with special programs to promote interest and develop expertise in the next generation of foreign policy leaders; convening meetings at its headquarters in New York and in Washington, DC, and other cities where senior government officials, members of Congress, global leaders, and prominent thinkers come together with CFR members to discuss and debate major international issues; supporting a Studies Program that fosters independent research, enabling CFR scholars to produce articles, reports, and books and hold roundtables that analyze foreign policy issues and make concrete policy recommendations; publishing *Foreign Affairs*, the preeminent journal on international affairs and U.S. foreign policy; sponsoring Independent Task Forces that produce reports with both findings and policy prescriptions on the most important foreign policy topics; and providing up-to-date information and analysis about world events and American foreign policy on its website, CFR.org.

The Council on Foreign Relations takes no institutional positions on policy issues and has no affiliation with the U.S. government. All views expressed in its publications and on its website are the sole responsibility of the author or authors.

For further information about CFR or this publication, please write to the Council on Foreign Relations, 58 East 68th Street, New York, NY 10065, or call Communications at 212.434.9888. Visit CFR's website, www.cfr.org.

Contents

Acknowledgments

An edited volume is by definition a collaborative project, and this one is no exception. We would like to thank all those who helped bring *Pathways to Freedom* to fruition.

First and foremost are the authors whose work appears in these pages: John Campbell, Grzegorz Ekiert, Joshua Kurlantzick, Shannon O'Neil, Carlos Pio, George Soroka, Jan Teorell, and Andrew Wilson. Managing drafts and deadlines is never easy—especially when participants come from different institutions and, indeed, different continents. All of these authors were a pleasure to work with, graciously accepting multiple rounds of feedback. We are grateful to them for helping us distill the complex lessons of history in a compelling and accessible way.

We also appreciate the contributions of several scholars who generously shared their time and feedback at various stages of the project, including Daron Acemoglu, Carol Adelman, Thomas Carothers, Larry Diamond, Jessica Einhorn, Stephan Haggard, Dani Kaufmann, Meghan O'Sullivan, and Katharina Pistor. In addition, we benefited from the wisdom of the advisory committee of the Council on Foreign Relations' (CFR) Civil Society, Markets, and Democracy initiative (CSM&D), which includes John Danilovich, Marlene Hess, Henrietta Holsman Fore, Reuben Jeffery, Elizabeth Keck, Rodney Nichols, Hutham Olayan, and William Priest.

We would like to thank Richard N. Haass, president of CFR, and James M. Lindsay, CFR's senior vice president and director of studies, for their support of the project. They provided invaluable guidance on the book's overall shape and insightful comments on drafts.

Many others at CFR were likewise indispensable to the book's completion. Patricia Dorff and Lia Norton of CFR's Publications team managed editing and production with patience and efficiency. Anya Schmemann and Amy Baker in the Studies Program offered sound advice and support. Lisa Shields, Iva Zoric, Tricia Miller, and others in the Global Communications and Media Relations department helped disseminate the book to a wide audience. Many staff members from CFR's Washington Program, National Program and Outreach, and Corporate Program made special efforts to share the book and its findings with constituencies in the United States and abroad. Tom Davey, Nate Freiberg, Andrei Henry, and others in the Web Management and Development department created an effective home for the project's outputs on CFR's website, CFR.org.

Inside CSM&D, we benefited from the project management and editing skills of Associate Director Charles Landow, the research and administrative support of Research Associate Thalia Beaty, and the efforts of Program Assistant Julia Knight, whose statistical acumen and good cheer enhanced the project from start to finish. Interns including Emily Apple, Naomi Fujiki, and Sam Gelb also helped along the way.

Pathways to Freedom: Political and Economic Lessons From Democratic Transitions was made possible by the generous support of the Bill & Melinda Gates Foundation, the Goldman Sachs Group, the Smith Richardson Foundation, the Hurford Foundation, the Alliance for Global Good, and an individual CFR donor. The views expressed in this book are the authors', and we take full responsibility for any errors or omissions.

Isobel Coleman and Terra Lawson-Remer

Political and Economic Lessons From Democratic Transitions

Isobel Coleman and Terra Lawson-Remer

Over the past three years, the world has witnessed a number of democratic transitions take root across the Middle East and Asia. Millions of oppressed people in countries once ruled by autocrats are struggling to realize freedom and shared opportunity. Other countries around the world also now teeter on the edge of transition to more free and open societies.

These movements for political freedom and broader prosperity come at a time when democracy appears to be receding, as experts such as Larry Diamond in *The Spirit of Democracy* and Joshua Kurlantzick in *Democracy in Retreat* have noted. After the fall of the Berlin Wall, democracy surged, reaching a high-water mark in the first years of the twenty-first century with various "colored revolutions" in former Soviet Bloc countries. But then democratic gains in eastern Europe, Africa, and Latin America stalled or even deteriorated as fragile democratic institutions buckled under the enormous challenges of governance. The failed U.S. attempts to impose democracy in Iraq and Afghanistan and the economic rise of autocratic China further undermined confidence in the inevitability and even desirability of democratization. As Freedom House reports in its *Freedom in the World 2013*, global levels of freedom have declined for the seventh straight year. Noted democracy scholars now talk about a "democratic recession."

If successful, the nascent democratic openings in Tunisia, Egypt, Libya, and Myanmar, along with steps toward greater freedom in other countries such as Georgia, Ivory Coast, Sierra Leone, and Malawi, could help reverse the recent regressions in democracy. Yet the transition from authoritarianism to democracy is notoriously difficult. Many countries that once seemed budding with democratic promise now appear mired in political infighting and power grabs by ousted elites, or trapped in downward spirals of poverty and unemployment. History suggests that many transitioning countries will move only slowly toward substantive democracy—one characterized not only by majority rule through free and fair elections, but also by strong minority and civil rights protections. For quite some time, many will remain in the democratic purgatory of what experts Steven Levitsky and Lucan Way call "competitive authoritarianism" in their book of the same name—hybrid regimes with elements of both democracy and authoritarianism.

Despite a vast academic literature on democratization, the factors that allow some democratic transitions to succeed as others stall or backslide remain poorly understood by policymakers. Since the fall of the Berlin Wall, the relative importance of economic development and modernization, economic structure, inequality, governance and rule of law, civil society and media, structure of government, and education have been exhaustively debated. Rather than advancing a new one-size-fits-all theory of democratization, this book looks carefully at the statistical evidence, and backward at eight landmark country transitions over the past twenty-five years—some successful, others not so successful—to distill practical lessons for reformers in transitioning countries and policymakers in supportive outside states. By understanding the trade-offs, sequencing, and critical economic and policy decisions that transitioning countries have faced in the past, policymakers can make smarter choices to improve the chances of successful democratization in states undergoing transitions today.

The eight studies presented in this volume—Mexico, Brazil, Poland, South Africa, Indonesia, Thailand, Ukraine, and Nigeria—are not intended to be a representative sample, but instead encompass a range of experiences and outcomes with geographic diversity and high geopolitical relevance. The authors highlight the critical inflection points of each transition, rather than present an exhaustive record of each country's trajectory. The tangible examples from the case studies, combined with insights from the statistical research, illuminate why some democratic transitions have succeeded while others have stumbled.

Each case study is organized around six themes that previous research indicates are clearly important to the process of democratization:

- socioeconomic exclusion and inclusion
- economic structure and policies
- civil society and media
- legal system and rule of law

- government structure and division of power
- education and demography

This structure allows the interested policymaker to easily compare an issue, such as rule of law, across each of the studies, and to understand the complex interplay of these themes. Through their focus on these issues, the studies illustrate a range of policy decisions and outcomes that can help guide other countries facing analogous challenges.

FACTORS THAT MATTER IN TRANSITIONS

Although policy options are inevitably constrained by context, as Stephan Haggard and Robert Kaufman explain in *The Political Economy of Democratic Transitions*, this book suggests seven major insights to assist those facing confusing and difficult trade-offs on the hard road to democracy and inclusive growth. Four of these concern initial circumstances; three involve critical policy choices once transitions begin to unfold. After laying out these insights, this chapter discusses their important implications for the pacing and sequencing of policy choices.

INITIAL CIRCUMSTANCES

Each country begins the process of democratic transition from a unique position based on its own political and economic development, but four initial circumstances play a critical role in shaping the trajectory of the transition.

Economic Growth and Crisis
Many experts once believed that economic growth inevitably led to democracy. But although most rich countries in the world today are relatively democratic, some—such as China and Saudi Arabia—have enjoyed growing economic prosperity without a commensurate increase in substantive political freedoms. In fact, history suggests that economic growth and prosperity do not necessarily lead to democracy, although a large middle class and higher overall wealth can help prevent backsliding to authoritarianism once democracy takes hold. On the other hand, short-term economic crises do trigger regime changes. Over the past three decades, many democratic transitions have been

precipitated by serious economic shocks that inflicted unacceptable costs on citizens, rupturing the authoritarian bargain.

Indonesia's remarkable and relatively sudden transition to democracy is a compelling example of economic crisis unleashing momentum for democratic freedom. With the onset of the Asian financial crisis in 1997, the frailties of Suharto's economic policies, such as corruption, debt, and a hands-off approach to corporate governance and financial regulation, became clear. The resulting discontent swept the long-ruling Suharto regime from power.

Likewise, in Brazil, almost two decades before Indonesia's transition, a structural economic crisis paved the way for the military government's fall. Brazil suffered skyrocketing inflation, plummeting reserves, and crushing debt following the global oil shock of 1979. These woes eroded confidence in the military's economic stewardship and raised questions about the authoritarian bargain of repression in return for economic growth. Protests erupted in the country's manufacturing belt, and the military embarked on a liberalization process that eventually led to the restoration of civilian rule.

Mexico had a similar trajectory as the 1982 debt crisis set off political and economic change. The governing Institutional Revolutionary Party (PRI) struggled to maintain the unity of its authoritarian coalition as government revenues fell sharply. Just as in Brazil, the crisis caused many Mexicans to rethink their authoritarian bargain—a sentiment that intensified as growth lagged and poverty increased in the ensuing decade. A devaluation forced by excessive spending and insufficient reserves during the 1994 peso crisis sparked another recession. These crises cost the PRI significant support from interest groups and the public.

The three cases of Indonesia, Brazil, and Mexico demonstrate that economic shocks under autocracy can trigger democratic transitions over a broad time frame. In Indonesia, crisis led quickly to Suharto's downfall. In Brazil, an economic shock starting in 1979 paved the way for the opposition's victory in the presidential election six years later. In Mexico, subpar economic performance, punctuated by two crises, began almost two decades before the long-ruling PRI eventually lost the presidency in 2000. In all three, however, deteriorating economic conditions were an unmistakable trigger of change. This continues to be the case around the world, as is clear from the Arab uprisings of recent years, which were sparked in part by rising food prices and frustrated economic ambitions.

Poland illustrates a related point: that a robust middle class and the other trappings of a solid middle-income country are instrumental to the consolidation of democracy once it emerges. Though Poland began its transition in 1989 with serious challenges, the communist era left a legacy of functioning and professionally staffed state institutions, a well-educated labor force, and a robust industrial base. Polish society was also relatively egalitarian. The country further bolstered these initial favorable endowments with economic policies that nurtured and expanded the middle class in the years following its transition. The relationship between economic growth, economic crisis, and political transition is by no means automatic, but the evidence is clear that shocks make regimes of all types vulnerable, whereas prosperity makes regimes of all types more stable. Statistical findings suggest, however, that democracies are less vulnerable to economic crises than are autocracies, though the reason for this is unclear. Argentina, for example, weathered an extremely severe economic crisis in 2001, but its democracy proved resilient.

Alternatively, it is clear that countries undergoing democratic transitions before achieving a sizeable middle class will face a steep road indeed. With this awareness, policymakers should be prepared for years of intensive but undoubtedly rocky economic and political engagement when lower-income countries such as Egypt embark on democratization. Leaders both inside and outside the country should insist that austerity measures be balanced with smart and effective safety nets. They should also work to educate the population about the challenges of economic restructuring and the time required to lift economic prospects.

Electoral Experience: "Fake It Till You Make It"
All but the most unapologetically totalitarian regimes now go through the motions of holding elections. Even autocrats perceive a need—both domestically and internationally—to legitimize their rule with the appearance of democratic participation. International observers often denounce these sham elections as meaningless attempts to dress authoritarian rule in the trappings of democracy with Orwellian double-speak. But the evidence suggests that the process of holding elections, even very flawed ones, creates a voting muscle memory that proves important when real elections finally occur. Elections also sow the seeds of public expectations that over time can blossom into democratic demands that cannot be ignored—and, contrary to the expectations of

elites, cannot always be controlled. In short, countries with some experience with elections tend to realize greater success in their transitions to substantive democracy.

Mexico's government in the 1970s, dominated by the PRI, took its quest for electoral legitimacy so far that when the loyal opposition failed to field a presidential candidate in 1976, the government revised the election laws to make it easier for the opposition to gain a few seats. To the PRI's surprise, when the economic crisis of the early 1980s hit, the opposition was able to use this opening to marshal civil society organizations in a campaign for more transparent elections. Although it still took many years to dislodge the PRI's single-party rule, the country's faux elections were the thin end of a wedge that helped pry open space for truly contested ones.

In Brazil, the military regime likewise tolerated an opposition it believed it could control. As economic crisis led to widespread discontent in the early 1980s, however, the military began to lose its grip on the political situation. The opposition won a surprisingly large victory in the 1982 elections for Congress and state governors, setting the stage for the military's ultimate downfall in the presidential election of 1985. Brazil's electoral process—highly constrained under military rule— took on a momentum of its own that the military could not stop.

The Round Table talks in Poland between the then-illegal Solidarity movement and the Communist government in early 1989 resulted in semi-free elections with rules designed to guarantee the Communists and their allies the majority of legislative seats. However, the Communists did not anticipate the level of voter support for the opposition or the defections that occurred from the Communist coalition. As a result, Solidarity was able to form the first noncommunist government in the region in decades.

In Ukraine, a crudely rigged election was the proximate cause for the Orange Revolution in 2004. The blatant electoral fraud by the regime provoked widespread public outcry and ignited long smoldering discontent. Although the Orange Revolution failed to produce lasting democracy, it further illustrates that even flawed elections can open the door to unexpected political change.

Finally, in Nigeria, which remains far from robust democracy, elections are one of the few political bright spots. Though flawed, the country's repeated elections are gradually fostering democratic attitudes. Even if elites are the real authorities in the selection of the president,

Nigerians today expect that they will have some kind of vote. Also crucially, it is understood that the president will be a civilian. This is a far cry from the days of military rule, when coups or threatened coups were the method of leadership change. It is unclear whether the "act" of voting will lead to a more substantive democratic opening in Nigeria, but history indicates that going through the motions better prepares citizens for that possibility. Quantitative evidence also confirms that those authoritarian regimes with partial political openness are the likeliest to become more democratic, especially if they provide for multiparty electoral competition. The lesson is that even imperfect elections can have unanticipated positive effects that foster more profound changes over the longer term.

Violence and Civil Society

Authoritarian governments, by definition, keep tight control over the levers of power in their countries. Overthrowing these autocratic systems is understandably difficult.

However, armed rebellions often fail to lead to democratization, even when regimes are overthrown. History is littered not only with failed uprisings, but also with coups d'état and violent revolutions that succeeded in nothing more than replacing one form of dictatorship with another, some of which were even worse than the autocracies they replaced—"'liberators' who turn out to be totalitarians," in the words of Jeane Kirkpatrick. Nonviolent, mass mobilizations, on the other hand, have a stronger track record of laying the groundwork for democratic change—especially when these mobilizations are broadly sustained through deep public participation over time. Proponents of nonviolence, from Mohandas Gandhi and Martin Luther King to Gene Sharp, have noted that sustained peaceful protests lead to a more engaged citizenry and a better-organized civil society with a deep stake in the outcome of the transition. This sustained engagement often proves critical for staying the course during the inevitable challenges of democratic transitions.

Large-scale peaceful protests also help undermine any remnants of legitimacy that authoritarian regimes still claim, and can exacerbate intra-elite divisions. With moral clarity and a refusal to acquiesce to injustice, mass nonviolent dissent challenges the inertia of the status quo. Additionally, if autocrats resort to force to put down peaceful demonstrations, the resulting bloodshed generates moral outrage, both domestically and internationally, further undermining the regime.

Poland's experience with its trade union federation Solidarity—a social-political movement that at its peak included a quarter of the population as members—strongly illustrates how a peaceful grassroots movement can be instrumental in a democratic transition. Solidarity exercised influence through its mass of citizens willing to engage in Poland's nascent democratic government. Many present-day Polish politicians were once prominent leaders of Solidarity. The group's broad reach helped spawn a robust civil society and strong, independent media, which provided critical foundations for democratic deepening, especially during the initial stages of the transition.

Similarly, South Africa's broad-based grassroots liberation movements, though not always peaceful, opposed apartheid over decades and bequeathed a strong legacy of civil society engagement. The liberation leadership included genuine democrats committed to human rights, most notably Nelson Mandela, but also Christian leaders such as Archbishop Desmond Tutu, who helped shape liberation thinking. Their legacy of peaceful resistance is still a touchstone for South African civil society today. Indeed, over the past decade, South Africa's civic organizations have gained strength in the townships. They now play an important role in agitating for better service delivery, more accountable governance, and policies to address poverty, inequality, and high unemployment. And the country's vibrant media, a core pillar of civil society, serves as something of an opposition to the dominant African National Congress (ANC).

Indonesia also benefited from massive popular participation in its shift to democracy. In 1997 and 1998, citizens protested against Suharto's rule en masse. The following year, huge numbers voted in the presidential election. This fostered a broad sense of involvement in Suharto's downfall and the transition to democracy, making Indonesians more tolerant of the economic and political turbulence that followed. In Thailand, by contrast, citizens generally saw their transition as a deal among elites.

Although Ukraine appeared to experience a peaceful mobilization during the Orange Revolution in 2004, when hundreds of thousands of protestors filled the streets of Kiev, the crowd was in some ways a passive force lacking the depth and vibrancy of a genuine grassroots movement. Pro-Orange support came largely from western and central Ukraine, and the movement never realized country-wide mobilization, allowing the Orange camp's opponents to claim that the revolution was a usurpation of power instead. Without sustained civil society pressure, Ukraine's political system did not undergo thorough change, and the new elites fell into the same corrupt patterns as their predecessors. Although the Orange Revolution was indeed a peaceful movement, its lack of depth and breadth contributed to a legacy of a weak civil society that has struggled to pose an effective counterweight to the country's entrenched oligarchs and democratic erosion.

Similarly, Nigeria's largely unsuccessful transition has never been grounded in a broad-based popular movement. Although the country did succeed in shifting peacefully from military to civilian rule, this was the result of a pact among leaders seeking to maintain their power and privileges inside an ostensibly democratic structure. The broader society was hardly involved. In the absence of significant popular resistance, elites have continued to use their positions for gain without promoting basic development. Given that the country's small middle class limits possibilities for sustained protest, the prospects for deeper reforms remain constrained. Had citizens been more involved in the initial transition, Nigeria might well have established a tradition of greater accountability that could have enabled more equitable enjoyment of the country's considerable resources.

Some countries, of course, have overcome violent beginnings to evolve along a path of democracy. And some dictatorships are so totalitarian that their end can come only through violence: Muammar al-Qaddafi, for example, was determined to fight his people to the bitter end. Libya's transition is not doomed by its violent birth, although the militias that helped overthrow Qaddafi—and the climate of lawlessness that resulted—now pose significant obstacles to stability. On the other hand, that such a large proportion of the population was involved in the overthrow of the regime offers hope for the long-term civic engagement so crucial for democratic consolidation, and, indeed, some civil society has begun to take root since Qaddafi's fall.

The takeaway for policymakers is not to write off countries born of violence, but to proceed with caution in abetting armed revolutions and, perhaps most important, to resist the great temptation of favoring pacted transitions—deals between elite groups—over the uncertainties and unpredictability of mass mobilizations. Foreign and multilateral policymakers should embrace the cause of populations that manage to launch and sustain a peaceful popular protest against an autocratic regime.

Neighborhood Effects

Neighborhoods are not merely geographic, although shared borders are an important element of interdependence between countries. Neighborhoods are also economic communities, such as the North American free trade bloc and the European Union; political-military alliances, such as the North Atlantic Treaty Organization; and cultural groups based on a common heritage. Neighbors exert a powerful force on the trajectory of countries with which they share interests and destinies.

Good neighbors can help fragile democracies succeed through tough times. Not only do they provide critical economic and technical assistance, they also exert constructive political pressure to bolster the democratic transition. Conversely, bad neighbors can undermine transitions by fostering power-grabbing, corruption, and authoritarian reversals—or simply by failing to provide moral, financial, and diplomatic support for democratic consolidation. These effects can come at the hands of a general neighborhood or of a single powerful neighbor, such as Russia in the case of Ukraine.

In Poland, Indonesia, and Mexico, positive neighborhood influences provided important leverage for internal reformers intent on challenging entrenched interests and proved a powerful bulwark against backsliding. Although transitions are always complex and depend on many factors, Poland clearly benefited from outside support. The International Monetary Fund, the World Bank, and various Western governments played a role. But the major influence was the European Union and its enticing prospect of membership. In addition to providing funds and expertise, these external players held Poland to conditions that cemented democratic gains, such as ensuring basic liberties and allowing oversight of government.

Likewise, outside pressure propelled Mexico's political opening. During the tenure of President Ernesto Zedillo—the last president of the PRI's long stretch in power—American business and political leaders, among others, called out Mexico's democratic shortcomings and advocated electoral reforms. Being next door to the enormous U.S. market also benefited the country, as did preferential U.S. trade policies. Indeed, Mexico's economy was transformed by the North American Free Trade Agreement, which accelerated trade and foreign direct investment. A broad middle class emerged as incomes rose and poverty and inequality declined, creating a positive feedback loop for the democratic changes under way.

Yet bad neighbors can exert an equally powerful but destructive influence. Poland's democratic success contrasts sharply with Ukraine's stagnation, in large part because of Ukraine's difficult geopolitical situation. While European countries have failed to effectively support democratic development in Ukraine, Russia has fostered its own style of business and politics there. It has backed nongovernmental organizations (NGOs) catering to Ukraine's Russian speakers, who generally opposed the Orange Revolution. Russia has also been instrumental in Ukraine's energy industry, including backing a shady gas-import scheme from which Ukrainian leaders drew hundreds of millions of dollars.

For policymakers, the lesson is to pay considerable attention to the influence of external forces—whether powerful neighbors or international organizations—on countries attempting transitions to democracy. With an understanding of the influence these forces can have, policymakers can work to leverage the impact of good neighbors while limiting and counteracting less savory forces.

CRITICAL POLICY CHOICES DURING TRANSITION

No matter what the initial starting point is of a country's transition, both qualitative and quantitative research underscore the need for policymakers to make smart choices and trade-offs in three critical areas.

Delivering on Expectations for Social and Economic Opportunities

The promise of political freedoms raises people's expectations for economic and social opportunities. The trajectory of emerging democracies depends fundamentally on whether political democratization can also deliver shared opportunity and inclusive growth to materially improve people's lives. The mere procedural freedoms of ballot box and marketplace participation are not enough to sustain nascent democracies over the longer term. Citizens—especially the poor—must also begin to realize the substantive social and economic freedoms that generate the capability to live full and meaningful lives. When they do enjoy such social inclusion and rising living standards, they reward the politicians who provide them, creating a powerful feedback loop that helps consolidate democracy. On the other hand, a return to autocracy, perhaps under a populist authoritarian, becomes more likely if the transition fails to deliver material benefits.

The challenge, or course, is that democratic transitions are inherently messy, with newly empowered groups often demanding different measures of justice and equity. Implementing economic reforms in this volatile mix is never easy, and politics often constrains economic choices. But underpinning successful democratic transitions is the imperative of not only expanding the pie, but also meeting expectations of fairness and delivering tangible benefits that materially improve the lives of those who for too long were excluded from power and prosperity.

Brazil's transition to democracy was legitimated and consolidated in large part by socially inclusive growth, which generated widely shared benefits. Starting around 1993, Presidents Fernando Henrique Cardoso and Luiz Inacio Lula da Silva managed the impressive jujitsu of unleashing new talent and investment through anti-inflationary, anti-monopoly, and pro-market economic reforms, while increasing social spending to improve equity and opportunity for the poor and middle class. Brazil had previously offered social protections for those with political connections. But as democratization proceeded, the government made safety nets universal and launched income distribution programs targeted to poor families. Among the effects was increased support for the democratic system among groups long marginalized by previous authoritarian regimes.

Brazil used two main strategies to improve the well-being of the poor: first, conditional cash transfers like Bolsa Familia that efficiently targeted the neediest while encouraging investments in human development, and, second, universal provision of social and economic rights (health care, education, and labor protections) to include blacks and other disadvantaged groups. Strong overall growth rates unlocked by market-oriented economic and legal reforms that promoted exports, ended government subsidies to crony industrialists, expanded opportunities for new entrepreneurs, and reined in inflation were also critical to Brazil's achievement of socially inclusive growth. The transition away from Brazil's long-held pursuit of import substitution industrialization and toward a market economy in the 1990s unleashed significant benefits, especially for consumers at the lower end of the income scale. Taken together, the commitment to both macroeconomic stability and socially inclusive spending laid the foundation for Brazil's sustained growth trajectory over the past decade.

Mexico, likewise, has consolidated democracy in the same period by delivering on economic opportunity for a broader cross section of citizens. This is a marked shift from earlier decades, when the government did very little to provide social and economic opportunities for the poorest and most vulnerable groups, even as political participation began to expand. Frustrations grew most sharply in the south, home to a higher percentage of indigenous people than other regions, prompting the Zapatista uprising in 1994. But the slow growth of the 1980s and the opening of the economy to international competition in the early 1990s pushed inequality up across the country.

More recently, however, targeted social spending and safety nets have expanded significantly in Mexico. Oportunidades, a program of cash stipends conditional on children's health care and attendance in school, has greatly expanded, now benefiting around 25 percent of all Mexicans. The government has managed to protect such programs from corruption, a change from social programs mounted previously by the PRI. Thanks to these efforts, poverty is on the retreat, dropping from 70 percent to less than 50 percent since the mid-1990s. In health care, a national program targeting informal and unemployed workers has reached forty-four million Mexicans who previously lacked insurance. In an important feedback mechanism, voters seem to appreciate these benefits and to express their approval at the ballot box.

When democracy fails to deliver on material expectations, by contrast, dissatisfied and excluded constituencies often embrace authoritarian populists who promise to fight against the rich. In Thailand, the economic and social policies of the nascent democratic government were widely perceived as exclusionary, benefiting foreign investors and domestic elites at the expense of regular Thais who continued to suffer after the 1997 Asian financial crisis. This widespread resentment swept into power the populist Thaksin Shinawatra, who promised to deliver equity and opportunity for ordinary Thais but put in place an electoral autocracy that led to a coup and a streak of violent unrest.

South Africa—two decades after the end of apartheid—also needs to deliver better for the disadvantaged. Though many South Africans expected fundamental socioeconomic change, very little has occurred. In 2008, for example, the total income earned by blacks was only 13 percent that of whites, down slightly from 13.5 percent in 1995. The government's failure to deliver for more citizens has given rise to populists like Julius Malema, the expelled ANC youth leader, whose firebrand rhetoric has tapped into the seething anger of disaffected groups such as South Africa's miners.

The past few years have also seen a reversion to populist authoritarianism in other countries where democracy failed to deliver on material hopes and expectations. In Serbia and Hungary, citizens exhausted by poverty and joblessness have embraced political leaders who promise economic opportunity at the cost of political freedom. In Venezuela, the poor saw Hugo Chavez as their champion, someone committed to their well-being over the interests of foreign investors, despite his abrogation of basic civil rights.

Statistical studies have to date provided weak support for a connection between socioeconomic inclusion-exclusion and democratization. This could be due to poor data; quantitative measures of wealth distribution and social cleavages are scarce, making reliable cross-country research on this topic challenging. Yet the case study evidence is compelling that inclusion supports durable economic and democratic gains.

For policymakers, the takeaway is simple: insufficient investment in social inclusion endangers democratic stability, whereas broadening economic opportunities creates positive feedback loops. Domestic reformers and their international supporters ignore these concerns at their peril.

Rule of Law and Economic Governance

Rule of law reforms that create a fair and level economic and political playing field and protect core rights—such as free speech, religious freedom, minority rights, predictable regulations, and secure property for all—are a linchpin of successful and sustainable transitions. The rule of law safeguards against corruption and nepotism, facilitates equal opportunity, and ensures government accountability. An effective, transparent, and predictable legal system prevents well-connected insiders from amassing wealth and public assets through shady backroom deals. It also encourages citizens to believe that legal systems and public institutions work for them, rather than against them and only for elites, and thus nurtures a public more willing to tolerate the inevitable turbulence of a transition. Citizens come to see that they have a stake in seeking justice and political change through the rule of law, rather than outside it.

Over the past two decades, Poland has emerged as a paragon of inclusive democracy and a market economy built from the ashes of an oppressive state. Poland's success can in part be attributed to the fact that structural economic reforms, particularly the privatization of state-owned assets, occurred only after policymakers had put in place a legal system that leveled the playing field for all aspirants and established strong safeguards against corruption. Initial attention to regulatory effectiveness, the rule of law, transparency, property rights, safety nets, and free speech helped ensure that privatization and other reforms proceeded smoothly.

In the economic realm, Mexico, too, has benefited from the strengthening of the rule of law, which includes obeying international treaties and following legal procedures to resolve disputes. This has helped the country attract substantial foreign direct investment, despite its challenges with corruption. Of course, Mexico's democracy faces a significant security threat that is exacerbated by a legal system not up to the challenge. Murder and other crimes related to the drug trade have spiked, with tens of thousands killed in recent years. Though the U.S. drug market plays a large role in fueling these security risks, so too does Mexico's subpar legal environment. Mexico is now taking significant strides to build a more open, transparent, and effective rule of law through efforts to professionalize the police force, combat corruption, strengthen due process, retrain lawyers, and expand forensic laboratories and evidence collection systems. Its democratic vibrancy and the sustainability of its economic and political gains hinge in large part on the successes and failures of its legal system.

Over the past two decades, Ukraine has failed spectacularly to establish a fair and impartial legal system, building a complicated and arbitrary one instead. Without equality before the law, predictability in legal enforcement, or any meaningful mechanisms of transparency, the vast majority of Ukraine's newly privatized wealth ended up in the hands of oligarchs. Although Ukraine passed privatization laws designed to ensure transparency and evenhandedness as early as 1992, these laws were never implemented. Instead, most big enterprises were sold in backroom deals at steep discounts to politically connected insiders. Small and medium enterprises (SMEs) have also shrunk in recent years. As a result, Ukrainian oligarchs have maintained a stranglehold on the country's politics, stymieing reforms that could spread opportunity to the broader population, even after the 2004 Orange Revolution brought hopes of genuine democratic progress. Ukraine's story mirrors Russia's tragedy: privatization in Russia, undertaken hastily and without an effective legal system, likewise led to the massive concentration of wealth, power, and privilege. A handful of oligarchs now control almost 40 percent of Russia's vast natural resources and industry.

The failure to build effective legal institutions also helped undermine Thailand's recent democratic aspirations. Thailand's system of commercial and family law was well established and relatively professional. However, when the courts dealt with political questions or matters involving well-connected firms, no such qualities were apparent. Even as democracy reached an apex in the 1990s, the judiciary overall remained under the control of Thailand's leaders, notably the king. Thailand's reformist constitution in 1997 was an attempt to strengthen the rule of law, but the king's continued behind-the-scenes role was more powerful than the laws on the books. Thaksin Shinawatra, elected prime minister in 2001, likewise undermined the country's new legal institutions. His opponents in the elite and middle classes then spurned official channels in the judiciary and other institutions and instead chose to fight Thaksin's rule in the streets. The result is low public trust in the judicial system, and the belief among many Thais that conflict might be the only way to resolve disagreements.

It is clear that attention to issues surrounding the rule of law is essential, especially at the early stages of a transition. If the economic and legal environments remain tilted toward elites, reforms will likely further consolidate wealth and power in the hands of well-connected insiders. Even well-intentioned reforms will not enjoy public confidence and trust in democratic institutions will suffer.

Decentralization of Government Power

Devolution of power to regional and local levels can be a critical ingredient in the process of consolidating an emerging democratic culture. Decentralization not only helps dilute the dangerous concentration of central authority often bequeathed by authoritarian regimes, but also increases grassroots accountability by bringing administration closer to the people and extends crucial bureaucratic capacity at a time when the central government's ability to deliver services often does not match the electorate's high expectations.

Decentralization can take various forms. In some cases, it can come through legislative changes that allow for the election of local and regional leaders with a concomitant devolution of fiscal and bureaucratic authority. In others, it can take the form of federalism, where power is constitutionally divided between the central authority and states or provinces, with appropriate checks and balances. In places with deep sectarian and/or regional differences, a move to federalism can be highly fraught and spark fears of state dissolution, but it can also be a way to hold a deeply fractured country together.

Though a system with significant decentralization seems an obvious fit for the vast and diverse archipelago of Indonesia, Jakarta-based elites long resisted giving up any control. The chaotic political and economic environment of the late 1990s and early 2000s, however, led them to grudgingly accept greater devolution as a way of maintaining national unity in the face of growing separatist demands. Many believed that regions such as Timor, Aceh, and Papua would seek independence, possibly leading to Indonesia's dissolution. Under the circumstances, leaders undertook devolution, including constitutional changes that provided greater autonomy to parts of the country, as a way to preserve a measure of peace, economic growth, and secular government in a unified Indonesia. The move brought clear benefits and, according to surveys, most Indonesians approved. Separatist agitation diminished as local and regional governments gained authority and government services were decentralized. In addition, decentralization improved budget transparency as more citizens gained access to budget data, and fostered competition at regional and local levels for domestic and foreign investment.

Devolution also had positive impacts in Poland, a far more homogenous country than Indonesia. After the failed economic and political centralization of the Communist government, Poland's early reformers prioritized effective local self-governance. A series of reforms gave local communities control over almost half of Poland's budget by the late 1990s, including education, health care, and infrastructure. Critically, increased municipal resources, including independent sources of revenue, accompanied this increase in local responsibility.

Mexico's democratization also entailed greater authority—and budgets—for its states. The country had long had a federal system under its constitution but hardly operated that way; instead, power was tightly held by the center. Democratization resulted in greater budgetary control at the state level—today, states receive about half their budgets directly from federal authorities in transfers that are outside the president's control—hindering the abuse of presidential power and enhancing local governance.

In recent years, Nigeria, too, has experienced a shift in influence away from the center and toward the states. This, however, has come not through conscious devolution but through the federal government's weakness. Nigeria's post-transition constitution, in theory, provided for federal power sharing, but in practice, the central government has retained control over oil revenue, making states dependent on Abuja. However, a decades-long neglect of federal institutions means that today the central government is increasingly unable to provide basic services. In some places, state and local institutions are filling the gaps by default. In an otherwise bleak political landscape, the creation of space for innovative economic and political initiatives at the more accountable state level is one positive result of declining central authority. In Lagos, Cross Rivers, and Rivers states, local political leaders have seized the opportunity created by the vacuum of federal power to strengthen administrative capacity and modernize their economies. Crucially, the economies of Lagos and Cross Rivers do not depend on oil.

Devolution is not a panacea, however. In Indonesia, devolution of power brought with it a decentralization of graft. Instead of a single corrupt administration, every local official can now demand payment to grease the wheels of government and commerce, and, increasingly, they do. With respect to Mexico, many believe devolution has stymied democratization in states where one party dominates. In Nigeria, feeble federal authorities lack the means to address ethnic and religious conflict effectively, and too often default to repression.

Devolution is clearly not a silver bullet for democratization, given that its effectiveness depends on the administrative capacity and political accountability of regions and localities, but the benefits that often follow from a more decentralized, bottom-up approach cannot be ignored.

PACING AND SEQUENCING OF POLICY CHOICES

Taken together, these insights have important implications for the pacing and sequencing of reforms. Policymakers and reformers interested in nurturing democracies that will stand the test of time should focus on building vibrant civil societies and a sufficiently strong middle class that can sustain a nonviolent democratic transition. Supporting violent overthrows and coups d'état may appeal as a quick fix to oust a bellicose dictator, but they will likely only replace one authoritarian ruler with another.

In this vein, policymakers in outside states trying to encourage democratization should advance economic strategies—including trade, small-business entrepreneurship, and investment policies—that foster the emergence of a middle class, while limiting economic measures, such as investments in extractive industries, that tend to concentrate economic gains in the hands of elites.

As a transition begins to unfold, policymakers should prioritize rule of law reforms that establish strong safeguards against corruption and insider dealing. They should also deter pacts that privilege incumbents and encourage domestic pressures for further reforms. Constructive measures include the public dissemination of revenues, expenditures, and important social and economic statistics; establishment of transparent auctions to privatize public assets; reform of laws constraining civil society organizations and NGOs; disclosure of the assets and income of public officials; and capacity building of the judiciary, parliament, and civil society. Once the rules of the game are roughly in place, with some basic mechanisms of accountability to ensure that they are enforced, the government can proceed with other structural economic reforms that could have significant distributional consequences, such as the privatization of state assets.

At the same time, it is critical to prioritize economic policies and social expenditures that can deliver highly visible and broadly realized social and economic benefits in the short term. These measures should be paired with other market-oriented reforms that could inflict short-term costs but that will lay the groundwork for economic gains for everyone in the medium term. For example, immediate implementation of a conditional cash transfer program that rapidly disburses funds to the poor could be paired with the reduction of expensive but inefficient fuel subsidies.

Of course, there is no one-size-fits-all solution for what is an inherently adaptive process, so policymakers interested in nurturing democracy must be resilient, flexible, and creative as they attempt to guide their countries from oppression to freedom.

Statistical Evidence

Jan Teorell

Many of the most fundamental factors thought to influence the trajectory of democratic transitions can in fact be quantified, either directly or indirectly. By looking across time at the statistical association of important variables with countries' movements toward and away from democracy, it is possible to discover the factors that make democratic transitions more or less likely to begin, more or less vulnerable to backsliding or stagnating once they are under way, and more or less likely to consolidate and endure. Given the inherently messy complexity of politics, statistical likelihoods are far from perfect predictors—even a country with all the "right" characteristics may very well stumble on the road to democracy. However, these likelihoods reveal what often matters, and can help those who would like to foster and nurture democracy make more informed policy choices.

For decades, researchers have been trying to identify the determinants of democratization through statistical analysis. Their studies can be grouped around major questions such as:

- Is democracy inevitable after countries reach a certain level of economic growth, modernization, and per capita income, and how does this affect the chances of sustaining democratic advancements?

- Are these structural issues irrelevant, and are strategic interactions among elites what really matter?

- Is democracy forged from below, through a power struggle among social forces with competing economic interests?

Before reviewing the evidence, it is important to understand what *democracy* means. The definition encompasses more than merely electoral procedures. It implies holding regular, free, fair, and effective elections to the legislative or executive offices of state, or both, together with a bundle of continually upheld political rights, most notably freedom of association and opinion.

MAJOR FINDINGS

Although much remains unknown, because of insufficient data, careful review of the statistical evidence reveals several major findings:

- A country's level of economic development is not a driver of democratization, but it is a safeguard against backsliding toward authoritarianism. Rising levels of gross domestic product (GDP) per capita should thus not be expected to produce democratic improvements on their own. However, when a democratic transition has been achieved, no matter how, richer countries are more likely to sustain it.

- In the short term, economic growth under autocracy impedes democratization. Conversely, economic crisis tends to trigger democratic transitions.

- Nonviolent mass mobilization against autocratic regimes is a strong trigger of democratic regime change. Armed rebellion, by contrast, typically does not lead to democratization.

- Authoritarian regimes with partial political openness, most important through multiparty electoral competition, are likeliest to grow even more democratic. It is thus worthwhile to promote elections in autocracies, even if flawed and fraudulent, as long as they permit some competition.

- The fate of new democracies does not appear to hinge on the choice of a presidential or a parliamentary system.

- Overall, quantitative studies are fairly successful at predicting long-term changes in the level of democracy. Eruptive short-term change, however, is less predictable.

As for the six analytical themes of this volume, not all topics have been covered equally in existing studies. The following sections summarize the main quantitative findings in the literature around each theme to the extent that such findings exist.

SOCIOECONOMIC EXCLUSION AND INCLUSION

Despite strong theoretical expectations, quantitative studies to date have provided only weak support for a connection between socioeconomic inequality and democratization. Part of the reason for this could, however, be poor measures of income distribution.

Socioeconomic distribution is typically expected to affect democratization in two ways. In highly unequal autocracies, average citizens have a greater incentive to revolt in order to gain power and redistribute wealth. Elites, however, also have a greater incentive to repress uprisings (or stage coups d'état in new democracies) to avoid this redistribution. On the other hand, in more equal societies, elites have less fear of democratic redistribution, but average citizens have less incentive to revolt. This implies that transitions to democracy should be most likely in countries with intermediate levels of inequality, where the dispersion of income is great enough to incite a desire for redistribution but not so great as to provoke severe repression.

Although examples exist of transitions in countries at intermediate levels of inequality, such as Indonesia in 1999, overall these predictions have not been systematically borne out by quantitative evidence. One possible explanation for the weak and contradictory findings could be poor data quality. Significant observations in the existing data on income inequality are missing, and comparing the data over time and place is difficult.

Another possibility is that the relationship between inequality and democratization should look different in right-wing autocracies, such as South Africa's apartheid regime, than in socialist dictatorships, such as in the former Soviet Union and Eastern Europe. In South Africa, evidence indicates that levels of income disparity were declining in the 1980s, which would be consistent with the theory that the rich white elites had less to lose from redistributing power to the poor black population. In countries such as Poland and Ukraine, on the other hand, income was already fairly evenly distributed, and yet transitions occurred. This is not to deny that distributional conflict could be one of the main drivers of democratization, but the more exact nature of the relationship with inequality remains unclear.

Similar to those of economic inequality, studies of ethno-linguistic or religious fractionalization tend to show essentially no net effects on democratization. This could again result from poor data quality. Most scholars argue that it is not cleavages per se that matter but the extent to which they are politicized, and existing data poorly reflect this.

ECONOMIC STRUCTURE AND POLICIES

The relationship between economic development and democracy is by far the most well studied one in quantitative analyses of democratization. What studies have shown, however, is that growth in GDP per capita does not in itself make an autocracy more likely to democratize, presumably because people are happy with their rising fortunes. Increased national income does, however, make democracy likelier to endure once it arises.

These findings help illuminate the chances of democratization in a country such as China. As opposed to traditional modernization theory, quantitative evidence indicates that China's impressive growth is not likely to lead to democracy. On the contrary, a serious economic contraction would be a major threat to China's one-party regime. But the prospects that enduring democracy will result from such an economic crisis improve as China reaches higher levels of economic development.

Interestingly, the quantitative evidence on development and democratization shows a relationship that has changed over time. The traditional view that higher GDP per capita makes democracy more likely seems to have been correct during the first wave of democratization in the nineteenth and early twentieth centuries. But the newer view—that rising income does not bring democratization, but only safeguards against democratic backsliding—is more in line with the empirical evidence from World War II onward.

The causal mechanisms connecting wealth and democracy remain largely unresolved. What is it about economic development that safeguards democratic achievements? And what aspect of development is most important: national income in itself, urbanization, the structure of the economy, or perhaps some other element of this broad-based phenomenon?

A second systematically tested economic determinant of democracy is short-term growth and contraction (as opposed to long-run levels of income). The most robust finding seems to be that economic crisis bodes ill for authoritarian regimes and makes a country more likely to democratize. As seen in the 1980s in several Latin American countries, such as Brazil, deteriorating economic performance and the austere policy measures it provokes undercut the power bases of authoritarian regimes. They drive a wedge between the regime and economic elites, encouraging the latter to withdraw from the authoritarian bargain, and between hard-liners and reformers within the regime elite. All this eventually subverts the regime's hold on power.

Some studies have also found a systematic relationship between economic performance and democratic survival, but the overall evidence seems to be that economic crisis is less likely to hurt democratic regimes than autocracies. There is no consensus, however, for why this is the case.

A third economic determinant that has figured prominently in the literature is natural resource wealth. Regimes that rely on vast national resources such as oil can use both the carrot (tax cuts and patronage) and the stick (repression) to hold movements toward democracy at bay. Another reason to expect autocratic stability in resource-rich states is that natural resource abundance decreases capital mobility. This tends to hurt democratization because it forces wealthy elites to keep their money in the country, increasing their incentive to control policymaking in their favor. In Nigeria, for example, oil has not been a blessing for the prospects of democracy. But although many quantitative studies have shown oil wealth to decrease the chances of democratization, the evidence for the relationship is not overwhelming, and critics have argued that flawed statistical techniques might explain it.

Other studies have examined the relationship between democracy and state involvement in the economy. Theory generally holds that less state intervention should lead to more democracy. The reasoning is that if economic actors (including capital and labor) depend on state subsidies, they will be less inclined to oppose an authoritarian regime. Although some studies claim to show a positive effect of economic liberalization on democratization, however, these findings have been difficult to replicate. They also rely on composite measures of state involvement that blend aspects of economic policy with the institutional setup of the legal system.

Finally, the study of trade dependence has a long pedigree within the quantitative literature on democratization. Most studies show that countries more dependent on international trade are less likely to democratize, but the exact reasons are unclear.

CIVIL SOCIETY AND MEDIA

Democracy, as defined here, is constituted by the freedom of organization and opinion, both of which are directly reflected in the presence of a vibrant civil society and an independent press. In this sense, both civil society and media freedoms are critical facets, but not necessarily drivers, of democracy.

Beyond these obvious relationships, however, civil society, broadly understood, has a critical impact on democratization in a more distinct way. Quantitative studies find that popular mobilization significantly influences democratization—but, critically, not all forms of mobilization have this effect. On the whole, peaceful demonstrations are powerful drivers of democratization, whereas violent rebellions have less effect. Violent opposition is usually a strategy used by small segments of the population, which helps autocracies rally the broader public behind the party line and legitimizes the state's use of repression. When the regime chooses to confront peaceful protest through the barrel of a gun, however, moral outrage spurs further counter-regime mobilization, both domestically and internationally. A successful popular challenge eventually disrupts the government's material and other support bases, exacerbating intra-elite divisions and paving the way for a democratic takeover.

Another important feature of many peaceful protests is the way they diffuse across country borders, spreading from one authoritarian regime to another. This was certainly the case for the popular mobilization efforts that toppled the Communist regimes in Eastern Europe and later spread to demands for reform in sub-Saharan Africa. The "colored revolutions" in the early twenty-first century in the former Soviet Union and the Arab uprisings that began in 2011 illustrate this phenomenon as well. To be sure, though, these mass popular protests do not necessarily signal the presence of durable civil societies. Also, as the parallel cases of Syria and Libya show, the extent to which a peaceful uprising can occur at all hinges on at least a modicum of political openness.

With respect to the media, the quantitative evidence is more speculative. According to one recent large-scale study, though, the proliferation of media outlets across society matters significantly in safeguarding democratic advances. Radio, television, the Internet, and newspapers spread information, helping preempt antidemocratic coups. However, for the media to exercise this effect, some freedom of the press has to exist. This means that widespread access to media outlets generally prevents backsliding rather than triggers movements toward more democracy.

LEGAL SYSTEM AND RULE OF LAW

Perhaps surprisingly, few quantitative studies have examined the relationship between the rule of law, or its absence, and democratization. As in the case of civil society and the media, certain aspects of the rule of law are inherent features of democracy. Civil liberties and political rights critical to the democratic process, such as freedom of opinion and organization, must be upheld by an effective legal framework and functioning court system. Promoting such legal institutions would thus appear a direct way of strengthening democracy. Beyond this, significant questions remain about whether strengthening state administrative capacity, combating corruption, bolstering property rights, and improving the court system can exert an independent influence on democracy. On all these issues there is a dearth of reliable and replicable quantitative studies, and thus more testing is needed.

GOVERNMENT STRUCTURE

The most important determinant of democratization in terms of government structure is the existence of multiparty electoral competition under autocracy. The choice between presidential and parliamentary structures in new democracies appears less consequential.

Recent years have seen a rise in quantitative studies examining how the institutional makeup of an authoritarian regime may shape its likelihood to democratize. The most conspicuous finding is that those regimes with the trappings of a democratic system—especially multiparty elections—are the likeliest to do so. Thus, even if elections are flawed or fraudulent, that they are even held gives these countries a better chance at democracy, unlike the situation in closed single-party regimes, military dictatorships, or absolute monarchies.

Why is this the case? First, elections that allow contestants from outside the ruling party offer a venue for rival party factions to credibly threaten to leave the party and join the opposition. As a consequence, these rival factions may voice their grievances more effectively. Multiparty elections, however controlled, rigged, and unfair they may be, thus fuel intra-regime divisions. Moreover, these divisions may improve the incentives for opposition parties to join forces and challenge the ruling party under a unified banner. These two processes—defections from the incumbent coalition and unification of opposition forces—reinforce each other and together make democratic breakthroughs more likely.

Mexico clearly illustrates these patterns. Multiparty competition was an institutional feature of the authoritarian regime maintained by the Institutional Revolutionary Party (PRI). Through a series of events from the election of 1988 through the mid-1990s, the PRI's grip on power was gradually shaken. In its tug-of-war with the regime, the opposition managed to get through a series of incremental reforms of the institutional framework governing elections, which had previously favored the ruling party alone. As a result, the opposition gained increasing support from the electorate and was able to oust the ruling party in the 2000 presidential election.

Several quantitative studies have also addressed the question of whether presidential or parliamentary democracies are more stable. The conventional argument is that presidential democracies are more vulnerable to breakdown because the executive rests on a narrow support base and tends to be caught in deadlock with the legislature. This leads to political stalemate and, eventually, a severe political crisis that can be resolved only by defeating the democratic system. The most careful empirical scrutiny to date, however, proves this view of presidential democracy to be inaccurate. Indeed, presidential democracies are more prone to break down than their parliamentary or semi-presidential counterparts, but not because of their presidential qualities per se. Instead, they look more vulnerable because of what often precedes them. Presidential systems are typically installed as a bulwark against previous military dictatorships, and it is this legacy that endangers new democracies. Absent a recent history of military interventions, presidential democracies are no less stable than the parliamentary variety.

Other facets of constitutional design are less well studied. Although countries with proportional electoral systems tend to be more democratic than those with plurality or majority voting, evidence is scant that the choice of electoral system in itself is an important driver of democratization or democratic stability. The choice of a unitary system of government over a federal one appears to exercise a similarly weak effect.

EDUCATION AND DEMOGRAPHY

Empirical studies on education and demography are numerous, but few offer robust findings or plausible theoretical explanations. Some quantitative studies argue that higher societal levels of education have a positive influence on democratization, but these studies have generally ignored the fact that rising education is part of a larger modernization process, which also includes increased income, industrialization, urbanization, and media proliferation. When these are controlled for, the effect of education on democracy weakens considerably. In an argument not unlike that about education, some contend that certain cultural values, including individual autonomy, self-expression, and free choice, affect democratization and democratic survival. The findings on this issue so far, however, are scattered, contradictory, and inconclusive.

Another unresolved argument concerns the role of religion. Many quantitative studies have found that having a predominantly Muslim population impedes the chances of democratization. This so-called Muslim gap is, however, mostly an Arab gap, separating the Middle East and North Africa from the rest of the world, suggesting that any apparent religious correlations with democracy are spurious. Even more important, individual Muslims in various parts of the world express no weaker democratic sentiments than people of other religions. Indeed, religious obstacles to democratization have been cited before, only to be disproved by history. In the early 1970s, for example, Catholicism was considered a cultural hindrance to democracy, but then southern Europe and Latin America democratized. In the 1980s, Confucianism was blamed for democracy's bleak prospects in eastern Asia, but then South Korea and Taiwan democratized. If the precarious democratic reforms ensuing from the recent Arab uprisings prove sustainable, the negative statistical relationship between Islam and democracy might soon disappear. At the very least, the uprisings reveal that many in the Arab world hold strong democratic sentiments.

CONCLUSION

In sum, an array of studies shows that several structural factors affect the likelihood that countries will become and remain democracies. Even when taken together, however, these factors cannot predict revolutions or coups in the short term. If, for example, one knew how quickly China's GDP would grow or whether any major protests would occur next year, quantitative estimates would still not predict the immediate fate of China's single-party regime. The quantitative evidence has been more successful at explaining a country's long-run democratic trajectory. Though it is possible to predict how democratic reforms might progress in China given its structural conditions, predictions about individual countries drawn from cross-country data are inherently imperfect, and it is not possible to know when (or how) these reforms might happen.

Although this may sound discouraging, it has an upside. If structural preconditions do not cause short-term regime change, promoting democracy can be seen as worthwhile because its primary goal is to lead to democratization by strengthening domestic actors. In other words, programs to educate and empower voters and strengthen political parties and civil society groups could bear fruit under a range of circumstances. But, of course, the converse is also true: these activities might not produce sustainable democracy in the long term when structural preconditions are unfavorable.

Quantitative studies may offer many guidelines for policy, but three priorities in particular emerge. The first is increasing the capacity of groups to mount nonviolent protests against autocratic regimes. This capacity will prove particularly rewarding when there are splits between hard-liners and reformers in the regime, and when protests can hurt the government's economy and undermine its psychological support base. The second is support for multiparty elections. Even flawed or fraudulent polls may set forces in motion that loosen the regime's grip over time, helping the opposition increase its power. This is especially true when the regime faces a shock, such as an economic crisis or peaceful popular mobilization. Finally, maximizing access to mass media is a sound strategy to safeguard democratic progress already achieved. Radio, television, Internet, and newspaper access works as an antidote to coups d'état once some freedom of the press exists.

What does not seem to promote democracy, however, is economic development in authoritarian states. Economic crises, not growth, spur democratization. And long-term development affects not the prospect of democratization but the chance of sustaining existing democratic progress. This suggests that, at least in the short run, promoting democracy and prosperity may be incompatible.

Mexico

Shannon K. O'Neil

For decades, Mexico was known as the "perfect dictatorship," a term coined by Peruvian novelist and Nobel laureate Mario Vargas Llosa to describe the seventy-plus-year reign of the Institutional Revolutionary Party (PRI). The PRI dates back to the years after the Mexican Revolution (1910–20), when strongmen worked to gain control of Mexico's restive cities and countryside. Publicly they vowed to fulfill the demands of the masses—land, educational reform, and labor rights. Behind the scenes, these leaders consolidated political power and control, slowly incorporating labor unions, peasant groups, business associations, and popular organizations into the party apparatus. They also firmly subordinated the military to civilian rule, to the point that later, during Mexico's political and economic transitions, the military played no real part, unlike the situation in so many other countries around the world. Through a patronage system, an expansive revolutionary ideology, and the capacity and willingness to use a heavy repressive hand when necessary, the PRI maintained its control over Mexico's politics for decades.

Unlike many other nondemocratic regimes, Mexico has long held the trappings of democracy—notably, through regular elections. Although the PRI dominated at nearly all levels, a systematically loyal opposition, led by the right-leaning and heavily Catholic National Action Party (PAN), persevered. Small leftist organizations and parties existed as well, though they faced more political repression and achieved less success at the ballot box. Nevertheless, elections were so important for maintaining the perceived legitimacy of the system that when the PAN failed to register a presidential candidate in the 1976 elections, mostly due to internal disagreements, the administration of President Jose Lopez Portillo reformed the electoral laws to make it easier for the opposition to gain and retain at least a few token seats. The new legislation eased the restrictions around forming official parties and expanded the Congress to include at least one hundred seats—of four hundred total—for minority parties. This need for electoral legitimacy and the willingness to reform electoral laws to foster it became important factors in Mexico's nearly two-decade-long political transition.

The PRI also maintained a strong presence in the economy. Complementing its political control was an import substitution industrialization (ISI) economic framework of high tariffs, subsidies, economic favoritism, and widespread state ownership and management. This corporatist system created vested interests in the economic status quo and for many years provided the financial and patronage resources necessary to keep the PRI in power. Benefiting from a large consumer base, second only to Brazil in the region, Mexico's inwardly oriented policies fueled strong economic growth and development for nearly four decades, in what is often dubbed the Mexican miracle. Manufacturing led this transformation, with production increasing some 10 percent per year to make up nearly a quarter of GDP in 1970.

In the 1970s, this subsidy- and investment-heavy economic development model began to founder because of high deficits, mounting international debt, rising inflation, and, finally, a severe devaluation. The discovery of large oil fields in 1976 lessened the fiscal challenge, but only temporarily, as the government reacted to the news by increasing spending. In fact, Mexico racked up sizable debts from international banks eager to lend in order to recycle the petrodollars flowing in from other oil-producing countries. But in the early 1980s, the world entered an economic downturn, U.S. interest rates rose, and Mexico's mounting foreign obligations effectively bankrupted the government. In August 1982, Mexico stopped payments on its debt, setting off what became known as the Latin American debt crisis.

INFLECTION POINTS
OF THE TRANSITION PERIOD

The 1982 debt crisis spurred Mexico's political and economic transitions. On a basic level, the country's plummeting public revenues made it much more difficult to satisfy the various PRI factions and to keep together the authoritarian political coalition. Patronage resources diminished further with the economic policy choices of Mexico's next two presidents—Miguel de la Madrid and Carlos Salinas de Gortari—who, seeing no viable economic alternatives and hoping to boost economic growth, used their terms to fundamentally transform the structure of the Mexican economy.

The economic crisis also invalidated the tacit bargain between the PRI and many Mexicans—economic betterment in exchange for limited political rights. The 1982 debt crisis and the ensuing "lost decade" of limited economic growth halted the previous decades' long upward trajectory, throwing millions into poverty. This subpar performance was repeated during the 1994 peso crisis, when poor economic choices, overspending, and dwindling international reserves forced a devaluation and initiated another severe economic recession, further eroding the trust and backing of Mexico's interest groups and population in general.

The economic crises created uncertainty and room for change within the government, setting the stage for Mexico's long-suffering political opposition to use the opening to press its limited advantage, galvanizing budding civil society groups around the call for free and transparent elections. By the early 1980s, both right- and left-wing opposition parties began institutionalizing and professionalizing their organizations. For instance, the PAN, once seen as a far-right, ideologically driven party, shifted toward the center, opening its ranks to the disaffected middle class. It also began to work seriously on the nuts and bolts of creating a professional political party structure. These party-building efforts soon bore fruit at the subnational level. In the north of the country, the PAN won important local and state-level elections in 1983 and 1986, some of which were even grudgingly recognized by the ruling party.

The greatest national electoral challenge to the PRI-dominated regime first came from the left. In 1988, an amalgamation of disaffected PRI members, long-standing leftist parties, and budding social organizations joined together in a loose alliance, the National Democratic Front. They put forth and backed Cuauhtemoc Cardenas—a former PRI politician and son of the revered 1930s president Lazaro Cardenas—in a historic bid for the presidency.

Although Cardenas officially lost the elections, the voting process was filled with purported computer failures, burnt ballots, and reports of fraud, leading many to believe that he had bested his PRI opponent. Whoever actually won the vote, the PRI won the count, Carlos Salinas de Gortari officially receiving 50.4 percent of the ballots cast. Cardenas's supporters initially took to the streets, protesting the alleged fraud. But with their candidate uneasy about fully confronting his former colleagues, and the PRI threatening to unleash its heavy-handed repressive arm (as it had against students and opposition activists in the 1960s and 1970s), the opposition retreated, leaving Salinas firmly in control.

Once in office, to placate (and further divide) the democratic opposition, Salinas recognized the PAN's triumph in the 1989 Baja California gubernatorial race. He also passed a 1990 electoral reform, creating the Federal Electoral Institute (IFE) to organize and manage elections. Although initially designed to maintain PRI control, and thus quite limited in its reach, this institution was transformed by subsequent reforms and developments into an autonomous and fairly powerful tool for political opening.

Salinas assumed the presidential mantle with a vision to transform Mexico's economy, not its politics. Building on the economic opening of his predecessor, Miguel de la Madrid, Salinas renegotiated Mexico's debt, privatized some nine hundred state-owned enterprises, changed traditional land ownership structures, and negotiated the North American Free Trade Agreement (NAFTA) with the United States and Canada—at the time, the most ambitious free trade agreement in the world.

The 1994 peso crisis pushed the economy open further. Once NAFTA was firmly in place, many multinationals came looking for bargains, buying up large retail chains, supermarkets, and banks, among other businesses. Others took advantage of the competitive labor supply and favorable exchange rates to open factories and production facilities, catering to U.S. producers and markets.

These combined crises and reforms opened Mexico's economy, bringing substantial foreign direct investment, some $330 billion over the past two decades. Trade also expanded exponentially, and Mexico's foreign trade exceeded $300 billion in the decade after NAFTA.

Overall, from 1980 to 2000, Mexico transformed from a closed economy driven by oil to one led by diversified services and exports. Many scholars and other observers criticize the unequal spread of benefits from this economic opening, but these changes made Mexico a top global competitor in some sectors, even with respect to much larger economies such as China.

Although the PRI's top leaders had thought they could open the economy and maintain political control, they found it difficult, as Soviet leader Mikhail Gorbachev had discovered several years before, to have perestroika without glasnost. The combination of economic opening, declining state resources, institutional reforms, stronger opposition parties, and an increasingly vibrant and independent press and civil society all came together, accelerating the move toward democracy. Added to the mix were international influences, from foreign investors to U.S. senators and representatives, a few of whom spoke openly about the PRI's undemocratic practices. These forces pushed Salinas's successor, Ernesto Zedillo, to further reform the electoral system. In 1996, Mexico passed legislation cementing the independence of the electoral court from the executive branch, mandating public financing for all political parties, and establishing citizen leadership at the helm of the IFE—making electoral manipulations increasingly difficult.

Some analysts date Mexico's democratization to 1997, when the PRI lost its majority in Congress. Others cite 2000, when the PRI lost control of the executive branch. Whatever the start date for Mexico's democracy, the long transition was a product of many factors, including political and economic structural changes, institutional reforms, and the intended and unintended consequences of individual choices.

LESSONS OF THE TRANSITION PERIOD

Now, more than a decade later, Mexico routinely holds competitive elections at the local, state, and national level that most see as free and fair. It boasts a free press, an emerging civil society, three competitive political parties, and an increasingly demanding voter base. But many still worry about the inclusiveness of Mexico's democracy, and whether it truly represents the people. Many of the gains, as well as the limits, stem from the dual transitions, the processes of economic and political opening.

SOCIOECONOMIC EXCLUSION AND INCLUSION

Mexico remains one of the most unequal countries in Latin America, and indeed the world. The country's Gini coefficient, a common measure of inequality in which 0 indicates the most equal society and 100 indicates the most unequal, was at 51.9 in 2000, double the level of Sweden's. During the protracted democratic transition inequality skyrocketed, first during the lost decade of the 1980s, and again during the early 1990s, as the economy opened.

Public policies during the transition years did little to alleviate the disparities, and only a modest amount was spent on public health, schooling, and social services for the poor. Real wages, too, declined with respect to pre-1982-crisis levels. In 1996, some 70 percent of the population—more than sixty-three million people—lived in poverty. Although the economic downturn and public neglect were country-wide, the more isolated and indigenous south felt them most acutely, helping foment the popular discontent that culminated in the Zapatista uprising in the southern state of Chiapas in 1994.

These economic disparities continue to play out in the political realm today. Researchers find that voting remains stratified, with Mexicans in the higher socioeconomic brackets being more apt to vote and be politically active. Since democratization, this trend has only increased. As a result, some scholars worry that these dynamics decrease the incentives for politicians to be responsive to less-advantaged constituents.

Nevertheless, there are some signs of change. Inequality has been falling in Mexico. The country's Gini coefficient declined nearly 1 percent a year from 2000 to 2006, reaching 48.3 in 2008. Poverty has also declined; less than 50 percent of the population is now defined as poor, versus 70 percent in the mid-1990s, according to 2008 and 2010 surveys by Mexico's National Evaluation Council for Social Development Policy (CONEVAL).

Mexico's middle class is also growing. Although Mexico is still known broadly as a country of haves and have-nots, its middle class is now by many accounts the majority of the population. Per capita incomes have risen steadily over the past two decades, increasing from some $3,500 in 1990 to $10,000 in 2011. Tens of millions now enjoy the consumer trappings of a middle-class lifestyle: owning cell phones, cars, and homes; going to the movies; sending children to private schools; and taking vacations.

A number of factors are behind these trends. First, macroeconomic stability, even with slow growth, has been particularly beneficial for the poor, who, studies show, are hit the hardest by economic crises. Real wages also improved in response to expanding education and increased worker productivity.

Social spending directed toward the poor also rose (see Figure 1). Programs such as Oportunidades, begun under President Zedillo as Progresa and greatly expanded under Presidents Vicente Fox and Felipe Calderon, give monthly stipends to low-income households that keep their children healthy and in school. From three hundred thousand recipients in 1997, the program now reaches nearly six million families, about a quarter of the population. And unlike previous social programs

FIGURE 1. POVERTY AND SOCIAL SPENDING IN MEXICO

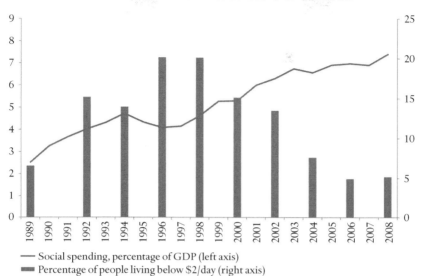

— Social spending, percentage of GDP (left axis)
▬ Percentage of people living below $2/day (right axis)

Sources: OECD (social spending data); World Bank (poverty data: purchasing power parity, 2005 international dollars).

under the PRI, these conditional cash transfer programs are found by most independent evaluations to be efficient, objective, and generally corruption-free. Mexico also made important gains in health care. In 2002, the Fox government started Seguro Popular, a national health insurance program designed to reach the country's informal and unemployed workers. By the end of 2011, the program covered some forty-four million previously uninsured Mexicans.

Evidence suggests an important democratic feedback loop. These programs lessen socioeconomic exclusion, providing a basic social safety net. Citizens who enjoy these benefits, in turn, tend to reward the politicians who provide them through voting. Studies show that these programs catalyze a larger turnout in favor of the incumbent party. According to one analysis, Oportunidades participants were 11 percent more likely than nonparticipants to vote for the incumbent PAN's presidential candidate, Felipe Calderon, in the 2006 election, making a significant difference in a race that Calderon won by fewer than three hundred thousand votes.

Mexico's political and economic opening left a legacy of strong patronage networks, high levels of poverty, and unequal wealth distribution. But after more than a decade of democracy, evidence indicates that these exclusionary economic structures are slowly being dismantled as electoral incentives encourage politicians to spread the wealth to cultivate votes.

ECONOMIC STRUCTURE AND POLICIES

The Mexican economy has transformed since NAFTA, which was the last time the PRI held a firm grip on both the legislature and the presidency. Today the public sector constitutes just 25 percent of GDP, much less than Brazil's or the United States' 40 percent. Oil, once the major source of trade revenue, now makes up less than 20 percent of total exports, though it remains vital to the federal budget, in which it accounts for nearly a third of federal funds. After decades of booms and busts, Mexico is now known for being a top foreign direct investment destination and for its strong macroeconomic and fiscal fundamentals, its independent central bank, and its solid privately managed banking system. Its manufacturing sector, which accounts for some 80 percent of exports and 20 percent of the overall economy, is tightly integrated with its neighbor and the world's largest consumer market, the United States (see Figure 2).

FIGURE 2. MEXICAN EXPORTS SINCE NAFTA

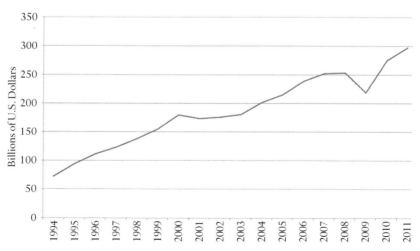

Source: World Bank

But the Mexican economy still faces significant structural challenges. Powerful monopolies, poor credit markets, and a large informal economy slow growth and hinder development. Monopolies and
oligopolies control not just energy, utilities, and telecommunications
(somewhat common in emerging and advanced economies alike) but
also sectors as diverse as bread, glass, media, tortillas, and soft drinks.
According to the Organization for Economic Cooperation and Development (OECD), the lack of competition in telecommunications alone
(see Figure 3) cost the Mexican economy some $129 billion between
2005 and 2009, or 1.9 percent of GDP per year.

Much of this concentration is a legacy of the decisions made during
the economic and political transitions—in particular, the widespread
privatizations in the late 1980s and early 1990s. Under the still-firm
control of the PRI, the transactions concentrated many of these economic sectors in the hands of just a few well-connected business leaders.

*FIGURE 3. ECONOMIC CONCENTRATION IN MEXICO'S MOBILE
TELEPHONE MARKET VS. OTHER OECD COUNTRIES'*

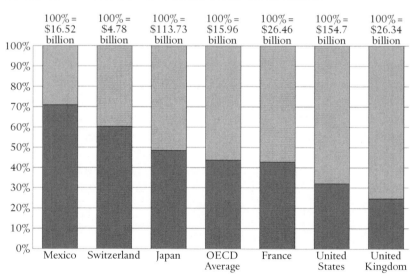

■ Largest mobile telephone network operator's share (with total market size)

Sources: Market share from *OECD Review of Telecommunication Policy and Regulation in Mexico*, revised
2012. All figures from 2009; OECD average from editors' calculations from data in the report. Market size
from *OECD Communications Outlook 2011*.

For instance, the bank privatization process included several inside deals in which buyers loaned themselves money from the banks being purchased, in part leading to and then deepening the 1994 crisis, in which many of these banks collapsed. Telmex is another example. In 1990, when President Salinas sold the state-owned telephone company to Carlos Slim (gaining his strong loyalty and political support), he also virtually guaranteed its monopoly status—closing the fixed-line telephone market for the next six years. In that time, Telmex became a dominant monopolistic power, controlling 90 percent of Mexico's phone lines, and Slim was well on his way to becoming the richest man in the world. More important for Mexico, its telecommunications industry suffered as a result, falling behind its Latin American neighbors in terms of infrastructure and investment. Today Mexico ranks last in the OECD for telecommunications investment per capita, although profit margins for telecommunications companies are double the OECD average.

Even as the Salinas administration quickly privatized sectors of the economy, it was slow to create and strengthen regulators. Mexico's main antitrust agency, the Federal Competition Commission (CFC), was established in 1993, and the Federal Commission of Telecommunications (COFETEL) was created only in 1996. This gave free rein to many of the newly privatized corporations for their first years, and left regulators the difficult task of catching up with their charges.

There are some indications that things are beginning to change. During President Calderon's administration, both houses of Congress unanimously approved a number of changes to antitrust laws designed to foster competition. The reforms put in place harsher punishments for those found guilty of monopolistic practices, including fines of up to 10 percent of their profits and, in the most serious cases (price fixing falls under this umbrella), up to ten years in jail. They also awarded more power to the CFC, including the right to conduct unannounced raids of companies under investigation. The courts, too, have jumped into the fray, striking down legislation in 2007 that gave unfair advantages to media giants, and more recently putting regulatory edicts into force immediately rather than waiting until after the companies exhausted all legal means and appeals. But regulating monopolies continues to be an uphill battle as companies resist efforts to foster greater transparency and competition.

Another sign of economic power translating into political influence can be seen in Mexico's tax code and collection. Mexicans pay some of the lowest taxes in the hemisphere, attesting not just to the oil wealth that pads public finances but also to the concentrated power of the economic elite. A few steps have been taken to increase non–oil tax revenues, but they still make up only about 10 percent of GDP. These revenue limitations leave little for publicly provided goods, whether infrastructure, social safety nets, or basic public safety.

CIVIL SOCIETY AND MEDIA

Mexico's civil society has grown substantially and been pivotal in many decisions that have pushed greater political opening. From the 2002 Freedom of Information law, which required that government documents be available for public scrutiny, to the 2008 judicial reform, which, when implemented, will fundamentally change Mexico's justice system, civil society organizations have been vital in pushing democracy forward. But compared with civil societies in other Latin American countries, Mexico's remains fairly weak when judged both by the sheer number of organizations and by their activity and influence.

This reflects in large part the legacy of the PRI. For decades, the dominant party actively organized workers, peasants, businesses, and popular organizations within the party structure. Autonomous organizations were not supported and at times were actively discouraged. It also results from Mexico's legal structure, in which donations to philanthropic organizations were not, until fairly recently, tax deductible. And it reveals traditions in which wealthy Mexicans donated to churches or their personal charitable organizations rather than to more professional advocacy-based organizations or civil society groups.

Some of this is changing. The first civil society movements and their successes came about during the political transition as hundreds of organizations rallied behind the goal of free and fair elections. Their activism attracted the interest and funding of international governments and foundations, which also helped with technical and organizational capacity building. Notably, the United Nations Electoral Assistance Division (UNEAD) financed and trained Mexican electoral observer groups from across the political spectrum, and the National Democratic Institute (NDI) helped implement a quick-count vote, important for dissuading ballot-box shenanigans by the ruling party. From there, and with democratization, other themes ranging from good governance to the environment to women's rights rose in prominence. In recent years, nonprofit efforts have successfully brought about a reformed tax code, encouraging domestic donations through tax-exempt status. Some organizations have also begun professionalizing their management. These are steps in the right direction, but the development of Mexico's civil society arguably remains a work in progress.

The media, too, have made great strides. Once virtually a propaganda arm for the ruling party, Mexico's newspapers, radio stations, and television networks are today fiercely independent. The media routinely question the official line, investigating and exposing corruption and helping hold the government accountable to the public. Yet challenges remain, especially with Mexico's network television (the dominant news source for the average Mexican), where coverage continues to be an effective "duopoly." Some in fact worry that the tables have turned, with the media controlling the movements of politicians afraid of bad press rather than the reverse.

LEGAL SYSTEM AND RULE OF LAW

Perhaps the greatest challenge to Mexico's democracy and economy today is security. Gruesome headlines attest to rising and spreading violence, fueled by the U.S. market for illegal drugs and an overall culture of impunity. In the past five years, there have been some fifty-five thousand drug-related killings. Other crimes—assaults, robberies, kidnapping, human trafficking, and extortion—have also escalated. This reflects not only U.S. demand for drugs (and supply of money and weapons) but also Mexico's weak rule of law.

According to Mexico Evalua, a Mexican public policy research center, only four thousand of 2010's twenty thousand homicides (20 percent) resulted in a conviction. Human Rights Watch reported an even lower figure for drug-related homicides, writing that the government opened investigations into fewer than 3 percent of the cases between 2006 and 2010. This widespread impunity stems in part from the weakness of the Office of the Attorney General, which has shown itself incapable of investigating and prosecuting the thousands of criminal complaints it receives each year. To improve security, Mexico will have to invest in and professionalize this vital link in the judicial process.

Corruption, too, permeates the country, hindering reforms and hurting average Mexicans. A 2011 study by Transparency International estimates that Mexicans pay some $2.5 billion a year in bribes. These costs hit the poor the hardest. Although some federal programs—including the postal service and utilities—have been cleaned up through reforms, such improvements are not consistent. Instead, the study suggests things are getting worse, with bribe amounts outpacing inflation. This culture of lawlessness permeates everyday life, eroding popular trust in the authorities and making the government's fight against bigger threats ever more difficult.

Impunity and corruption are in many ways legacies of PRI rule. For decades, the judiciary and law enforcement were generally just arms of the political party, useful for social control rather than for justice and protection. Corruption was so common, in fact, that Mexicans developed the phrase "Él que no transa, no avanza," which roughly translates to "If you don't cheat, you won't get ahead." Today's challenge is to counter the culture of lawlessness through the professionalization of justice and law enforcement systems, and through targeted social programs to get citizens and civil society organizations on board, even while addressing the threat of sophisticated and well-armed organized criminal groups. Mexico's democratic governments are just beginning to take these steps.

Further advanced are reforms to Mexico's federal police force. The force has been beefed up since 2006 to some thirty-five thousand members. New officers undergo restructured recruiting, vetting, and training processes, and receive career training and higher salaries. Although encouraging, this force amounts to just 10 percent of Mexico's total corps; state and local forces make up the other 90 percent. It is this challenge Mexico must now take on.

Another area undergoing change is the judicial system. In 2008, Mexico's Congress passed a judicial reform package that will, when implemented, fundamentally transform the entire court system. It includes many of the components that civil society groups pushed for, such as oral trials, reinforcement of the presumption of innocence, and mechanisms for strengthening due process and the role of defense attorneys. It also incorporates many of the crime-fighting tools that the executive branch supported, including the controversial *arraigo* provision, which allows organized crime suspects to be held for up to eighty days without being charged.

The reforms gave Mexico an eight-year transition period, until 2016, to renovate its courtrooms, retrain its lawyers, change its law school curriculum, and expand its forensic laboratories and evidence collection systems. So far, not enough progress has been made. The question remains whether Mexico will meet the deadline and create a more open, transparent, and effective legal system.

In the economic realm, the rule of law is more solid. Although issues of corruption and fraud are routine, Mexico's adherence to international treaties and arbitration ensures that most disputes are settled through institutionalized channels. Its ranking in the top third of countries in the World Bank's Doing Business surveys reflects this relatively favorable business environment and the steps that Mexico has taken to improve the ease of doing business within its borders. Still, strengthening the rule of law will only benefit Mexico's current market-based democracy.

GOVERNMENT STRUCTURE AND DIVISION OF POWER

On the books, Mexico has for decades been a federal democracy. But only with the political transition has it become one in practice. Under the PRI, the president held ultimate and rarely questioned authority, appointing the thousands-strong bureaucracy, choosing candidates for Congress (who were almost sure to win), and selecting and dismissing governors at will. Negotiations occurred behind closed doors and between the PRI's organized factions; Congress was simply a rubber stamp, and edicts were handed down to the state and local level.

Democratization has changed all this. Today the legislative and judicial branches routinely provide effective checks on presidential power. Since 1997, Mexico's top executive has worked with a divided Congress, which has led to slower, more incremental policymaking, as well as legislative gridlock, forcing coalition building for any legislative (not to mention constitutional) reforms.

The Supreme Court, too, has become influential. In the 1990s, President Zedillo reorganized the court in reaction to the growing probability of an opposition victory, believing that an independent court would be in the best interest of the PRI if and when it was voted out of power. Today, because of his reforms, the professionalized court provides a check on overreaching presidential power and on vested interests. In 2007, it overturned what is known as the Televisa law, which would have virtually assured the continuing duopoly of the Televisa and TV Azteca television networks by automatically renewing their licenses, giving them preferential access to new bandwidth, and limiting the president's and regulators' ability to foster competition. More recently, the Supreme Court gave regulatory agencies stronger tools to tackle powerful business interests.

Democratic opening also devolved more power to the states, increasing the autonomy and importance of Mexico's thirty-two governors. Indeed, many now see them as de facto veto players on national policy. Much of this has to do with their control over budgets. Roughly half of federal revenue is sent to the states. The executive has no discretion over these flows, fiscally empowering local politicians vis-à-vis their national counterparts. Power, too, stems from the influence they wield over the state's senators and representatives. To be sure, this transfer of power from the center limits the presidential abuses typical of the past. But many feel it also hinders democratic deepening, with some of the less electorally competitive states becoming the last bastions of authoritarianism.

Finally, Mexico's unusual no-reelection laws significantly shape politics and political parties. Instituted nearly a century ago in the aftermath of the Mexican Revolution, the laws hold that no elected official, from the president down to the local city council member or mayor, can remain in his or her office beyond one term. Perhaps designed to limit the control of *caudillos*, or strongmen, this legislation makes politicians more dependent on party bosses, who will nominate them for the next post, and less accountable to voters, who will not get the opportunity to vote for them again.

Since democratization, many prominent scholars and commentators have pushed for political reforms, including enabling reelection, allowing independent candidates to run for office, permitting ordinary Mexicans to propose bills, and reducing or eliminating the *plurinominales* in Congress (seats assigned not by direct vote but by the proportional percentage of votes that each political party receives). Many of these changes have merit, but they also run against the interest of powerful party leaders, diminishing their chances for success. And even these changes will not be a panacea for Mexico's democratic challenges.

EDUCATION AND DEMOGRAPHY

Mexico has done a good job of getting children into school and enticing them to stay there longer. In 1950, only one million Mexicans were enrolled in school; by 2000, thirty million were. Primary education enrollment has advanced the most dramatically, to almost universal attendance. But work remains to be done, especially at the secondary and high school levels, where Mexico falls behind its peers. The World Bank reports that only 75 percent of Mexicans of secondary school age (grades seven through nine), are enrolled. Just 30 percent will graduate from high school (grades nine through twelve). Mexicanos Primero, a Mexican nonprofit dedicated to improving the country's education system, notes that fewer than half of these high school graduates (13 percent of all students this age), will continue directly on to study at a university (although others will return later, bringing the total percentage of Mexicans with a university degree to just under 30 percent, a large improvement from just 1 percent in 1950). Some 2 to 3 percent of Mexican university graduates will continue on to postgraduate work.

Another question today is the quality of the education. Mexico ranks at the bottom of the OECD in terms of test scores, again outpaced by other emerging economies such as Chile, South Korea, and China. Part of the problem is the teachers' union. More than one million strong, it has proved better at protecting teachers than students. There is anecdotal evidence of schools selling teacher posts to the highest bidder, and the secretary of education has admitted that the government often does not even know how many teachers are assigned to a school, much less whether they show up. This issue is in many ways part of the PRI's legacy, which built up the politically strong union. It is also now part of the democratic dynamic. The teachers' union's political party, PANAL, delivers roughly 3 percent of the general vote, giving it the ability to swing what have recently been close presidential and legislative elections. As a result, few politicians outwardly challenge this power base.

In response to this political stalemate, Mexico has seen a rise in private schools at all economic levels, attesting to parents' ambitions and desires for their children. By some estimates, roughly 10 percent of all Mexican children are in private schools. At the university level, more than half of the institutions are now private. Real challenges remain for the education sector, but the opportunities for average Mexican children have improved.

Demography has helped. Whereas forty years ago Mexican families had on average six children, today it is closer to two. This is due to increasing education (especially for girls); more women entering the workplace; and, since the 1970s, widespread family-planning initiatives. Combined with rising incomes, smaller families can invest more in their children's future through education.

Mexico's current demography could also boost economic development, though the country has yet to really take advantage of its so-called demographic bonus, a period when workers outnumber dependents (those either retired or not yet in the labor force). This is an important time for economies because the workforce boom can enhance the productive capacity of the population, increase savings and investment, and lead to rapid growth.

This is a potentially auspicious time for Mexico, but the country needs to grow rich before it grows old. And the window is closing fast: Mexico's projected demographic bonus will peak in 2025. To take advantage and become a democratic and economic leader, Mexico needs to reform many sectors of its economy; implement labor, energy, and fiscal reforms; and expand financing, increase competition, and take on the corruption that permeates economic, political, and daily social life. Mexico has consolidated many political and economic gains, but it now needs to address this unfinished business.

Mexico will also need to keep its workers at home. Mexican immigration to the United States is a centuries-old phenomenon, but over the past thirty years it has reached unprecedented levels. The Mexicans who have gone north have sent hundreds of billions of dollars back in remittances, helping millions of Mexican families pay for education, medical treatment, and household expenses, and stimulating local economies at the same time. But Mexico has also suffered from the loss of its risk-takers and entrepreneurs, as well as its most educated: nearly 17 percent of all its college graduates and 50 percent of all Mexicans with PhDs live north of the border. The challenge for Mexico is to create opportunities for these citizens at home, and thus to make the most of their skills and energy.

CONCLUSION

Mexico benefited from a protracted transition to democracy. The gradual opening allowed for a steady strengthening of Mexico's democratic institutions and a peaceful power shift in 2000. Electoral legitimacy, which had been a powerful tool in maintaining the authoritarian regime for decades, also provided a space for the opposition—political parties and civil society organizations—to successfully push open the system.

Mexico's economy has also benefited from a relatively slow opening. The reforms of the 1980s and 1990s, cemented with NAFTA, accelerated trade and brought billions of dollars in foreign direct investment. These steps helped transform Mexico from a closed, commodity-based economy to a diversified and mature one based on manufacturing and services. As Mexico benefited from proximity to and preferential treatment by the largest economy in the world, per capita incomes rose substantially, poverty and inequality fell, and millions of Mexicans entered the middle class.

But the slow pace and tight control of the dual transitions also left less positive legacies. Politically, these included entrenched patronage systems, less-than-accountable politicians and political parties, and a relatively weak civil society. The country remains weighed down by the legacy of no reelection, which gives politicians the incentive to be responsive to their parties first and their constituencies second. Mexico's democratic challenges today show that though clean elections are necessary, they are far from sufficient. And while many scholars and politicians alike have pushed for change, their proposed reforms run up against strong interest groups and shifting administrations. Added to this is the more recent security challenge. Spiraling violence has exposed and overwhelmed Mexico's weak law enforcement and judicial institutions, also legacies of the PRI's seventy-year rule.

Economically, the process of opening left many sectors in the hands of a privileged few. This has raised operational costs for Mexican businesses, as basic inputs—electricity, communications, raw materials, and the like—are more costly and often less available than in other emerging markets. The economic concentration has also stifled entrepreneurship, leaving little room for new ideas or more agile operations. The relatively limited business credit available in the economy accentuates the hurdles for those not part of the privileged economic circle. In the aggregate, these barriers hamper productivity and ultimately the overall competitiveness of Mexico's economy.

What Mexico's experience shows is that transitions to democracy and open economies are not over when the executive or legislative branch changes hands, or when tariffs fall. Much more is needed to consolidate both and to erode the hold of remaining authoritarian legacies and vested economic interests. Mexico, like so many emerging nations, is a work in progress. The initial transitions successfully changed both the political and economic structures in the country. But much still needs to be done to ensure that what Mexico has achieved does not erode, and that it continues to move forward, consolidating and expanding on the democratic and economic gains of the past three decades.

MEXICO TIMELINE

1929: National Revolutionary Party Established, Becomes Institutional Revolutionary Party (PRI)

The National Revolutionary Party is formed in 1929 to bring together competing leaders from the Mexican Revolution. In 1938, the party is renamed the Mexican Revolutionary Party; in 1946, it becomes the Institutional Revolutionary Party (PRI). Throughout the rest of the century, all Mexican presidents and most elected officials belong to the PRI.

1976: Cantarell Oil Field Discovered

A massive oil field that comes to be called Cantarell is discovered offshore. Oil becomes one of Mexico's major exports, although its importance later declines (it now makes up less than 20 percent of total exports). Oil revenue continues to remain vital for the federal budget, however, accounting for nearly a third of federal funds.

1982: Mexico Sparks Latin American Debt Crisis

In the context of a global economic downturn, Mexico's mounting foreign debt obligations effectively bankrupt the government in the early 1980s. In August 1982, Mexico stops payments on its debt, setting off what becomes known as the Latin American debt crisis. GDP per capita plunges from about $4,200 in 1981 to about $3,000 in 1982. The debt crisis and the ensuing "lost decade" of limited economic growth throw millions of Mexicans into poverty and create political uncertainty, setting the stage for the political opposition and civil society to press for free and transparent elections.

1988: Electoral Challenge to the PRI

In 1988, an amalgamation of disaffected PRI members, leftist parties, and social organizations form a loose alliance called the National Democratic Front to challenge the PRI regime. They support Cuauhtemoc Cardenas, a former PRI politician, in a bid for the presidency. PRI candidate Carlos Salinas de Gortari wins the July 6 presidential election. However, reports of irregularities lead many to believe that Cardenas actually won. Cardenas supporters initially protest the results, but with Cardenas uneasy about confronting the PRI and the party putting the government's weight behind its candidate, the protestors retreat, leaving Salinas firmly in control.

1989: National Action Party (PAN) Wins Gubernatorial Race

The conservative PAN wins a governor's race in June. Seeking to placate (and further divide) the democratic opposition, President Salinas recognizes the PAN's victory, marking the first gubernatorial defeat in the PRI's six-decade rule. Salinas also passes a 1990 electoral reform, creating the Federal Electoral Institute to organize and manage elections. Although initially designed to maintain PRI control, and thus quite limited in its reach, this institution is transformed by subsequent reforms and developments into an autonomous and fairly powerful tool for political opening.

1994: Chiapas Uprising

The PRI's neglect of citizens outside its main interest groups is countrywide, but the more isolated and indigenous south feels it most acutely. This frustration helps foment the popular discontent that culminates in the Zapatista uprising in the southern state of Chiapas in 1994.

1994: NAFTA and Peso Crisis Push Economic Opening

NAFTA, a landmark agreement that creates a free trade bloc of the United States, Mexico, and Canada, enters into force on January 1. Later in the year, Mexico experiences a peso crisis when poor economic choices, overspending, and dwindling international reserves force a devaluation of the currency and initiate a severe recession. The peso crisis, however, also pushes Mexico's economy open further, encouraging foreign investment. Over the following decade, Mexico's trade booms. These developments, along with other reforms in the 1980s and 1990s, help transform Mexico from a closed, commodity-based economy to a diversified one based on manufacturing and services.

1997: PRI Loses Majority in Congress

In the July 6 election, the PRI loses its majority in the Chamber of Deputies, the lower house of Mexico's Congress, for the first time. The shift comes from the disillusionment of many voters after the peso crisis, as well as various electoral law reforms passed by President Ernesto Zedillo of the PRI that make electoral manipulations increasingly difficult. These reforms also cemented the electoral court's independence from the executive branch, mandated public financing for all political parties, and established citizen leadership at the helm of the Federal Electoral Institute.

2000: Fox Wins Presidency, Ending PRI Control

The PRI loses control of the executive branch for the first time in seventy-one years as Vicente Fox, leader of the conservative National Action Party, wins the July 2 presidential election.

2002: Social Safety Net Expanded

Oportunidades, a social protection program originally launched as Progresa under President Zedillo in 1997, is greatly expanded under President Fox starting in 2002. It provides monthly stipends to low-income households that keep their children healthy and in school. From three hundred thousand recipients in 1997, the program has extended to nearly six million families—or about a quarter of the population. Also in 2002, the Fox government starts Seguro Popular, a national health insurance program designed to reach the country's informal and unemployed workers. By the end of 2011 the program covers some forty-four million previously uninsured Mexicans. This social spending, as well as overall economic growth, reduces poverty and inequality and bolsters Mexico's emerging middle class. Recent surveys show that less than 50 percent of the population is defined as poor today, down from a poverty rate of nearly 70 percent in the mid-1990s. GDP per capita has increased steadily from $3,500 in 1990 to $10,000 in 2011.

2006: Calderon Elected President, Intensifies War on Drugs

President Felipe Calderon, inaugurated in December, quickly intensifies a campaign to combat violence related to Mexico's extensive drug trade. Gruesome headlines attest to rising and spreading violence, fueled by the U.S. market for illegal drugs and an overall culture of impunity. During Calderon's term, there are some seventy thousand drug-related killings, with other crimes also escalating. Mexico's weak rule of law contributes to the problem; only four thousand out of twenty thousand homicides in 2010 result in a conviction.

2012: PRI Candidate Elected President

PRI candidate Enrique Pena Nieto handily defeats two rivals in the presidential election on July 1, ending twelve years of PAN rule and retaking the presidency for the PRI. Pena Nieto takes office in December 2012. Though some worry about the return of the PRI, the widespread recognition of competitive free and fair elections is generally seen as a sign of Mexico's deepening democracy.

Brazil

Carlos Pio

During much of the twentieth century, Brazil alternated between quasi-representative government and authoritarianism. It was governed by a constitutional monarchy from its independence in 1822 until the founding of the republic in 1889 by a military coup. The country's nominal democracy (only a small percentage of the population could vote) of 1889 through 1930 ended with a coup that put Getulio Vargas in power. Fifteen years later, Vargas's dictatorship gave way to another period of democracy, between 1945 and 1964, this time more robust. That, in turn, ended with the military dictatorship of 1964 through 1985. Since the country's transition to civilian rule in 1985, Brazil has experienced an increasingly vigorous democracy, combined over the past decade with strong economic growth and greater socioeconomic inclusion.

Beginning in the 1930s, Brazil's governments pursued policies of industrialization. Under democracy as well as authoritarianism, Brazil made import substitution industrialization (ISI) its cornerstone economic policy until the late 1980s. The government promoted domestic manufacturing and industrial growth through state-owned enterprises (SOEs); significant investment in infrastructure; and special incentives to favored private companies in chosen industries, including subsidized credit, tax discounts, and protection from domestic competition and imports via licensing requirements and prohibitive tariffs. For urban workers in the formal manufacturing and public sectors, the state provided a strong social safety net, protective labor legislation, state-financed pensions, subsidized housing, and state-funded health care. These social protections were not generalized, but were instead provided on a case-by-case basis as the result of political bargains with the strongest trade unions in exchange for votes—a so-called corporatist arrangement.

For forty years, this strategy delivered strong, if uneven, economic benefits. The country went from a rural society ruled by a coalition of agrarian groups from the southeastern states to a complex political system and economy consisting of roughly 65 percent services, 25 percent manufacturing, and less than 10 percent agriculture. Relatively inclusive economic growth during this period generated support for ISI among influential constituencies and acquiescence to authoritarian rule. An alliance including business groups, trade unions, and the emerging middle class of public sector workers and liberal professionals supported the state's economic modernization policies and the rise of a semiautonomous technocratic elite to rule at the discretion of military or civilian leaders.

Brazil's economy performed relatively well between the mid-1950s and the mid-1970s, but only through a reliance on large coffee export revenues, a growing internal market, lax monetary and fiscal policies, and rising external debt. Indeed, ISI imposed a heavy fiscal burden on the Brazilian state. Brazil attempted to address its budget restrictions by printing money and assuming foreign debt; it also tried to avoid current account deficits by restricting imports. Both approaches proved to be roads to nowhere. Increasingly regressive taxation harmed the living standards of the politically powerless poor, particularly in rural areas, where labor protections and social policies were almost nonexistent before 1988. Loose monetary policies inevitably prompted inflation, hurting the very poor, and caused Brazil's currency, which was pegged to the dollar, to become overvalued. This combination of high taxation, appreciation of the real exchange rate, and protectionism created a significant anti-export bias, which caused a recurring balance-of-payments challenge. Financial insolvency became almost inevitable.

A severe external debt crisis, triggered by the second global oil crisis of 1978–79, was the immediate catalyst of Brazil's democratic opening. The country's external debt had soared from $5.3 billion in 1972 to $31 billion in 1978 as international banks, eager to recycle the petrodollars they accumulated after the 1973–74 oil shock, lent to Brazil at low but variable interest rates. When global interest rates increased suddenly and steeply after 1979 following the U.S. reaction to the second oil shock, higher interest rates led to an automatic increase in the service on Brazil's external debt and an increase in the principal every time the country failed to come up with the full payment. At the same time, the government's ability to service the foreign debt shrank as a result of deficits in the trade account for most of the 1970s. Unable to pay international creditors and facing rising inflation, Brazil's military rulers were forced to negotiate a stabilization package with the International

Monetary Fund (IMF) to prevent insolvency. Between 1979 and 1983, restrictive fiscal and monetary policies, mandated by the IMF, plunged the country into recession, provoking widespread social and political turmoil and profoundly damaging the economic performance rationale on which authoritarian rule was built.

The military did not respond to these social and political mobilizations with aggressive moves to retain power. As the economic crisis deepened, congressional elections, which had been held at regular intervals throughout the military dictatorship, laid the groundwork for the opposition party's eventual triumph at the ballot box and a transition to a vibrant and robust democracy. In short, Brazil's longtime economic strategies, although initially delivering strong growth that, to some, justified political repression during the military dictatorship, sowed the seeds of economic crisis and the military's resulting handover of power.

Brazil's transition to democracy, initiated by the military in 1979, proved a gradual, reasonably peaceful, and steady process. This outcome, however, was by no means a given. Many doubted that democracy could deliver better living standards than military rule. Brazil's earlier experiences with democracy had notoriously failed to foster political stability. Moreover, democratic periods had seen little progress on social and economic rights; autocrats had been more successful in distributing social entitlements. Consequently, when the transition began, important segments of the elite did not believe in the intrinsic advantages of democracy and defended the economic and social records of the Vargas dictatorship and the military regime.

INFLECTION POINTS
OF THE TRANSITION PERIOD

Five essential turning points marked Brazil's democratic transition. First, declining economic performance in 1978 and 1979 sparked waves of political and social mobilizations and triggered macroeconomic structural adjustment policies to satisfy international creditors. These policies, in turn, exacerbated the recession and generated widespread economic dislocation, fueling social turmoil in Brazil's major cities throughout 1982 and 1983. Second, and at the same time, the successful electoral performance of the opposition in state and national elections in 1982 consolidated and legitimized opposition forces. Third, internal fights led a group of regional bosses of the ruling party to formally dissent and support the opposition candidate in the run-up to the 1985 presidential election. Fourth, the successful 1992 impeachment of President Fernando Collor signaled the new regime's stability and resilience. And, fifth, the 2003 inauguration of President Luiz Inacio Lula da Silva brought Brazil into the current era.

The inauguration of General Ernesto Geisel as Brazil's president in 1974 marked the end of the most violent and repressive phase of the military dictatorship. Geisel was a soft-liner in the Brazilian army who, in the late 1960s, had resisted the most brutal impulses of the new authoritarian regime. Following Geisel's ascension to power, the state began to loosen its tight grip on the political process, and particularly on the press.

The economic and financial crisis of 1979 that followed the second global oil shock damaged the image of the military as a competent organization capable of steering economic growth better than civilian politicians under democratic rule, and undermined the trade-off of repression for economic growth. Brazil's economy staggered under an external debt crisis, the rapid depletion of international reserves, and spiraling inflation. A 30 percent devaluation of the currency mandated by the government to counter this debt and currency crisis by boosting exports made a bad situation even worse. As a result of the ensuing harsh economic conditions, a wave of social mobilizations blossomed in the nation's manufacturing heartland near Sao Paulo. A new political faction took control of the trade unions and began to organize strikes and mass gatherings, refusing to play ball within the old corporatist structure.

Under these circumstances, the military began Brazil's democratic transition in 1979 as a gradual process of liberalization. The generals expected that this would advance in a controlled way toward an increasingly open electoral competition between the party that supported the regime, the National Renovating Alliance (ARENA), and the permitted opposition, the Brazilian Democratic Movement (MDB). In anticipation of some type of transition, military leaders had Congress pass the 1979 Amnesty Law, which granted a full pardon for all actions committed on duty by the military, as well as by the civilian protesters. They also liberalized laws governing elections and parties in 1981, allowing for the creation of three new parties, and instituted direct elections for state governors in 1982 and for executives of large cities and state capitals in 1985.

The regime came under further pressure in the second half of 1982 when faced with a sudden halt in international financing. International interest rates had already climbed sharply as the United States and Europe moved to tame their own inflation through monetary contraction. Mexico then defaulted on its external payments, roiling international financial markets. Brazil's only alternative to default was a loan from the IMF. The loan was conditioned on the adoption of an orthodox stabilization program, including devaluations of the currency, high interest rates, and fiscal consolidation (higher revenues plus spending cuts). But the peculiar indexation of contracts in the Brazilian economy automatically transformed the IMF-mandated devaluations into inflation. As the devaluations increased prices of energy and food imports, they also increased production costs for finished goods and the overall cost of living. This painful period of stagflation threw economic production into disarray, provoked social turmoil, and further undermined support for the official military party.

The opposition party won a surprisingly big victory in the 1982 elections for Congress and for state governors. It captured 42 percent of seats in the House of Representatives and 40 percent in the Senate, and elected nine of twenty-two governors. That the military did not interfere with these results seems to indicate that it was resigned to restoring civilian order—not necessarily in the 1985 presidential election, as ultimately occurred, but certainly in the early 1990s.

In 1983 and 1984, continued economic malaise and rising social discontent swelled the previous wave of political protests into a tsunami, and peaceful mass demonstrations in favor of direct presidential elections swept the country. This intense discontent with the economy and agitation for democracy led the military establishment to adopt a hands-off approach in the nomination of the ruling party's candidate for the 1985 election. The final overthrow of the dictatorship with the victory of the opposition candidate, in January 1985, resulted from a surprising sequence of events over the second half of 1984. In reaction to the selection of a divisive businessman-turned-politician as the regime party's candidate, important regional bosses and longtime supporters of the authoritarian regime abandoned the party and sponsored the opposition candidate, Tancredo Neves. Even former president Geisel and incumbent vice president Aureliano Chaves encouraged Neves. At the time, Neves was the elected governor of Minas Gerais, a critical state, and an experienced politician who was fully trusted by the military.

This development turned the (indirect) election from an almost certain triumph for the regime into a surprising victory for Neves. However, Neves fell ill before his inauguration and died in April, never serving a day of his term. Ironically, this made Jose Sarney, the vice president and former leader of the pro-military ARENA party, Brazil's first civilian president since 1964. During his presidency, Sarney worked hard to consolidate democratic practices, respecting all demands advanced by the opposition MDB throughout the dictatorial period. He immediately opened the party system, called a constitutional assembly to write a new constitution, and liberalized controls over trade unions. In the presidential elections of 1989, in which Sarney was ineligible to seek reelection, he neither supported any candidate nor tried to interfere. Fernando Collor, a conservative politician running on an anticorruption platform, beat Lula da Silva by a margin of 53 to 47 percent in a runoff vote.

The 1992 impeachment of President Collor, together with the 2003 inauguration of President Lula, signaled the consolidation of Brazil's new democracy. Collor's impeachment was based on a combination of corruption allegations and a fragile support base in Congress. Collor's campaign treasurer was accused of selling his privileged influence over top officials to firms interested in obtaining government contracts, and of paying personal expenses for both the president and first lady. In September 1992, after a wave of popular mobilizations led by left-wing parties and the Union of College Students, Brazil's House of Representatives agreed by a vote of 441 to 38 that the Senate should start formal impeachment hearings. President Collor was then suspended from the presidency for 180 days. He would never return. Instead, he resigned from the presidency on December 29, the last day of the Senate proceedings, trying to avoid a formal impeachment vote, but the Senate voted for the impeachment anyway. Throughout the investigation and impeachment, only minor allegations of irregularities were lodged, and the federal police fully cooperated to provide all the information requested. Finally, and most important, the military did not threaten to intervene.

The period between Collor's impeachment and Lula's inauguration was economically difficult but politically calm. Vice President Itamar Franco finished Collor's term. Under Franco, Fernando Henrique Cardoso became finance minister and implemented an effective structural adjustment policy. The success of this so-called Real Plan catapulted him to the presidency after he beat Lula in the first round of the vote in 1994. He was reelected in 1998. As president, Cardoso sponsored a constitutional amendment that allowed all incumbents to run for reelection once; he also instituted a civilian-run Ministry of Defense in charge of military affairs. At the end of his tenure, he backed his party's candidate but did not meddle with the electoral process. When Lula won the 2002 race in the midst of an acute confidence crisis that led to a 60 percent devaluation of the (floating) currency in ten months, President Cardoso helped smooth the transition. In the forty days before Lula's inauguration, his top economic advisers were allowed to participate in high-level decision-making.

Lula's inauguration culminated Brazil's two-decade transition to democratic rule. Lula had been a leading political agitator throughout the transition, initially as a union leader and later as the Workers' Party candidate in all presidential elections since 1989. He had also opposed many of the major economic and social reforms implemented since 1990 and had threatened to reverse some of them—mainly the privatization of SOEs and the rescheduling of external debt. In the run-up to the 2002 vote, Lula built a broad electoral coalition in an effort to avoid a fourth defeat, including choosing a conservative vice presidential candidate. Six months before the vote, Lula's campaign released a formal letter committing to macroeconomic stability and, most important, to honor all existing contracts signed by previous administrations.

LESSONS OF THE TRANSITION PERIOD

SOCIOECONOMIC EXCLUSION AND INCLUSION

As Brazil transitioned to a more democratic society, it moved away from corporatist social protections for the politically powerful and toward a mix of universal safety nets and targeted income distribution schemes. This reinforced support for the democratic transition among the poor by providing palpable benefits to previously marginalized groups.

Until 1988, the bulk of social policies benefited only the families of urban, unionized workers under formal employment contracts. This made workers in some sectors vastly better off than others. Benefits were the product of direct political bargaining between government officials and politicians on the one hand and leaders of powerful trade unions on the other. Health care, pensions, and housing were provided to specific segments of the urban workforce, the quality and generosity depending on each segment's political strength. At the same time, the labor code required firms to grant unionized workers a series of benefits: a forty-four-hour workweek, premium payment for work exceeding eight hours per day, one premium salary a year (called the thirteenth wage), thirty days' paid vacation, and a vacation premium. The extra cost imposed by these requirements, equivalent to 105 percent of the wage paid to the worker, caused firms to resist formal employment contracts, thereby reducing workers' access to legislated social benefits. Thus, social protection never reached more than 70 percent of the workforce.

This all changed with the adoption of a new democratic constitution in 1988. The new constitution universalized access to the existing (corporatist) network of hospitals and health facilities. To fulfill the promise of universal education, it also imposed on states and municipalities minimum spending requirements for primary education.

Likewise, starting in 1995, Brazil's maturing democratic government adopted a series of targeted social spending policies (see Figure 4) called conditional cash transfers (CCTs). Targeted at the poorest families, CCTs were first used to encourage them to enroll their children in schools and maintain attendance. This new approach to income distribution was introduced in 1995 at the local level, in the city of Campinas, and gradually adopted by the Cardoso administration. Soon CCTs were also used to encourage pregnant women to seek prenatal care. In 1996, the federal government launched a CCT program specially designed to reduce child labor; by 2000, the program covered four hundred thousand vulnerable children. Expanding these efforts in 2001, the Cardoso administration launched Bolsa Escola Federal (school stipend), Bolsa Alimentacao (food stipend), and Vale Gas (cooking gas stipend), all targeting the poorest families. After 2003, President Lula unified all such programs under the brand Bolsa Familia (family stipend) and significantly expanded its coverage until it reached twelve million families.

In short, the adoption of a mix of universal safety nets and targeted income distribution schemes effectively extended social protection to rural and non-unionized sectors of the workforce that had been long excluded. Perhaps the biggest impact was on Brazil's black population. More than a hundred years after the end of slavery, 61 percent of Brazil's poor today are blacks, yet they make up less than 10 percent of the population. In 2003, 43 percent of all blacks were poor, versus

FIGURE 4: POVERTY AND SOCIAL SPENDING IN BRAZIL

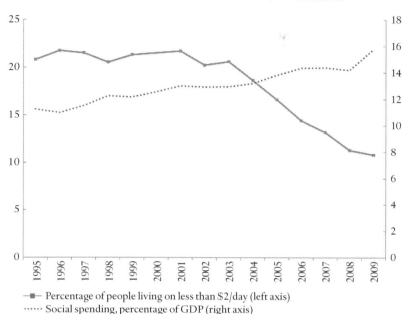

—■— Percentage of people living on less than $2/day (left axis)

······ Social spending, percentage of GDP (right axis)

Sources: Brazilian Instituto de Pesquisa Econômica Aplicada (Ipea) publication *15 Anos de Gasto Social Federal Notos Sobre o Período de 1995 a 2009*, http://bit.ly/ntpifc (social spending data); World Bank (poverty data: purchasing power parity, 2005 international dollars).

20 percent of whites. Politically, too, blacks were long excluded. They were completely shut out from political participation until slavery was abolished in 1888 and mostly excluded thereafter because, starting in 1891, the right to vote was denied to illiterates. At the same time, black children's access to schools was long delayed due to poorly functioning public education and the need for poor families to send their children to work. The move toward universal social protection expanded health, education, and other benefits to include black Brazilians and other disadvantaged groups, and today blacks are the heaviest users of both public education and public health systems.

Beyond targeted policies, social inclusion also increased in the wake of pro-market reforms introduced in the 1990s. First, the move away from ISI policies benefited Brazilian consumers in general, and especially boosted the living standards of the lower-middle classes and the poor. Trade liberalization directly increased their purchasing power by cutting red tape and reducing tariffs on most imported items, from food and medicine to fertilizers, footwear, consumer goods, and technologies. At the same time, stronger competition from abroad encouraged businesses to cut prices, reduce production costs, and increase productivity.

Second, as firms were exposed to global competition, they moved away from the more industrialized southeastern states, particularly Sao Paulo, and into the countryside, where production and labor costs were lower. This spread the benefits of employment to the rural poor and increased demand for lower-skilled workers. In addition, local tax collection rose in small and mid-sized municipalities, making possible social spending that further benefited the poor.

ECONOMIC STRUCTURE AND POLICIES

The end of military rule was precipitated in large part by a deep structural economic crisis—a legacy that also created significant challenges for the incoming civilian governments as they attempted to promote economic growth and social inclusion simultaneously. ISI brought on a hangover of high and intractable inflation, a huge external debt, stifling rules and procedures, and minimal funds to spend on more inclusive social policies. The need to generate positive economic and social outcomes—either to strengthen support for democracy overall or for electoral reasons—initially motivated several failed attempts by new civilian administrations to fight inflation without reducing government spending.

The first of these attempts was the 1986 Cruzado Plan, which tried to curtail inflation without addressing its underlying structural causes. Based on wage and price freezes and the adoption of a new currency, it began with astounding success: the economy grew swiftly as aggregate demand boomed, poverty levels fell significantly, and the popularity of the president (and of the new democratic regime) skyrocketed. But soon the core inconsistencies of the strategy made a bad situation worse. Rising demand increased the bargaining power of trade unions, pushing production costs up. To bypass strict price controls, firms developed innovative strategies, such as making minor changes to product designs to escape controls and charge higher prices. Even with price controls, inflation took hold.

The consumption euphoria triggered by the Cruzado Plan led the incumbent party to a significant victory in the 1986 elections for

Congress, the Constitutional Assembly, and state governors. As a result, the plan was widely viewed by later politicians as an attractive strategy to simultaneously fight inflation and promote social inclusion. Its disastrous longer-term consequences—ever-higher inflation, disrupted production chains, and current account imbalances—were ignored. The appealing illusion that inflation could be controlled by government decree was repeatedly indulged in 1988, 1990, and 1991. Indeed, following the return to civilian rule, Brazil changed its currency five times. After each round of wage and price controls, overall inflation rose even more sharply, going from 200 percent at the start of the transition period in 1985 to more than 2,000 percent in 1993, on the eve of the adoption of the Real Plan, Brazil's most successful stabilization attempt to date.

Fernando Henrique Cardoso, appointed finance minister in 1993, put in place a team to design and implement more sound economic ideas in the Real Plan. The plan differed from all previous attempts to curb inflation. First, it was launched after the Collor administration had already begun to implement market-oriented reforms. Restrictions on imports had been significantly relaxed, Congress had passed a privatization law, and the exchange rate regime had been partially liberalized. Therefore, the structural basis for an anti-inflation program differed radically from the one that had existed. Second, Cardoso piloted a two-step process of currency replacement to get rid of core inflation created by wage and contract indexation, which had undermined the previous stabilization attempts. Third, the economic team that designed the Real Plan knew it needed to overcome politicians' natural resistance to required budget cuts. Therefore, in contrast to previous stabilization attempts, the team insisted that the government drastically reduce spending before launching the less orthodox program to de-index contracts. This meant that inflationary pressures were partially subdued before the less orthodox, and more politically appealing, phase of the program occurred.

Overall, the market-oriented reforms launched and implemented between 1990 and 2002 were a fundamental departure from Brazil's ISI development model. The economists and politicians who pushed in this direction understood the structural requirements for long-term economic growth in the post–Cold War era of global capitalism, democratic government, and increasing demands for poverty alleviation and social inclusion. The linchpin of the strategy was not simply to withdraw the state from its previous role of directly steering the private economy;

especially after 1994, it was also to empower new agencies and regulatory bodies so that the goal of socially inclusive growth could be realized.

President Lula's inauguration in 2003 marked the consolidation of Brazil's new economic strategy to promote sustained and inclusive growth. Previously fierce critics of both the Real Plan and the Collor and Cardoso market-oriented reforms, Lula and his Workers' Party begrudgingly accepted most of these reforms once elected. Lula had been forced to build a diverse electoral coalition to win power and needed to keep this coalition together to govern. He therefore broadly maintained the economic course established during the 1990s. He left the Central Bank relatively free to set interest rates in accordance with inflation targets and to sustain a floating exchange rate regime. He also kept fiscal balance as a central policy commitment. At the same time, as discussed, he worked to expand targeted income distribution schemes, universalize social safety nets, and invest in health and education for the poor.

Taken together, the commitment to both macroeconomic stability and socially inclusive spending and development priorities laid the foundation for Brazil's sustained growth trajectory over the past decade. This moderation in Lula's agenda had naturally evolved as his Workers' Party gained administrative experience, particularly in rich and politically complex states and municipalities. Moderation was also imposed on the Lula administration by two external forces: the crisis of confidence that threatened to wreak havoc as the currency declined during the 2002 presidential campaign, and the necessity of forming a congressional majority that included centrist and right-wing parties. Lula's cabinet and policy choices reflected those conditions.

In sum, the structural changes implemented after 1990 were fundamental to stimulating strong macroeconomic growth and creating economic opportunities that have benefited the poor, both as workers and as consumers, and increased their satisfaction with democratic governance. Nevertheless, structural obstacles to sustained economic growth and social inclusion still abound.

CIVIL SOCIETY AND MEDIA

Throughout the authoritarian period, a few international civil society organizations played important roles in denouncing violations of human rights, attempting to minimize them, and championing the reinstatement of democratic rule. As early as 1969, Amnesty

International denounced torture in Brazil, and, the following year, the Vatican's Pontifical Commission for Justice and Peace solemnly condemned "deplorable violations of human rights" taking place in Brazil. During a period marked by severe limitations in international communications and travel, networks of human rights activists were hard to form and operate within the country. Despite such difficulties, domestic human rights activists were occasionally able to gather sensitive information regarding political repression and the mistreatment of political prisoners and distribute it outside the country via informal networks. The media in the United States, France, and the United Kingdom were instrumental.

The Catholic Church, the Brazilian Bar Association, and the Brazilian Press Association were the most active civil society organizations in Brazil until the end of the 1970s. The church in particular could draw on a vast web of connections to exchange information and personnel between remote areas of the Brazilian territory and the outside world. However, the church had also been deeply divided since the 1960s between those who favored and those who opposed military rule. During the early 1970s, as the authoritarian regime grew more repressive and violent, the church gradually assumed a leading role in denouncing human rights violations and directly negotiating with the military for the release of political prisoners. After 1978, the Diocese of Sao Paulo set up Brasil: Nunca Mais (Brazil: Never Again), a research group that specialized in tracking and cataloging civil rights violations disclosed in official documents.

Journalists fought for the right to report on cases involving political repression and abuses perpetrated by the military, and distinguished lawyers increasingly defended political prisoners in military courts. Like the church, the Brazilian Bar Association had been divided among supporters and opponents of the military regime, but it gradually grew strongly supportive of the restoration of civil and political liberties, particularly the reinstatement of habeas data and habeas corpus rights. These organizations were small in structure and membership, but some of their leaders were well-known and respected, either locally or nationally, and so could leverage their public stature and the perceived legitimacy of their cause to exercise significant influence.

Trade unions were also active in Brazil's democratic transition. As a direct consequence of the difficult economic conditions following the second oil shock, social mobilizations blossomed in the nation's manufacturing heartland of Sao Paulo beginning in 1979. Starting in the metalworkers' union, a new political faction began to organize strikes and mass gatherings in favor of loosening rigid labor codes and the long-standing submission of unions to state controls. In 1982, this new faction created the Workers' Party and an independent trade union, which became essential players in the transition process. They were instrumental in organizing the mass rallies in 1984 calling for direct presidential elections. The independent union grew steadily to become the most powerful labor association in Brazil, benefiting immensely from the upsurge in public sector unionization that followed the establishment of union protections in the 1988 constitution. With President Lula's election in 2002 at the head of the Workers' Party, the movement's leaders ascended to Congress or to cabinet positions in the administration, boosting their influence but weakening the organization's independence from the state.

The Movement of Landless Workers (MST), created to push for radical agrarian land reform, followed a similar trajectory. At one point, MST units across Brazil peacefully occupied both private farmland and government grounds. The movement gained more adherents and legitimacy as the occupations succeeded in accelerating agrarian reform; it also expanded its political influence by denouncing "the system" and its coercive apparatus when forced to abandon occupied land or public buildings. It is essential to note, though, that despite its disrespect for private property and disobedience of court rulings, MST never embraced violent or armed resistance.

Left-wing parties used associations of college students, mainly in state-run universities, as leadership recruitment and training grounds. The primary association of college students, Uniao Nacional dos Estudantes (UNE), was instrumental in gathering the support of middle- and upper-class college students and their families for the mass demonstrations against President Collor, which led to his impeachment in 1992. After President Lula's election, UNE became an instrumental arm to increase support for the administration among urban youth.

Media outlets, which had been put under strict political surveillance during the 1970s, were allowed to report somewhat freely on the wave of trade union activism that exploded in Sao Paulo state. Intense media coverage spread information about the growing anger with the regime and its policies. In 1984, the media were also partially free to report on the internal struggle that led to the pivotal defection of senior ruling party figures to support the opposition candidate in the 1985 presidential election.

When compared with newspapers, television networks were traditionally less critical of the regime. The three largest networks had built privileged relationships with the most powerful government agencies and competed to caress the military. However, once a civilian president was installed, the entire media establishment wholeheartedly embraced the new freedoms extended to them.

Yet, contrary to expectations, the transition to democracy has not entirely delinked the media from the government. Indeed, one of the most important effects of the transition on the media was the sharp increase in the number of radio and television station licenses granted by the administration to individuals in exchange for political support in Congress. Many politicians now own stations, allowing them to manipulate media coverage. For instance, former presidents Sarney and Collor own the most important television and radio networks as well as the largest newspapers in their home states of Maranhao and Alagoas, respectively. Political bosses control a large chunk of the media in many other states as well.

LEGAL SYSTEM AND RULE OF LAW

Despite Brazil's relatively robust democratic transition, the rule of law continues to be applied inequitably, and with too little regard for due process, human rights, and the fundamental principle of equality before the law. In Brazil, justice is not blind. The country is marked by a generalized culture of impunity, which shields special categories of citizens—police and law-enforcement officers, upper-middle-class and rich individuals, and politicians—from the severity of the law. For example, Brazil's current constitution, like previous ones, holds that a citizen with an undergraduate diploma is entitled to "special, individual cells" in police stations and penitentiaries.

The judicial system is distinguished by a large circuit court of appeals, which benefits those who can pay to manipulate its many formalities to their advantage. Cases can reach the Supreme Court in any one of thirty-seven ways, from special appeals to allegations of unconstitutionality. As a result, the Supreme Court is perpetually overcrowded: for example, it issued rulings on 80,565 cases between January 2009 and June 2010. Everyone able to pay for a competent lawyer, no matter how serious the case, is able to avoid detention for many years, to speed up or slow down routine police procedures, and to influence the content of decisions by judges, especially in the lower courts.

According to Freedom House, the Brazilian "prison system is anarchic, overcrowded, and largely unfit for human habitation." According
to official estimates, Brazil's prisons hold more than 490,000 inmates,
50 percent over the system's intended capacity. Amnesty International
reports that "severe overcrowding, poor sanitary conditions, gang violence, and riots continue to blight the prison system, where ill-treatment,
including beatings and torture, are commonplace." Since Brazil has
signed the American Convention on Human Rights, the general conditions in prisons and jails have been subject to intense investigations and
censures by the Inter-American Commission on Human Rights and the
Inter-American Court of Human Rights.

Even today, torture and nonjudicial executions are practiced by
military police forces, which are the state corps responsible for civilian
crime prevention and law enforcement. The constitution establishes
a separate system for the trial of military police personnel and a military criminal law. The state military justice system has been subject to
intense criticism from nongovernmental human rights organizations
and the Inter-American Human Rights System over the years, with allegations of endemic impunity. Military court cases are often delayed for
years due to the heavy workload, the scarcity of judges and prosecutors,
and excessive red tape, among other things.

The major institutional change set forth by the 1988 constitution in
the structure of the legal system was the definition of the prosecutor's
office (Ministerio Publico) as an independent agency. Its full autonomy
from all major branches of the state—executive, legislative, and judicial—is a defining part of the structure of the Brazilian state, and the
constitution declares that it cannot be changed. The office has played
an increasingly active role in defense of many interests in society, but it
has especially tried to fight the overall culture of impunity that endures
in Brazil. Although promising, these efforts have been subject to pitfalls: there is strong criticism of an apparent tendency of prosecutors
to lead ideological crusades, which are normally in tune with left-wing
party agendas.

Finally, early in 2010, the Supreme Court upheld the 1979 Amnesty
Law in the face of domestic challenges from public prosecutors. Yet,
later that same year, the Inter-American Court of Human Rights found
that the law was not compatible with the American Convention on
Human Rights and should not be used to prevent investigations into
alleged violations committed during the military dictatorship. This
legal lacuna is still unresolved.

GOVERNMENT STRUCTURE AND DIVISION OF POWER

To understand the mechanics of the Brazilian federation, it is essential to note that Brazil was a unitary country until 1889. In that year, the founding of the republic coincided with the establishment of a federal system in which the central government shares fiscal and administrative responsibilities with states. As a result of this history, the union is quite powerful in relation to the states. Nowadays, Brazil has twenty-six states plus the Federal District. Most governors try to influence the political process at the national level to advance their state's agendas. Central issues of interest to the governors involve the allocation of the federal budget through policies that benefit particular constituencies in states competing for scarce resources. In the past two decades, and given the straitjacket imposed by Brazil's federal constitution, federalism has been increasingly expressed in the design of public policies by national agencies that take states' particularities into account. This normally involves states' accepting federal conditions on their policies in exchange for larger budget allocations.

The Brazilian Chamber of Deputies and state and local legislatures have been elected through an open-list, proportional representation system since the constitution of 1945. The electoral system encourages the proliferation of parties, several of which are based in just a few of the twenty-seven states, and more than twenty parties are currently represented in Congress. Given the large number of mid-sized parties holding seats in Congress, no Brazilian president can expect to govern effectively without building a large coalition after being elected.

This feature of the political system favors compromise over ideology. Large coalitions can promote the gradual accommodation of political and ideological differences, leading to increasing political tolerance and trust among opposing forces.

Inescapably, though, the need to build and constantly manage heterogeneous coalitions makes it harder for the party in command to honor electoral promises and even govern in a consistent way. This challenge is exacerbated because all parties are internally fractured, around either regional bosses or ideological differences, so coalitions are fundamentally collections of factions with conflicting loyalties and divergent policy priorities.

At the same time, the structural fragmentation of party membership and political representation can also lead to stalemate and confrontation—something that marked the Collor presidency and led to his impeachment once a corruption scandal during a deep recession dented his popularity.

The constitutions of 1967 and 1988 made some changes to the political system, but only on the margins.

EDUCATION AND DEMOGRAPHY

In 1997, Brazil reached 98 percent school enrollment of children aged five to fourteen, a fundamental step in increasing human capital and economic opportunities for the poor and disadvantaged—particularly for blacks and residents of neglected rural areas.

This impressive expansion of educational opportunities in the decade following the democratic transition can be attributed largely to two things: new constitutional guarantees protecting the right to education, and new federal policies and expenditures that helped translate these guarantees into widespread opportunities (see Figure 5). The 1988 constitution fixed minimum spending levels in education for all three tiers of government: municipalities were required to spend a minimum of 18 percent of their budget on education, states at least 25 percent, and the federal government no less than 18 percent. Less than a decade later, the Cardoso administration launched a new set of programs to vigorously promote universal primary enrollment. These programs provided robust financial incentives for municipal authorities to promote attendance, to adopt a minimum salary benchmark for primary school teachers (triggering substantial raises in rural areas), to invest in teacher training, to effectively assess the performance of both students and teachers, and to establish parent-teacher monitoring boards at every school. Cardoso's programs were not solely responses to domestic political pressures; they also mirrored international best-practice trends promoted by multilateral organizations like the World Bank. The combination of policy and constitutional reforms effectively catalyzed the virtual universalization of primary schooling.

Despite their potential importance for improving teachers' standards of living in the poorest areas and promoting better performance, these programs were strongly resisted by the left-leaning opposition in Congress and the teachers' trade unions at the state level. In Congress, the opposition pursued a strategy of noncooperation with the administration, demanding higher teacher pay raises and refusing to discuss

FIGURE 5. ILLITERACY AND EDUCATION SPENDING IN BRAZIL

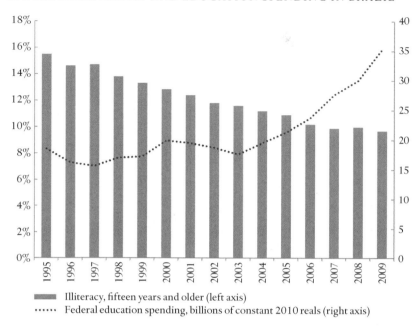

    ▭   Illiteracy, fifteen years and older (left axis)

    ······ Federal education spending, billions of constant 2010 reals (right axis)

Sources: Federal spending on education in billions of constant 2010 reals comes from the Brazilian Instituto de Pesquisa Econômica Aplicada (Ipea) publication *15 Anos de Gasto Social Federal Notos Sobre o Período de 1995 a 2009* (http://bit.ly/ntpifc). Illiteracy statistics are from the Instituto Brasileiro de Geografia e Estatística (IGBE) "Séries Estatísticas" (http://bit.ly/SRxDRO). No illiteracy data was available for 2000, so that year is an average of 1999 and 2001 data.

anything else; meanwhile, the unions questioned the utility of assessing teachers' skills and establishing national tests for students.

Although primary school enrollment has been addressed effectively, significant challenges remain in the realms of infrastructure and education quality. School infrastructure, provided by states and municipalities, varies significantly across the country and tends to be better in urban areas than in the countryside, where 6 percent of schools still lack electricity, 12 percent lack clean drinking water, and 40 percent lack adequate sanitation.

The quality of the education provided is another major problem. In 2010, Brazilian fifteen-year-olds from both private and public schools ranked fifty-third of sixty-five countries in reading and fifty-seventh of sixty-five countries in math on the Program for International Student Assessment (PISA) index of the Organization for Economic

Cooperation and Development. Throughout the twentieth century, average years of schooling among Brazil's workforce have consistently increased, but whites still have a higher average than blacks. Illiteracy, meanwhile, is almost three times higher in rural areas than in urban areas, and the rural northeastern states have the worst averages in the country. Twenty-four percent of black men are illiterate in the northeast, compared with only 9 percent in the south.

CONCLUSION

Brazil's twentieth-century transition to democracy was long and complex. It was managed by neither a single individual nor a single political group. From the start, the military establishment was deeply divided between a liberal faction, which favored a limited intervention to neutralize radical politicians and parties, and hard-line generals who favored a longer hold on power. Meanwhile, electoral competition had never been completely erased from Brazil's political landscape, although rules related to parties and elections were subjected to constant manipulation by the regime. It was not until 1982 that the system was partially liberalized.

The socioeconomic performance of the regime helped determine the course of democratic transition and consolidation. The military chiefs decided to launch and deepen the transition only when besieged by a severe financial crisis. As public discontent intensified, the military declined to interfere in the 1985 presidential election, and opposition candidate Tancredo Neves was elected with essential backing from former top supporters of the authoritarian regime. Once it had withdrawn to the barracks, the military command was reorganized, and the institution never again threatened to meddle with the political process.

The emergent Brazilian democracy struggled to tackle the steep economic crisis left behind by the military. The political transition occurred in tandem with two other processes intrinsically associated with the quality and depth of democratic politics—the launch of reforms aimed at promoting sustainable economic growth and the expansion of social and economic inclusion. In a country long marked by a feeble commitment to social, economic, and political inclusion, even relative democracy offered privileged social groups institutional mechanisms to block or delay structural reforms. It took Brazil almost a decade to accept—and then only partially—the prevailing consensus in the global financial community that a long-term solution to the crisis would require a complete reversal of the economic regulations and policies then in place. But Brazil needed not only to balance its budget and pursue market-oriented reforms. It also needed to aggressively pursue social policies to benefit the poor, who had been excluded from opportunity for decades. In sum, the implementation of politically sensitive reforms and social measures proved difficult and, despite important progress, has not been fully accomplished.

Brazil's democratic transition suffered from many delays and pitfalls; at times, implementing reforms that were both effective and politically feasible appeared nearly impossible. But Brazilians persevered, and by pursuing a strategy of growth with equity, they have managed to simultaneously consolidate Brazil's once fragile democracy and extend social and economic opportunity to an ever-widening cross section of rural, urban, black, white, and pardo (mestizo) Brazilians.

BRAZIL TIMELINE

1930: Vargas Gains Power, Pursues Industrialization

On October 24, a coalition of civilian leaders and military officers overthrows the government and Getulio Dornelles Vargas takes power. He rules as a dictator until 1945 and again as an elected president from 1951 to 1954. Beginning under Vargas in the 1930s, Brazil makes ISI its cornerstone economic policy. For forty years, this strategy delivers strong, if uneven, economic growth.

1964: Military Dictatorship Begins

After a democratic interlude (1945–64), Brazil's military mounts another coup d'état on March 31. The economy continues its strong performance for the first decade of military rule, but only through a reliance on large coffee-export revenues, a growing internal market, lax monetary and fiscal policies, and rising external debt. Indeed, the ISI strategy imposes a heavy fiscal burden, and financial insolvency becomes almost inevitable.

1978: Global Oil Crisis Rocks Brazil

A severe external debt crisis, triggered by the global oil shock of 1978–79, serves as the immediate cause for Brazil's democratic opening. After an explosion of external debt in previous years, declining economic performance sparks waves of political and social mobilizations and triggers macroeconomic stabilization policies to satisfy international creditors. The image of the military's competence is damaged. Social unrest blossoms in the nation's manufacturing heartland near Sao Paulo.

1979: Military Begins Transition to Democracy

Faced with an ongoing economic crisis, the military begins Brazil's democratic transition in 1979 as a gradual process of liberalization. In anticipation of some type of transition, military leaders prevail on Congress to pass the 1979 Amnesty Law, which grants a full pardon for all actions committed on duty by the military, as well as by civilian guerrillas. The military liberalizes laws governing elections and parties in 1981 and institutes direct elections for various state and local offices to occur in 1982 and 1985. The opposition party wins a surprisingly big victory in the 1982 elections.

1982: Debt Crisis Forces IMF Loan

The military government comes under further pressure in the second half of 1982 when faced with a sudden halt in international financing. Brazil's only alternative to default is a loan from the International Monetary Fund. The loan is conditioned on the adoption of an orthodox stabilization program, including currency devaluation, high interest rates, and fiscal consolidation. However, the devaluation increases energy and food prices, resulting in painful stagflation that throws economic production into disarray, provokes social turmoil, and further undermines support for the military. The devaluation, along with tight import restraints and generous export subsidies, leads to large trade surpluses between 1984 and 1986, but this allows for the delay of deeper, long-term structural adjustments. Inflation picks up.

1985: Opposition Leader Neves Wins Presidential Election

Opposition candidate Tancredo Neves wins a surprising victory in the presidential election of January 15 after longtime supporters of the authoritarian government abandon the regime party and support him. However, Neves falls ill before his inauguration and dies in April. Ironically, this makes Jose Sarney, the vice president and former leader of the pro-military party, Brazil's first civilian president since 1964. Sarney immediately opens the party system, calls an assembly to write a new constitution, and liberalizes controls over trade unions. He also inaugurates a long list of stabilization programs, which are implemented between 1986 and 1991. After initially dropping, inflation tends to resurge each time.

1988: Brazil Adopts New Constitution

Brazil adopts a new democratic constitution on October 5. It universalizes access to hospitals and health facilities and imposes minimum spending requirements for primary education. Along with new federal policies and expenditures, this paves the way for steep improvements in human capital and economic opportunities for the poor and disadvantaged—particularly for blacks and residents of neglected rural areas. By 1997, 98 percent of children aged five to fourteen are enrolled in school.

1992: Collor Impeached

Brazil's House of Representatives overwhelmingly decides on September 29 that the Senate should start formal impeachment proceedings against President Fernando Collor. He is suspended from the presidency and never returns. Collor's downfall results from a combination of corruption allegations and fragile support in Congress. His impeachment and the subsequent peaceful instatement of Vice President Itamar Franco signal the consolidation of Brazil's new democracy. Collor leaves office with a mixed legacy. Despite his failed attempts at price stabilization, his structural reforms help pave the way for the success of the Real Plan.

1993–94: Cardoso Launches Real Plan

Fernando Henrique Cardoso, appointed finance minister in 1993, implements a macroeconomic stabilization program known as the Real Plan. It includes a two-step process resulting in the launch of a new currency, the real, on July 1, 1994. Benefiting heavily from the market-oriented reforms implemented by Collor and Franco, the Real Plan succeeds in taming inflation, which had reached more than 2,000 percent in 1993. This success catapults Cardoso to the presidency in October 1994.

1995: Brazil Begins Social Spending for the Poor

Starting in 1995, Brazil's maturing democratic government adopts a series of targeted social spending policies called conditional cash transfers (CCTs). CCTs are used to encourage school enrollment, bolster health, discourage child labor, and advance other goals. In 2003, several CCT programs are unified under the brand Bolsa Familia (family stipend), which expands until it reaches 12 million families. Along with universal safety nets written into the 1988 constitution and gradually implemented thereafter, these targeted income distribution schemes extend social protection to rural and nonunionized workers, who had long been excluded.

2002: Lula Elected President

Luiz Inacio Lula da Silva is elected to lead Brazil on October 27 in his fourth attempt at the presidency. His inauguration on January 1, 2003, deepens Brazil's new strategy to promote sustained and inclusive growth. Previously a fierce critic of market-oriented reforms, Lula grudgingly accepts most of them once elected. At the same time, he works to expand targeted income distribution schemes, universalize social safety nets, and improve health and education for the poor. Lula oversees the robust expansion of Brazil's economy but does not match his predecessors' reformist zeal. GDP exceeds $1 trillion in 2006 for the first time ever, on its way to more than $2 trillion by 2010. Despite these gains, structural obstacles to sustained economic growth and social inclusion abound.

2010: Rousseff Elected to Succeed Lula

Dilma Rousseff, a former energy minister and chief of staff to President Lula, is elected Brazil's first female president on October 31. Her victory is seen as a vote for continuity by Brazilians satisfied with socioeconomic gains under Lula. Before entering politics, Rousseff had been involved in a Communist guerrilla movement opposed to Brazil's military regime, and she was arrested in 1970 and subjected to torture. In the first years of her term, she is surprised by a series of corruption scandals involving several ministers from the cabinet she inherited from Lula. In sharp contrast to her former boss, she fires all of those accused of improprieties. In an attempt to avoid market-oriented reforms, she also pursues a traditional state-led approach to economic stimulus to boost slowing growth in 2011–2012. These efforts bear meager results, leading Rousseff to sell concessions for private firms to modernize and manage important infrastructure.

Poland

Grzegorz Ekiert and George Soroka

More than two decades after the collapse of Europe's Communist regimes, Poland has emerged as a model of how to successfully build democracy and a free-market economy. Today the country is a stable, smoothly functioning state with fair and competitive elections, robust representative institutions, an independent and assertive media, and a vigorous civil society. Firmly anchored within the European Union, Poland features a rapidly growing economy, an extensive welfare system, a technocratic bureaucracy, a professional political elite, and an institutionalized party system catering to a reliably divided electorate.

This political and economic success is remarkable given conditions at the outset of the transformation. Poland's extrication from communism was predicated on the abandonment of a system that had attempted, for more than four decades, to fundamentally remake state and society. The imposition of Communist rule entailed radical social and institutional upheaval, including nationalizing and centralizing the economy, partially collectivizing agriculture, and rapidly industrializing and urbanizing what before World War II had been a predominantly agrarian population. Achieving these ends required political dictatorship, the destruction of civil society, mass ideological indoctrination, and widespread political repression.

Consequently, in stark contrast to Third Wave democratizations in which market economies existed prior to the change of regime and survived the transition largely unscathed, Poland was characterized by a glaring absence of many of the economic, political, legal, and social preconditions typically deemed necessary for capitalism and democracy to flourish. Not only were the middle and entrepreneurial classes virtually nonexistent in Communist Poland, but the country also featured distorted property rights, a lack of governmental accountability, and a political culture unaccustomed to electoral competition. Moreover, Polish citizens were viewed by outside observers as being passively reliant on the state, as having expectations of cradle-to-grave welfare provisioning and lacking in personal responsibility and initiative. Given this backdrop, the Communist past appeared to be an entrenched negative burden that would be extremely difficult to undo or overcome.

Further complicating matters, the transition from communism involved the simultaneous initiation of seemingly incompatible political and economic transformations. Such weighty changes would necessarily exact a considerable toll, causing profound uncertainty and creating fundamental challenges for political elites and wider society. An electoral backlash against these reforms could have easily derailed Poland's nascent democracy had voters judged that the burdens being placed on them were too great.

In reality, however, the complex legacies of communism were not uniformly detrimental to the establishment of a liberal political and economic order. Despite the significant negatives associated with its previous regime, postcommunist Poland inherited comprehensive state institutions run by professional bureaucracies, an egalitarian social order, an educated and skilled labor force, and a diversified industrial base—all factors that helped ease the transformation in the aftermath of 1989.

Similarly, managing concurrent economic and political transitions did not prove as daunting a task as initially feared. Thanks to the effective design and implementation of reforms and a durable elite consensus favoring democratic norms and procedures, successive governments were able to handle these changes despite often fierce challenges from the most affected segments of the population. Getting the sequencing of reforms "right" in the Polish case involved, first, rapidly increasing the state's regulatory effectiveness, reinforcing the rule of law, and putting into place institutional safeguards (for example, securing the right to free speech, supporting public debate and ensuring legislative transparency, and instituting property rights guarantees and social welfare safety nets) that would allow for subsequent reforms, such as privatization, to proceed at a more measured and less politically destabilizing pace. Therefore, once the most pressing challenges had been addressed, paying attention to the sequencing of reforms often meant prioritizing debate and consensus-building over achieving specific economic and political objectives immediately. Doing so not only allowed for a wider range of input but also guaranteed that more Poles would feel invested in the reform process.

To be sure, Poland was not a typical example of a postcommunist transformation. Even the most cursory glance at the record of democratization and economic reforms across the postcommunist region reveals striking differences in outcomes, by and large corresponding to traditional historical and geographic divisions within this area of Europe. Such an observation suggests that deeper structural factors played a major role in determining the diverging trajectories evident across the former Soviet Bloc. In this regard, Poland's success may be seen as stemming from the country's cultural and political affinity for the West, memories of its failed democratic experiment in the interwar period, the staggering human and infrastructural losses suffered during World War II (which dramatically shifted borders and led to a far more ethnically homogenous polity), and the cumulative influences of the modernization and state building experienced throughout the twentieth century.

Poland's successful transition was also the direct result of massive external support, including that offered by Western states, multilateral institutions such as the International Monetary Fund (IMF) and the World Bank, and—most significant of all—the European Union (EU), which exerted influence by holding out the credible possibility that Poland might someday gain full membership. Engagement with external actors not only brought extensive financial aid and expertise but also introduced leverage and conditionality mechanisms tied to fulfilling foreign aid conditions ranging from ensuring basic civil rights and liberties to permitting oversight of policymaking and implementation on the local level.

Finally, although the Polish transition may at first glance appear to be an elite-centered affair resembling the power transfers that took place in Latin America or southern Europe during the 1970s and 1980s, it was in fact the outcome of a decade-long struggle whose essence was the formation, destruction, and resurrection of Solidarity, a sociopolitical movement that at its peak numbered nearly ten million members—about one-fourth of Poland's population—and was capable of bringing the entire country to a standstill. Solidarity mounted a sustained challenge to Communist Party rule by deploying a wide variety of methods to mobilize supporters and maintain high levels of confrontational activity. The Polish transition thus combined top-down elite negotiations with the indispensable bottom-up pressure provided by a grassroots political movement. As a result, postcommunist Poland inherited vocal and well-organized citizens eager to oversee and influence its new democratic institutions.

INFLECTION POINTS
OF THE TRANSITION PERIOD

Poland's late-Communist-era political and economic crisis, punctuated by the rise of the Solidarity trade union in 1980 and the imposition of martial law in 1981, simmered for more than a decade before political leaders decided to seek accommodation with societal forces opposed to Communist Party rule. During this time, profound economic challenges emerged, the roots of which extended back to the excessive borrowing of the 1970s and the failure of subsequent economic reform efforts. Since the mid-1970s, the Polish economy had been beset by severe imbalances, no real growth, and an unsustainable foreign debt load. In the 1980s, the situation deteriorated even further, leading to rising inflation, massive shortages in the consumer market, and, after 1981, international sanctions against the regime. During this time, an estimated 750,000 people emigrated from Poland. The resulting crisis unleashed an inflationary spiral, with inflation increasing from 60.2 percent in 1988 to 251.1 percent in 1989 and to an all-time high of 584.7 percent in 1990. Such catastrophic economic performance produced a marked decline in state efficacy, effectively delegitimizing Communist Party elites.

Poland's transformation, once initiated, unfolded at a faster pace than either government or opposition leaders had anticipated. Officially, it commenced with the Round Table talks in early 1989 between Communist Party officials and the then-illegal Solidarity movement. These discussions took place in a highly uncertain environment, with Communist regimes in power across east-central Europe and Soviet troops still stationed in Poland. The Polish transition consequently had no precedent to guide it; strategies had to be invented along the way, making compromise a guiding principle. This sustained bargaining between old and new political elites, along with the reaffirmation of Poland's institutional and legal continuity, made the transition to democracy less threatening to forces associated with the previous regime and went a long way toward securing their cooperation and support.

As a direct result of these talks, semi-free parliamentary elections were held on June 4, 1989. Although the agreed-upon electoral rules were designed to guarantee the Communists and their allies the majority of legislative seats (thereby granting them the prerogative to form the government), the unexpectedly high level of electoral support for the opposition and the unanticipated defection of two minor partners from the Communist camp paved the way for the formation of the first noncommunist government in east-central Europe since the 1940s. Led by longtime Solidarity activist Tadeusz Mazowiecki, the new government was sworn in on August 24, 1989.

Under Mazowiecki's tenure, the legislature began a fundamental overhaul of the political system. The resulting liberalization not only brought about guarantees of political and property rights but also introduced the institutional groundwork necessary for systemic reforms to eventually be undertaken across virtually all areas of public life. The most important of these was the comprehensive economic reform package that came to be known as the Balcerowicz Plan, named after its chief architect, Leszek Balcerowicz, then deputy prime minister and minister of finance.

The transfer of political power to the Solidarity-led opposition in 1989 brought about the formation of a political scene characterized by the emergence of a dizzying array of parties. Instability and uncertainty defined this initial stage. Post-Solidarity forces dominated the early transition, though internecine competition soon emerged among factions within the former opposition. Attesting to this, more than one hundred parties and electoral alliances competed in the first fully free parliamentary election in 1991, with twenty-nine winning legislative seats. By the end of 1993, Poland had already held five national-level elections, rotated through six prime ministers, and witnessed the political resurrection of the ex–Communist Party, which returned to power with a clear electoral mandate after early elections were called that year. Due to the initiation of its economic adjustment program, during the same period the country also experienced a sharp contraction in gross domestic product (GDP), large declines in industrial output as inefficient factories were idled, and a rapidly rising unemployment rate (at the height of the crisis some 20 percent of the work-eligible population was unemployed). The resulting economic hardship contributed significantly to a radicalization of labor demands, reflected in waves of strikes and protests across the country.

By contrast, between 1993 and 2004, Poland witnessed a rapid economic recovery and the stabilization of its political and economic situation. Whereas the introduction of democracy and a market economy were the principal challenges facing the country in the first reform stage, the EU accession process dominated the second. Politically, these years were marked by repeated democratic turnovers in which power oscillated between post-Solidarity and postcommunist forces. A tenuous political balance between the two emerged, fostering a middle-of-the-road approach to reforms. Polish civil society, meanwhile, continued to display its vitality by engaging in large-scale protest actions challenging the social and economic positions of successive governments, encouraging transparency, and pushing political actors to seek solutions acceptable to their constituents. This stretch of time also witnessed the negotiation of EU accession conditions, which led to Poland's becoming a full EU member in 2004.

The third and final transition period, which began with the Polish entry into the EU and extends to the present, has been marked by the stabilization of the country's institutions and the consolidation of its party system. Thus far it has revealed a diminished role for the political forces inherited from the old regime, a general weakness of the ideological left, and the emergence of fierce competition between two major post-Solidarity political parties: the center-right/liberal Civic Union and the nationalist/populist Law and Justice. Economically, meanwhile, these years have proved to be a time of remarkable growth, as reflected by Poland's steadily rising GDP and living standards. Attesting to this, the global economic crisis that continues to batter Europe has so far largely bypassed the country. Signaling the maturation of the Polish electoral system, since 2004 there has been a noteworthy decline in protest activities sponsored by civil society organizations, political contestation having begun to take place primarily through institutionalized party channels. That Poland's constitutional arrangements were not threatened by the April 2010 Smolensk airplane crash, which claimed the lives of President Lech Kaczynski and dozens of other leading political and cultural luminaries, testifies to the institutional stability the state has achieved over the course of the past two decades.

LESSONS OF THE TRANSITION PERIOD

The trajectory and outcome of Poland's democratization underscore the importance of its historical and structural endowments, the country's location in Europe, and the policy choices of central political and economic actors.

SOCIOECONOMIC EXCLUSION AND INCLUSION

Social welfare questions haunt regime transitions, and the failure of democracy is often caused by unresolved problems associated with underdevelopment, poverty, uneven resource distribution, and a lack of employment opportunities. Democracy certainly can take root in poorer countries, but extreme and systemic inequalities do not bode well for its survival. In this respect, Poland after 1989 had some important structural factors in its favor. For one, given the leveling effect of communism and its redistribution policies, income disparities were relatively minimal across the population. Likewise, the country's economic sectors were diversified, linked to the regional economy, and not overly tied to natural resource bases prone to oligopolistic exploitation. Moreover, government policies explicitly aimed to attenuate socioeconomic dislocation and the rampant poverty that might otherwise have followed from these economic transformations; this was absolutely necessary to maintain a critical mass of popular support for the overall thrust, if not always the specifics, of the reform effort. As a result, Poland entered a virtuous cycle: by promoting sound economic policies, it created a burgeoning middle class secure in its forward-looking prospects, a group essential for consolidating democracy and sustaining it over time.

Since 1989, Poland has become a comprehensive welfare state (see Figure 6). In 1991, for example, it spent 21.2 percent of its GDP on social expenditures, and this rate increased in the years that followed, reaching almost 25 percent at one point during the early transition period. In comparison, spending within the countries of the Organization for Economic Cooperation and Development (OECD) as a whole was 18.5 percent for 1991. Since then, outlays as a percentage of GDP have averaged well over 20 percent.

Attention paid to rising socioeconomic inequalities, particularly in the first few years of transition, is therefore a defining characteristic of Poland's democratization. Polish political leaders managed to promote democratization and market reforms by consistently favoring policies that would cushion the economic shocks experienced by the potential or actual losers of the transition, the most vulnerable groups being pensioners, the rural poor, and workers in restructured industries. Such policies were informed by a broad consensus on the state's responsibilities to its citizens harking back to the interwar period and the central European

FIGURE 6. INCOME AND SOCIAL SPENDING IN POLAND

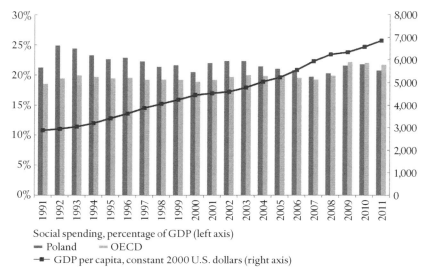

Social spending, percentage of GDP (left axis)
➤ Poland   ▬ OECD
➤■ GDP per capita, constant 2000 U.S. dollars (right axis)

Sources: OECD (social spending) and World Bank (GDP per capita).

tradition of expansive social rights and welfare guarantees. Postcommunist Poland's carefully crafted welfare policies and its ability to make and follow through on its promises (such as maintaining generous unemployment benefits, introducing a national antipoverty program, propping up those regions most affected by unemployment, indexing wages to inflation, paying pensions on time, and improving health services) were instrumental in overcoming opposition to reforms and mitigating the appeal of populism and xenophobic extremism.

Social inclusion was likewise furthered by comprehensive reforms of the pension, health-care, and education systems. Questions over how to revise these programs had been hotly debated since 1989, and consecutive governments developed competing policy proposals. The details of these reforms were eventually finalized in 1998, when a political consensus was reached about their design, merits, and necessity. The Solidarity-led government that succeeded the ex-Communists in 1997 was instrumental in vigorously moving these projects through parliament and pushing ahead with their implementation.

By 1999, Poland had embarked on a comprehensive overhaul of its pension system. The existing underfunded pay-as-you-go schema was transformed into a three-pillar system that married state-run basic coverage with a defined contribution plan and voluntary individual retirement accounts. Concurrently, health-care reform was introduced. Responsibility for funding and delivering medical services was decentralized, allowing patients to choose their doctors and hospitals but requiring payment of mandatory premiums. The new system was intended to inject competition into the sector and, at the same time, reduce waste and mismanagement by establishing more rigorous control over health expenditures. Educational reforms were also far-ranging and comprehensive.

Poland was in a better position to pursue such policies than many other countries. Despite facing daunting economic challenges, by 1989 it was a middle-income nation, with a GDP per capita of almost $6,200 (in purchasing power parity terms). Critically, it could also count on extensive economic aid and technical support from Western states and multilateral institutions. As a result, Poland experienced the fastest recovery of all the former Warsaw Pact countries from the deep recession that gripped the region after the collapse of communism, providing it with a solid foundation on which to build future economic growth.

ECONOMIC STRUCTURE AND POLICIES

Poland's post-1989 governments not only were forced to deal with severe fiscal imbalances and hyperinflation but also needed to privatize an inefficient, state-dominated economic system and build the institutional and legal infrastructure of a market-based economy. Realizing the dire nature of this predicament, the architects of the Polish transition opted for a shock therapy approach to economic restructuring. This was intended to promote development as well as undermine old interests and power networks in order to prevent them from sabotaging the transformation process.

In consultation with Western experts, the first post-transition government introduced the Balcerowicz Plan, a radical macroeconomic adjustment and stabilization program. This approach had the backing of the IMF and World Bank, as well as that of the United States and major European states. Time was of the essence, because by 1989 Poland's foreign debt had reached $42.3 billion, or 64.8 percent of its GDP. What resulted was the negotiation of a comprehensive program of debt restructuring and forgiveness among Western donors. Additionally, the IMF granted Poland a $1 billion emergency stabilization fund, with a further $720 million credit available if needed (neither was used), and the World Bank extended credits for modernizing trade infrastructure so that Polish goods would be more competitive on the export market. In the short term, however, these reforms—which, among other things, allowed inefficient companies to declare bankruptcy, reformed the banking laws and tied interest rates to inflation, limited wage increases among state companies to tamp down hyperinflation, allowed foreign direct investment, and protected workers in state-owned firms from blanket layoffs while guaranteeing them unemployment benefits should they be terminated—produced a sizable economic contraction: GDP declined by 11.6 percent in 1990 and a further 7.6 percent in 1991. Meanwhile, industrial output declined by 24.2 percent in 1990 and another 11.9 percent in 1991. During this time, unemployment increased from 6.1 percent in 1990 to 11.5 percent in 1991, 13.6 percent in 1992, and 16.4 percent in 1993.

As these numbers indicate, in its initial stages this strategy exacted large social costs and led to a precipitous decline in living standards. Poland's militant trade unions and professional associations responded predictably, with wave upon wave of strikes and protest. Yet successive democratically elected governments were able to withstand this political pressure and maintain the momentum of economic reforms despite frequent elections and changes of ruling coalitions. Even though specific measures were variously prioritized by successive governments, the overall objectives of political actors remained remarkably consistent during the transition. Moreover, when political conflicts arose, they generally centered on questions of institutional design and strategies of implementing new policies when the dominant neoliberal vision clashed with traditional Polish social-democratic and Christian-democratic inclinations. That these were largely differences of degree, not kind, was critical to the reform effort.

Yet, though political will among elites was crucial, it must be recalled that what was happening in Poland was not occurring in isolation—the entire former Warsaw Bloc was involved in political and economic transitions during the 1990s, making the situation in Poland seem more routine and allowing politicians to learn from the successes and failures of their regional compatriots. The political legitimacy of the postcommunist state was also reinforced by a societal consensus regarding the ultimate goals of these transformations: a stable liberal democracy with expansive welfare protections, a market economy, and integration into a wider Europe. Because no viable "third way" was articulated between communism and capitalism, or between West and East, protesters tended to oppose the manner in which reforms were proceeding rather than the reforms' substance. In this respect, societal contention contributed to ensuring political accountability without unduly threatening the essential logic behind the reforms. Likewise, the highly partisan policymaking environment had a rather counterintuitive but ultimately beneficial stabilizing effect, since politicians were aware that any perceived carelessness in the design or implementation of reforms would be fully exploited by their competitors to gain political advantage.

External financial support for the Polish transition should also not be underestimated. Beginning with the signing of a trade agreement between Poland and what was then still the European Community (the precursor to the EU) in 1989, and followed shortly by the ratification of its European Association Agreement, Poland was from a very early point in time eligible for pre-accession European aid under three programs—Poland and Hungary: Assistance for Restructuring their Economies (PHARE), Instrument for Structural Policies for Pre-Accession (ISPA), and Special Accession Programme for Agriculture and Rural Development (SAPARD). EU membership brought even greater monetary transfers. Between 2004 and 2006 alone, Poland received 12.8 billion euros in structural and cohesion funding from the EU, more than half of the total EU funding available to the ten 2004 accession states. For 2007 through 2013, 67.3 billion euros has been earmarked for Poland, making the country the largest nonemergency aid recipient of all EU member states.

Macroeconomic stabilization, however, was only part of the challenge. The Communist legacy also meant that Poland needed to introduce far-reaching privatization programs, as by 1990 it had 8,453 medium and large state-owned enterprises on the books, and newly formed private companies were contributing only 15 percent of GDP. To this end, a government ministry was created that same year to manage the privatization process. By 2010, Poland had privatized or liquidated 5,975 medium and large firms, and all small enterprises had been transferred to local authorities and either leased out or auctioned off. Although the privatization process was highly contentious and comparatively slow, it was conducted in an orderly and transparent fashion, allowing it to avoid many of the pitfalls that plagued other post-communist states, such as Russia.

As a consequence of these reforms, in two decades' time Poland managed to remake itself into one of the most dynamic markets in Europe. Its debt load and balance of payments are quite healthy by European standards, and its economy has been expanding at a rate above Europe's average since 1991. As a result, Polish per capita income has quadrupled since 1990 and the country has managed to attract impressive levels of foreign direct investment (FDI) in recent years ($23.6 billion in 2007, $12.9 billion in 2009, and $15.1 billion in 2011), putting Poland second only to Russia in terms of recent FDI inflows among postcommunist states. (It took much-larger Russia until the mid-2000s to displace Poland from the top position.) Moreover, Poland is the only European nation that avoided lapsing into recession as a result of the latest global financial and sovereign debt crisis. Consequently, since 2007 Poland's real GDP growth has exceeded that of all the other thirty-three OECD countries, contributing to a sizable decline in the income gap between it and western European economies.

Poland has also benefited from being located near Germany and other major European markets. Membership in the EU (and eventually the Schengen zone) allowed Polish workers to freely move across much of Europe, providing an important economic safety valve for a country with a long tradition of relying on financial flows from abroad. Remittances spiked dramatically after Poland joined the EU, rising from $2.28 billion in 2003 to $4.73 billion in 2004 and more than $10 billion by 2007–2008. Even in the midst of one of the worst economic crises in memory, in 2009 officially reported remittances from Poles living or working abroad made up 2 percent of Poland's GDP (the actual figure is undoubtedly much higher).

Quickly putting into place institutional safeguards that would allow subsequent implementation of more comprehensive economic reforms, expanding the power and authority of state bureaucracies charged with making fiscal and economic policy, and reinforcing the determination of central decision-makers to see these reforms through (including by leveraging mechanisms such as EU conditionality) were all critical to Poland's economic transformation. The government seized the window of opportunity that opened in the immediate aftermath of the regime change—when societal optimism was running high and harsh economic realities had yet to set in—to enact the most politically difficult measures while allowing others to be thoroughly discussed before being put into place. This created a point of political no return and allowed the government to forestall the emergence of powerful interest groups with incentives to block further reforms.

Assuring transparency in the policymaking process, guaranteeing the accountability of public officials, and paying attention to distributional effects were all hallmarks of the Polish transition. So too were efforts to increase the capacity of the state and the power and independence of its regulatory institutions. However, it was the ability of Polish lawmakers to demonstrate that economic austerity measures would eventually raise living standards that proved most instrumental in sustaining electoral support for the reforms. It is therefore no surprise that today the majority of Poles believe that democracy is a good political system and that the economic transformation resulting from the collapse of communism in 1989 changed their lives for the better.

CIVIL SOCIETY AND MEDIA

Poles have a history of mass protest against the Communist state dating back to the 1950s. Nevertheless, it was the imposition of martial law in 1981 and Solidarity's subsequent revival and eventual disintegration between 1989 and 1991 that had the most formative impact on transitional politics. This decade-long struggle bequeathed to Poland a well-organized labor movement, a strong Catholic Church imbued with considerable political capital, and experienced opposition leaders. The composition of the postcommunist elite and their networks dates from this period (many present-day politicians were prominent in the Solidarity movement), as do seminal political cleavages and ideological divisions.

The collapse of the Communist regime in Poland opened space for the reconstitution of civil society and unleashed massive societal mobilization. The first postcommunist government aided this process by liberalizing the media, introducing extensive political freedoms, and simplifying registration procedures for parties and nongovernmental organizations (NGOs). Two parallel developments followed. First, the state-controlled associations and media outlets of the old regime underwent substantive transformations, with most managing to quickly incorporate themselves into the new democratic system. Second, civil society and media sectors representing views that had been banned or suppressed under communism were reinvented. Postcommunist Poland thus experienced a rapid emergence of a wide spectrum of new movements, including NGOs, charities, foundations, religious-ethnic organizations, and employer-business associations. Since 1989, an average of five thousand new NGOs and five hundred foundations have been created in Poland each year.

In short, the growth of Polish associational life during the past two decades has been impressive, resulting in a dense civil society network. And despite regional differences in the distribution of organizations across Poland, the countryside is as much the site of vibrant associational activity as are large cities and industrial centers. Moreover, while growth in most types of civil society involvement in Poland has been steady, the rise in volunteerism has been nothing short of spectacular: in 2008, some 20 percent of adults declared that they had performed unpaid work during the previous year and more than 50 percent reported that they had done so in the past.

Poland also enjoys a highly politicized but thriving media market. After 1989, the print, radio, and television sectors all expanded dramatically. Increases in the number of periodicals published were particularly notable; the European Press Centre estimates that more than five thousand are currently issued in Poland. Book production has also been trending upward since the end of communism (when some 10,000 titles were released annually), reaching a record 31,500 new books in 2010. No longer fettered by ideological constraints, print and digital journalism have likewise flourished over the course of the past two decades. As a consequence, the 2010–2012 Press Freedom Index ranks Poland twenty-fourth in the world, ahead of such countries as the United Kingdom, France, and Spain.

As Poland's experience attests, a robust civil society and lively, independent media provide important underpinnings for democracy. Especially during the initial stages of the Polish transition, civil society was instrumental in representing diverse interests and identities, providing services for disadvantaged sectors of the population, and offering resources for political mobilization. Media outlets played a crucial role as well, exemplified by their ability to catalyze public debate and signal social problems.

LEGAL SYSTEM AND RULE OF LAW

The Polish legal system under communism, despite its politicization and distortions, was comprehensive and based on the continental tradition. One of the most critical decisions of Poland's transition was to reaffirm the rule of law and the validity of inherited legal arrangements while acknowledging the need for speedily removing the most antiliberal and repressive regulations.

After 1989, Poland's legal institutions underwent two main phases of alteration. The first centered on abolishing preferential treatment for the Polish United Workers' Party (PZPR), Poland's communist party at the time, and removing restrictions on political rights and civil liberties, as well as implementing private property protections and restoring an independent judiciary to Polish courtrooms.

The second was part and parcel of the Polish EU accession bid. In early 1994, Poland signed an association treaty with the EU, the first step in membership negotiations. Talks were completed by 2002, a referendum on accession was held in 2003, and Poland entered the EU on May 1, 2004. Between 2001 and 2003, far-ranging legal reforms took place. These consisted of implementing the EU's demanding accession conditions, which not only introduced profound changes to existing domestic laws and regulations but also placed certain policy domains outside the realm of political contestation. In many instances, this was accomplished by bureaucrats, without public debate or consultation. The process was not particularly democratic, but it had the virtue of being efficient and producing an outcome favorable to liberal norms.

This is not to suggest that the Polish state did not face significant challenges along the way. Prominent among these was the increase of both public and private corruption in the immediate aftermath of its transformation. However, societal opprobrium and aggressive governmental efforts to counter this trend have yielded positive results: the rate of corruption has been in a downward spiral since the 1990s. More specifically, prominent antibribery campaigns, oversight by the EU, and sensationalistic media revelations have all had an impact. Consequently, the 2011 Transition Report of the European Bank for Reconstruction and Development finds not only that Poles have become more trusting of public institutions in recent years but also that corruption perception levels among the public are falling, having nearly converged with the western European average.

Another recurrent issue that has plagued Polish society and politics is the question of transitional justice and how Communist-era officials and secret police informants are to be dealt with. Symbolically, the divide over this dates back to a speech Prime Minister Mazowiecki delivered in 1989, when he declared that his government intended to draw a "thick line" at the past so as to focus on forward-looking reforms. This statement was spun politically by more conservative and nationalistic forces as an indication that the liberal faction of Solidarity (of which Mazowiecki was a part) and its ideological heirs favored the nonpunishment of Communist crimes. Whether individuals should be held accountable for their actions under the past regime—a process that came to be known throughout the postcommunist world as *lustration*, after the ancient Roman rite of expiation—quickly became a highly polarized issue.

As a result, Poland only belatedly passed a so-called vetting law in 1997 requiring high-level public officials to admit any collaboration with the Communist-era secret police. Penalties applied only for lying, ensuring that the law was circumscribed in scope and effect. However, signaling the unresolved nature of this issue, in March 2007 a revised lustration law came into force. The changes it wrought were substantial, including greatly expanding the list of professions subject to vetting procedures. But just two months later, the Constitutional Tribunal struck down crucial provisions of the new statute, leaving the final disposition of the matter unresolved. Related and similarly protracted arguments surround the question of what should be done with Poland's secret police files, which were not immediately released to the public in the wake of 1989. The result of all this is that the past is an ongoing source of political disquietude in Poland, revisited regularly by legislators and the courts.

Poland's decision to maintain the continuity of the previous legal system while installing an independent judiciary and emphasizing respect for property rights and the rule of law facilitated the transformation by creating a sense of predictability and stability amidst the chaos of reforms. Meanwhile, extensive external monitoring (chiefly by the EU, but also involving such entities as the Council of Europe) improved adherence to international legal and electoral standards and promoted law-abiding behavior among political and economic actors. The expansion of the police force also increased the state's ability to combat illegal activities, and postcommunist Poland's integration into Europe allowed it to more effectively disrupt cross-border links between criminal groups. In sum, Poland's enforcement of its revamped legal code, combined with extensive coverage of large-scale infractions by the media, reduced the level of corruption in the country and led to a drop in crime after an initial and predictable uptick during the early years of transition. Yet a free electoral system and judiciary have also unwittingly ensured that legal issues related to the Communist past remain significant points of political contestation.

GOVERNMENT STRUCTURE AND DIVISION OF POWER

Four factors played a pivotal role in the reform of Poland's governmental structure and the resulting division of power: return to a bicameral parliament, which Poland had in the interwar period, and the adoption of semi-presidentialism, with competencies divided between prime minister and president; decentralization and the transfer of resources and responsibility for the provision of many social services to local-level authorities; reform and expansion of core national-level bureaucracies, improving and consolidating the state's regulatory capacity and fiscal effectiveness (for example, in tax collection); and establishment of an autonomous central bank authority to oversee monetary policy.

The Round Table negotiations brought about an agreement on how to modify Poland's Communist-era constitutional arrangement, adding a directly elected president with relatively broad powers and restoring an upper chamber to the legislature. Poland thereby became a semi-presidential regime, avoiding the excessive concentration of power in the executive that frequently plagues pure presidential systems. Meanwhile, proportional representation in the lower house (*Sejm*) ensured that a multiplicity of ideological positions and societal views would be represented in the parliament, even though this arrangement initially produced striking political fragmentation and coalitional instability. The aim of these reforms was to prevent power from becoming overly concentrated in the hands of any individual or political institution. This tacit system of checks and balances has on the whole achieved its goal of fostering robust electoral contestation and offering the public a range of policy options. At the same time, such demanding political realities also explain why it took most of a decade before Poland embraced a permanent new constitution in 1997. Cognizance of the highly competitive environment in which they found themselves led politicians to pick their battles carefully and think hard about the sequencing of reforms.

This is not to suggest that consensus was unreachable. Early on, the creation of effective local self-governance structures was determined to be a political priority, and it became the first legislative initiative of the newly established upper chamber (*Senat*) of the Polish parliament. Beginning in the early 1990s, municipalities were granted considerable power and resources, including an independent revenue base, and charged with handling many of the tasks previously performed by the central state administration (such as the maintenance of infrastructure and provision of education and health services). These changes were followed by a second round of reforms in 1998, which when completed left nearly 50 percent of the Polish budget in the hands of local communities, transferred additional social responsibilities to municipal governments, and streamlined the structure and prerogatives of the state.

Only after power had significantly devolved to local administrative organs and the most essential redesign of the electoral and legislative systems had been undertaken was attention turned to reforming Warsaw's revenue-generating capabilities. This task involved a new system of taxation (personal income tax was introduced in 1992 and the value-added tax in 1993) and the design of effective collection mechanisms.

Legislation enacted in 1996 introduced additional changes in the structure and operation of the state apparatus. Among other things, it strengthened the ministries responsible for macroeconomic regulation (especially the Ministry of Finance), created a better system of managing public property, and improved the quality and efficiency of the civil service.

Building on this, the 1997 Act on the National Bank of Poland considerably extended the authority and autonomy of the central bank, enabling it to emerge as a powerful and independent actor. The bank's resulting political clout, coupled with its conservative fiscal policy, allowed Poland to maintain the stability of its currency and control inflation throughout critical periods, including during the 2008 financial crisis.

The Polish experience strongly argues that the formal codification of new constitutional arrangements is not as important as the broader democratic transitions literature suggests, provided basic freedoms and liberties are respected and laws reliably enforced. Increasing the capacity of the state was therefore a seminal component of Poland's far-ranging reforms. To this end, the Polish bureaucracy doubled between 1988 and 1995 and the state became better organized, developing more infrastructural power than its Communist predecessor ever had. Poland's example suggests that a capable and efficient (but not necessarily small) state apparatus is indispensable as the backbone of a working democracy.

EDUCATION AND DEMOGRAPHY

Until the 1999 reforms were initiated, Poland's education system relied on a traditional European dual track, in which students spend eight years in primary school before being channeled either into an academic track lasting four years or a vocational one lasting three or five (depending on the specialization and qualification sought). Now, after the reforms, students study for six years at the primary level and three at the lower secondary level before they are segregated into vocational training or further academic instruction, adding one more year to the comprehensive education requirement for those pursuing the vocational route.

Accompanying these measures was a shift in policy toward giving schools additional autonomy and responsibility for educational outcomes. Along with the devolution of state funding to local-level authorities, EU structural funds were made available to underwrite the reforms. Taken together, these changes produced substantial performance improvements across subject areas as measured by the OECD's Program for International Student Assessment (PISA). For example, between 2000 and 2006 Poland went from lagging the OECD average in comprehensive reading assessments to placing ninth among countries using PISA, the only transition state to achieve such a significant advance (see Figure 7 for achievements in science assessments).

Paralleling these developments, postcommunist Poland's integration into pan-European structures has also resulted in a significant expansion of opportunity for Polish students eager to study in other countries under initiatives such as the European Community Action Scheme for the Mobility of University Students (Erasmus). This has produced a subset of younger Poles who are multilingual and increasingly comfortable in thinking of themselves as citizens of a wider Europe.

After 1989, the institutional composition of the Polish educational landscape changed markedly as well. Church-run and other privately administered schools have not proved a significant factor in primary and secondary education (currently some 98 percent of Polish students attend state-run schools), but the expansion of private higher education has been astounding. Liberal policies adopted in the 1990s and 2000s

FIGURE 7. EDUCATION ACHIEVEMENT AND EXPENDITURE
IN POLAND

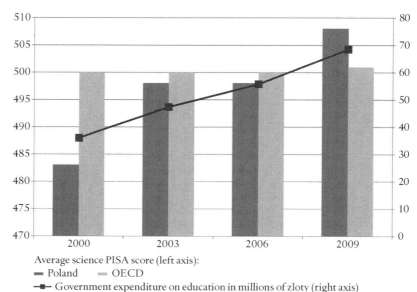

Average science PISA score (left axis):
■ Poland   ■ OECD
■ Government expenditure on education in millions of zloty (right axis)

Source: OECD. The Program for International Student Assessment (PISA) measures the literacy of fifteen-year-olds in math, science, and reading.

concerning the entry of nonstate players into the tertiary educational market produced dramatic growth in that sector, with more than three hundred private institutions of higher education established between 1991 and 2011 (during this period the number of state institutions grew more modestly, from 96 to 135).

Meanwhile, the number of students enrolled in higher education (including part-time studies) roughly quintupled between 1990 and 2009, approaching two million. According to Poland's Central Statistical Office, the percentage of full-time students in higher education programs has also steadily increased over the past decade, finally making up more than half of all enrollees in 2010 and 2011. Partly this has been the result of demographic growth in the critical nineteen- to twenty-four-year-old segment of the population during the 1990s and early 2000s, but enrollment overall has outpaced this increase, indicating that more Poles are availing themselves of tertiary credentialing. Among higher education students, 32 percent are enrolled in private institutions. However, the results of this expansion have not been all positive. Poland has had to deal with vexing quality-control issues related to the private (and often for-profit) educational sector, and it faces a looming population contraction that will dramatically reduce the university-age population in coming decades.

Regarding other demographic measures, Polish citizens are universally literate and predominantly (60 percent) urban. Both trends are legacies of the Communist period. Poland is also similar to developed European democracies in that it features low growth and a rapidly aging society. Population statistics were essentially flat between 1990 and 2009, and are expected to become slightly negative (-0.1 percent per annum) for 2009 through 2015, according to estimates by the United Nations Educational, Scientific, and Cultural Organization. And with a birthrate of 1.40 children per woman, Polish fertility is lower than in the rest of the OECD, where the mean is 1.74. Yet while the labor force contracted somewhat between 1990 and 2009 (-0.2 percent annual growth), the population structure at present remains weighted toward the working-age fifteen- to sixty-four-year-old demographic (72 percent of Poles, versus 15 percent in the fourteen and younger range and 13 percent in the sixty-five and older range). These figures have proved to be a political asset as well as a liability throughout the transition; aging societies are less prone to radicalization, but they also face significant economic and social challenges going forward.

Poland, like much of the developed world, experienced an uptick in birthrates after World War II, with population growth falling off into the 1970s but then picking up again in the 1980s. The result was that by 1990 Poland had a roughly triangular age distribution, with a small elderly pinnacle and prominent bulges among the thirty- to thirty-nine-year-old and the five- to fourteen-year-old demographics (reflecting the postwar baby boomers and their children). This distribution guaranteed that the working-age population would remain high for at least the next two decades relative to the number of pensioners, a critical but often overlooked demographic advantage Poland brought to the transition.

What remains to be seen is how Poland deals with negative population growth over the next several decades. Statistical models suggest that the Polish population may drop from its current 38.2 million by as much as 20 percent by 2050. Meanwhile, the Germany-based Max Planck Institute is predicting that the median age of Poles will increase from 35.7 in 2004 to 51.8 by 2050, a factor that will place significant stress on the health-care and pension systems.

One final observation: Poland has historically been an emigrant nation. Between 1990 and 2000, for instance, an average of more than twenty-two thousand Poles emigrated each year, but immigration to Poland averaged just less than seven thousand. The trend toward out-migration strengthened after Poland's accession to the EU, permanent emigration (defined as leaving for at least one year) peaking in 2006, when nearly forty-seven thousand Poles went abroad, mainly for economic reasons. (European countries widened their labor markets at staggered rates, ranging from the United Kingdom, Ireland, and Sweden, which began allowing free labor migration in 2004, to Germany and Austria, which opened their borders only in 2011.) And although the current economic crisis has caused many Poles residing internationally to start returning home, according to World Bank data, 8.2 percent of Poland's population as of 2010 was still living outside its borders.

CONCLUSION

Poland's successful transition offers a number of lessons. First, it demonstrates that institutional engineering has definite limits. However, this does not mean that the design of institutions should be neglected. As the Polish case shows, simultaneously promoting the dispersion of political and economic power and the inclusion of diverse actors in policymaking processes is highly conducive to democratic consolidation. But trying to find institutional solutions for every problem is self-defeating. Attempting to secure a multitude of well-intended outcomes not only creates unnecessary complexity but may have just the opposite of the desired effect, reifying boundaries among groups and discouraging cooperation.

Second, the Polish experience argues that an efficient and accountable state is essential to democratic consolidation and the rule of law. Democracy-building in Poland was functionally tied to reform efforts that increased Warsaw's ability to fulfill its legal responsibilities and fiduciary functions.

Third, the Polish case reveals that it is not only the timing and sequencing of reforms that matters but also the alacrity of their implementation. An inherent irony of democratic transformations is that if the costs of transformation become too onerous for society to bear, the people always have the option of voting reform-minded politicians out of office. Policymakers should realize that there is often a short honey-moon phase once reforms are begun, when expectations are still high and during which the electorate will tolerate increased levels of eco-nomic hardship, provided they have reasonable expectations that the situation will soon improve. This initial goodwill should not be squan-dered, as it usually lasts months rather than years. At the same time, care must be taken to not let reforms get ahead of the state's ability to effectively regulate them.

Reformers should therefore not fear embarking upon concurrent social, economic, and political changes, provided that social welfare safety nets are put into place beforehand to ensure that the most vulner-able within society do not become the transition's unintended victims. As to the ordering of reforms, Poland teaches us that ensuring the rule of law and securing property rights ought to be priorities.

Fourth, geographic proximity to democratic neighbors and histori-cally friendly relations with the West were all critical components of the Polish transformation. As a result, Poland quickly joined such influential international bodies as the World Trade Organization (1995) and the North Atlantic Treaty Organization (1999). It also benefited from Euro-pean aid and monitoring, institutional and knowledge transfers, foreign investment, and, above all, the tangible prospect of EU membership. Incentives and constraints offered by the EU and Western donors shaped the contours of domestic political competition, informed the agendas of political and economic actors, and expanded opportunities for reform. Consequently, while offering substantive economic support (for exam-ple, guaranteed stabilization funds) imposes very real short-term costs on foreign governments, the potential long-term benefits far exceed these. Poland's success is directly proportional to the aid, resources, and opportunities offered it by other states and multilateral entities.

It should be underscored that Poland's geographic, historic, and cul-tural relationship to Europe allowed for particularly effective carrot-and-stick offers by outside entities. Still, the essential point remains valid: comprehensive efforts to support regime change through political and economic instruments and long-term commitments by foreign gov-ernments and organizations are vital to ensuring democratic outcomes. Even so, the effectiveness of external actors will always be limited.

Finally, having previous democratic experience helps. Poland is an example of what the political scientist Samuel Huntington labeled a second-try pattern of democratization. The country experienced both democratic episodes and associated reversals, and it struggled to build and maintain democratic institutions. Political as well as societal learning takes far longer than is commonly imagined, often involving multigenerational spans of time. Failures to sustain democracy in the past may therefore actually help consolidate it in the future. Authoritarian reversals, though regrettable, should consequently only increase efforts to support the political opposition and civil society actors. In the struggle for democracy, there are no lost causes, only frustrated short-term expectations.

In conclusion, Poland's success is the result of a unique combination of factors. On the one hand, postcommunist Poland enjoyed many structural conditions and proximate legacies conducive to democratization. On the other hand, Poland exemplifies a democratic transition based on a broad consensus regarding the ultimate goals and underlying values of the reform process. This combination set in motion a dynamic, and self-reinforcing, transformative process. Of course, Poland's transition unfolded in highly favorable global conditions, both economic and geopolitical. *Fortuna* was thus a significant part of Poland's story, and the Polish "formula" is neither foolproof nor easily replicable in other contexts.

POLAND TIMELINE

1945: End of World War II and Imposition of Communism

The leaders of the United States, the United Kingdom, and the Soviet Union outline the shape of post–World War II Poland at the Yalta and Potsdam conferences in 1945. Poland is forced to give up a considerable portion of its eastern territories to the Soviet Union, but in return it gains more economically developed territory from Germany. These changes make the population more ethnically homogeneous. Communist leaders backed by Moscow quickly gain the upper hand in the country's postwar government. The emerging Communist regime harasses and constrains opposition parties, using a referendum in 1946 and an election in 1947 to consolidate its power. The Polish United Workers' Party is formed in 1948; it goes on to govern Poland as a Communist state until 1989.

1980: Solidarity Trade Union Founded

Solidarity, the first noncommunist trade union in Poland, is founded at the Gdansk shipyard on August 31. The union's formation follows a summer of widespread strikes and protests over rising consumer prices. Solidarity transforms into a sociopolitical movement that at its peak numbers nearly ten million members—about one-fourth of Poland's population—and that is capable of bringing the entire country to a standstill. Throughout the 1980s, it mounts a sustained challenge to Communist Party rule.

1981: Martial Law Imposed

Communist general secretary Wojciech Jaruzelski imposes martial law on December 13 in an attempt to suppress political opposition. Solidarity is banned, and its leader, Lech Walesa, is jailed along with other activists. Solidarity goes underground and continues to agitate for democratic change for the remainder of the decade.

1989: Round Table Talks Begin

In response to Poland's economic woes and social unrest, the Communist government initiates the Round Table negotiations with the still-illegal Solidarity movement in Warsaw in February. The discussions take place in a highly uncertain environment, with Communist regimes in power across east-central Europe and Soviet troops stationed in Poland. They lead to an April 6 agreement for political reforms, including the legalization of Solidarity and other independent trade unions.

1989: Parliamentary Elections Lead to Noncommunist Government

Following the Round Table talks, partially free parliamentary elections are held on June 4. The electoral rules are designed to guarantee the Communists and their allies the majority of legislative seats (and thus the prerogative to form the government). However, unexpectedly high support for the opposition and the unanticipated defection of two partners from the Communist camp pave the way for the formation of the first noncommunist government in east-central Europe since the 1940s. Longtime Solidarity activist Tadeusz Mazowiecki becomes prime minister. Under his tenure, the legislature begins a fundamental overhaul of the political system and lays the groundwork for systemic reforms across virtually all areas of public life.

1989: Balcerowicz Plan Adopted

In consultation with Western experts, Poland's first post-transition government introduces a radical macroeconomic adjustment and stabilization program on December 31. Known as the Balcerowicz Plan, the program affects bankruptcy laws, banking laws, interest rates, wages, foreign direct investment, and workers in state-owned firms, among other things. In the short term, the plan produces a sizable economic contraction. Strikes and unrest break out, but successive governments are able to withstand these pressures and maintain the momentum of reforms. Starting in 1993, Poland witnesses a rapid economic recovery and the stabilization of its political and economic situation.

1990: Privatization Ministry Created

Poland creates the Ministry of Privatization in 1990 and introduces far-reaching privatization measures as part of its transition to a market economy. By 2010, thousands of firms are privatized, liquidated, leased, or auctioned off. Although the privatization process is highly contentious and comparatively slow, it is conducted in an orderly and transparent fashion, allowing it to avoid many of the pitfalls that plague other postcommunist states, such as Russia.

1990: Walesa Elected President

After his predecessor resigns, Lech Walesa is elected as the first president of postcommunist Poland on December 9. Walesa had been a longtime labor leader at the Gdansk shipyard, chairman of the Solidarity movement, and winner of the 1983 Nobel Peace Prize. He serves as president until his 1995 defeat by former Communist official Aleksander Kwasniewski.

1997: New Constitution Adopted

The Polish legislature adopts a permanent new constitution on April 2. Poland's demanding political realities—which stem from post-transition reforms that aimed to prevent power from being overly concentrated in the hands of any individual or institution— explain why it took most of a decade before the country embraced a permanent charter. The constitution is approved in a popular referendum on May 25.

1999: Poland Joins NATO

Poland, along with the Czech Republic and Hungary, joins the North Atlantic Treaty Organization on March 13. Poland's accession to the alliance, ten years after the Round Table talks, helps cement its transition from a Communist state to a Western-oriented democracy.

2004: Poland Joins the European Union (EU)

Poland, along with seven other east-central European postcommunist states, joins the European Union on May 1. Between 2001 and 2004, Poland had undertaken far-ranging legal reforms as it prepared for EU accession. The EU's demanding conditions not only introduced profound changes to existing domestic laws and regulations but also placed certain policy domains outside the realm of political contestation. This process was not particularly democratic, but it had the virtue of being efficient and producing an outcome favorable to liberal norms.

2010: Plane Crash Kills Kaczynski and Senior Officials

On April 10, a plane crash kills President Lech Kaczynski and ninety-five other dignitaries traveling to Smolensk, Russia, to commemorate the seventieth anniversary of the 1940 Katyn Massacre. With President Kaczynski's death, parliamentary speaker Bronislaw Komorowski becomes acting president. Komorowski wins a full term in the election of July 4, defeating Jaroslaw Kaczynski, the late president's twin brother. That Poland's constitutional arrangements are not threatened by the crash testifies to the institutional stability the state achieved over the previous two decades.

2012: Economy Stays Robust Through Global Downturn

Poland is the only European nation that avoids lapsing into recession as a result of the global financial crisis. Between 2008 and 2011, it achieves total GDP growth of more than 15 percent. Indeed, since 2007, Poland's real GDP growth has exceeded that of the other thirty-three countries in the OECD, contributing to a sizable decline in the income gap between it and west European economies.

South Africa

John Campbell

With the end of apartheid and subsequent elections in 1994, South Africa became a nonracial democracy. The rule of law and representative government were extended to all its peoples—black, "colored," Indian, and white. Subsequently, the country adopted a new constitution that provides perhaps the most elaborate protection for human rights anywhere in the world. But the postapartheid government has largely failed to deliver on expectations of shared economic opportunity.

For most South Africans today, there is more economic and social continuity with the past than had been anticipated twenty years ago. South Africa has the continent's largest economy, but, as before 1994, it remains characterized by gross inequality. For example, in 2008, the aggregate income of blacks was 13 percent that of whites; in 1995, it was 13.5 percent. The black middle class has grown to approximately 2.6 million in a population of about fifty million, and among the country's millionaires are high-visibility blacks. Some commentators argue, indeed, that the country's fault lines are becoming those of class rather than race. But race remains the predominant predictor of destiny, including access to education, health services, and middle-class status.

In fact, the 1994 transition was a negotiated settlement between the incumbent government and the liberation movements, not a capitulation of the former to the latter. Although formal apartheid ended and the government became largely black, wholesale transfer of wealth from the privileged to the poor was not a realistic option then and has not happened since.

Today, despite the growth of a black middle class employed primarily in the public sector, and a handful of black millionaires closely linked to the governing African National Congress (ANC), whites remain much wealthier than other racial groups and continue to dominate the private sector of the economy. Race even continues to be defined by law, as it was under apartheid. Only now, racial classification is used to access

Black Economic Empowerment (BEE) and affirmative action programs rather than to solidify white privilege. Indeed, with the help of
BEE, black, colored, and Indian investors now own 28 percent of the
Johannesburg Stock Exchange's one hundred biggest companies—an
improvement but also a reminder of the disproportionate economic
power of white South Africans.

For the overwhelming majority of blacks, poverty and limited
upward mobility remain the enduring reality, even with the right to vote
and political representation at the highest level. Despite increased black
participation in the modern economy, the life expectancy of blacks has
declined from 64.8 years in 1994 to 47 years in 2010, largely because of
HIV/AIDS.

Apartheid's victims expect more. But demographic pressures are
building because of a high (though declining) black birthrate and massive immigration from the rest of the African continent. Population
growth risks outrunning economic growth and opportunity for average
blacks, despite the HIV/AIDS demographic disaster. Still unresolved is
whether South Africa's democratic institutions can address the mounting demands for transformative change for the black majority against
the background of low and unequal economic growth and rapid population expansion.

The Dutch settled Kaapstad (Cape Town) in 1652. In the decades that
followed, they were joined by other northern Europeans, most of whom
were seeking religious freedom. The descendants of these seventeenth-
century settlers amalgamated into the Afrikaner people, often called
Boers (farmers). They remained Calvinist in religion, and developed
their own language, Afrikaans, from Dutch.

South Africa was far from empty when the Dutch arrived. From
the beginning, warfare was typical and cooperation scant between
the Dutch and the indigenous black peoples, who far outnumbered
the white settlers. But black Africans were also divided into numerous ethnic groups, with frequent intertribal warfare. With their more
advanced weapons, the Dutch slowly pushed the boundaries of settlement out from Kaapstad.

The Dutch were also major slave traders. However, Dutch enslave-
ment of indigenous people in their Cape of Good Hope colony was
difficult, because the newly enslaved escaped easily into a familiar
environment close at hand. So, within the first years of settlement, the
Dutch began to import South Asians from their East Indies possessions

for agriculture and viniculture. These South Asians intermarried with whites and indigenous peoples. Over time, they gradually became a separate and distinct people, called coloreds. (They see themselves today as a separate, not a mixed, race.)

After the British captured the Cape from the Netherlands in 1795, small waves of British immigration into the colony continued periodically. Later in the nineteenth century, the British imported large numbers of South Asians to work newly established sugar plantations. Over time, they too evolved into a separate racially defined community, called Indians.

By the late nineteenth century, the racial hierarchy was fixed. Whites were at the top, coloreds and Indians in the middle, and blacks at the bottom. Whites were divided by language, between English and Dutch (later Afrikaans), and blacks by ethnic group and language. Whites often used coloreds and Indians as "bosses" over Africans and extended certain privileges to them within a framework of increasingly rigid racial segregation. Africans, in turn, often resented the two intermediary peoples as much as they did whites.

Apartheid arose primarily from Afrikaner fear of being swamped by the far larger black population. But a parallel sense of grievance against the British following their victory in the Boer War (1899–1902) also played a significant role. From an Afrikaner perspective, blacks and English each in their own way imperiled Afrikaner identity, the former through their numbers, the latter through their wealth and links to the British Empire. After the war, it was the English who controlled the modern economy. Afrikaners remained poorer and less educated than the English. Even now, it is estimated that their average income is about 30 percent less than that of the English. Afrikaner economic resentment is compounded by the perception that the English can always go "home," whereas they are already home and have no alternative.

Nevertheless, despite the bitterness, the British Empire and the Afrikaner leadership concluded a post–Boer War bargain at the expense of nonwhites. In return for continued English domination of the modern economy, the British ceded control of political life to the Afrikaners. All the British territories were incorporated with two former independent Afrikaner states to become a new entity: the Union of South Africa. In 1910, it became a self-governing dominion similar to Canada and Australia, with universal suffrage for white males. Demography ensured that one white man–one vote meant Afrikaner domination. No provision was made for black African political life, the few exceptions being mostly for coloreds, and in only one province, the Cape. South Africa was a parliamentary democracy—for whites only.

Fueled by gold and diamonds, the South African economy in the late nineteenth and early twentieth centuries evolved into a type of unbridled booty capitalism, dominated by big, privately owned corporations seeking quick profits and dependent on cheap black labor. Rates of economic growth were high, as was income inequality. South Africa rapidly acquired the infrastructure of a modern industrial state. The economy was dominated by extractive industries, but white commercial farming and manufacturing also developed rapidly. By the 1960s, it was often said that white South Africans had the highest material standard of living in the world, whereas blacks were on par with citizens of Cameroon.

Apartheid as a formal system of legislation segregating races dates from 1948, when the radically conservative Afrikaner political party, the Nationalists, narrowly won the elections. With an ideology that was anticommunist, overtly racist, and suffused with a sense of colonial grievance by Afrikaners against English speakers, apartheid offered few new ideas but was systematically organized and rigidly enforced. Its primary feature, the physical separation of races into different territories, caused untold misery. Rural black Africans were increasingly squeezed into lands of marginal fertility, and coloreds and Indians gradually lost their already limited political rights. Urban blacks were consigned to townships and informal settlements, usually without electricity and often with limited access to water.

An elaborate system of labor regulation reserved jobs for whites and, to a lesser extent, for coloreds and Indians. It systematically excluded blacks from many occupations. The National Party also developed a publicly financed affirmative action program for Afrikaners, thereby largely eliminating white poverty.

As apartheid evolved, the government established tribally defined "self-governing homelands." Over time, the expectation was that they would become fully independent states. Africans would be stripped of their South African citizenship and assume that of the independent homeland to which they "belonged." The goal was a white and, to a much lesser extent, coloreds and Indian South Africa, but with millions of black sojourners, their movements regulated by hated "pass laws" to provide the labor necessary for a modern industrial state.

Black opposition movements arose in response starting in the early twentieth century. The African National Congress (ANC), probably the largest liberation movement throughout the period, was multiracial in its early years and dominated by middle-class black professionals.

When it became exclusively black in the face of official intransigence, whites opposed to apartheid gravitated to the South African Communist Party (SACP), which also attracted support from the other racial groups. Other liberation movements included the Pan African Congress (PAC) and the Black Consciousness Movement, led by the activist Steve Biko and influenced by American civil rights activists.

Until the 1980s, all of these groups usually saw socialism or communism as the most important element to ending apartheid and establishing nonracial democracy, and they received significant support from the Soviet Bloc. Among many in the antiapartheid movement, East Germany in particular was admired as a developed, socialist economy.

Black organized labor also played an important role in the struggle against apartheid. Black trade unions were recognized by the apartheid state in 1979 and wrested concessions for nonwhite workers. From its founding, the Congress of South African Trade Unions (COSATU) has also politically mobilized working Africans. But highly skilled white workers often supported apartheid. They were organized into their own trade unions, which were not usually sympathetic to any expansion of black employment opportunities.

The government responded to the antiapartheid movement with repression. Prominent African leaders such as Nelson Mandela were imprisoned. Black Consciousness leader Steve Biko was murdered while in police custody. Popular insurrections were met with bullets, notably the Sharpeville massacre in 1960 and the Soweto School Boycott of 1976, both of which marked stages in the escalation of government repression. The world came to associate apartheid with official violence, and South Africa gradually became a pariah state.

INFLECTION POINTS
OF THE TRANSITION PERIOD

Apartheid began to collapse in the late 1980s. The South African courts overturned some apartheid statutes as unconstitutional; other aspects were ended in response to pressure from the liberation movements. A few clergy in South Africa played a significant role convincing Afrikaners that apartheid could not be morally justified. Western countries intensified a variety of economic and sports-related sanctions against South Africa, and many Western corporations disinvested from the South African economy. For whites especially, exclusion from international sporting competitions was particularly bitter. Meanwhile, the ANC and other black liberation organizations fueled unrest in townships.

Whites came to acquiesce both to the legalization of the liberation movements under F. W. de Klerk's National government in 1990 and to the release of imprisoned liberation leaders. The ANC, led by the newly released Nelson Mandela, gradually abandoned socialism and embraced free-market capitalism. Multiple causes prompted this ideological shift, including growing economic sophistication on the part of the ANC leadership, encouraged by their participation in various international economic forums; the collapse of the Soviet Union and the further discrediting of Communist systems; and the anticipation of governing a country with a big, highly developed economy.

Free elections in 1994, stemming from prolonged negotiations between the government and the liberation movements, resulted in a black-majority government under President Nelson Mandela. The state was somewhat decentralized, and newly created provinces enjoyed some authority. The last two white governments before the nonracial elections had privatized certain state-owned enterprises, and de Klerk dismantled South Africa's nuclear weapons capability.

In the last years of apartheid, few would have predicted that South Africa would undergo a negotiated transition from its white-dominated security state to nonracial democracy. Yet the geopolitical circumstances in the decade before 1994 were propitious. The internationally brokered independence of Namibia resulted in the departure of Communist Cubans who had supported the indigenous liberation movement, the South West Africa People's Organization; free Namibia proved to pose no threat to either South Africa's whites or the capitalist economic system. The collapse of the Soviet Union dried up a source of support for the South African liberation movements and discredited communism, depriving supporters of the status quo with the justification for apartheid as a bulwark against the Red Menace in Africa.

The liberation struggle had also stalled. Although it could make the townships ungovernable, it lacked the military strength to defeat the government, even with guerrilla tactics. Critically, the liberation leadership included genuine democrats devoted to human rights, not least Nelson Mandela. Christian leaders such as Archbishop Desmond Tutu also helped shape liberation thinking. As the liberation movements became more open to negotiation, the role of Nelson Mandela and his close associates was critical to building the bridge between the liberation movements and the de Klerk government that made a negotiated settlement possible.

As for whites, even among strong supporters of the National Party, apartheid no longer seemed to work. Some saw parallels between the radical racial segregation that culminated in apartheid and the European anti-Semitism that culminated in the Holocaust. Gradually, to an increasing number of whites, a society organized along rigid racial lines began to appear incompatible with the Christian beliefs that most whites (and blacks) held.

And white pocketbooks were hurting. In part because of international sanctions, low direct investment, and labor unrest, the economy was in the doldrums. Whites were weary of being treated as pariahs by the rest of the world.

President F. W. de Klerk and other white leaders concluded that change was inevitable, and the liberation movements recognized they could not defeat the white government. So, after prolonged negotiations, they struck a deal at Kempton Park, a conference center outside Johannesburg, in 1993. This provided both for nonracial elections in 1994 with a transition period wherein the largest parties would share executive authority for five years, and ultimately for a new constitution with far-reaching human rights protections, proportional representation, and a mild form of federalism.

This wholesale political reorganization, however, was not matched by economic restructuring. Indeed, a possible reorganization of the economy was never on the table, and the economy continued to be dominated by white-owned corporations. It was widely assumed that in a nonracial, democratic South Africa, massive foreign investment would stimulate rapid growth of the economy that would lift millions out of poverty without requiring significant redistribution of wealth. Those within the liberation movements who advocated radical redistribution did not have widespread popular support and were sidelined by the ANC leadership.

Under Mandela's successors, Thabo Mbeki and subsequently Jacob Zuma, government policy tied South Africa closely to the global, liberal economic system. Government-mandated BEE and affirmative action did little for the majority of blacks mired in poverty and high unemployment in an environment of globalization and the decline of extractive industries. More important for the growth of the black middle class was access to employment in the public sector. The civil service became predominately—although not exclusively—black, encouraged by a system of racial preferences. The ANC government significantly improved black housing and access to water and electricity. The education sector saw limited progress in overcoming the heritage of formal apartheid—and its consequences. Moreover, health services for nonwhites went into free fall in the face of the HIV/AIDS epidemic, which the Mandela and Mbeki governments largely ignored for too long.

Under the provisions of the new constitution, credible elections were held in 1994, 1999, 2004, and 2009. The ANC consistently polled almost two-thirds of the vote, ensuring them an overwhelming majority in parliament. The National Party collapsed, and most white voters (as well as Indians and coloreds) moved to the Democratic Alliance, which became the formal parliamentary opposition.

Although South Africa was now a nonracial democracy, race remained the usual determinant of party support, and blacks overwhelmingly voted for the ANC. Nevertheless, the ANC and the Democratic Alliance remained genuinely multiracial in their leadership. Other small political parties retained a parliamentary presence because of proportional representation. Increasingly, they have cooperated with the Democratic Alliance.

LESSONS OF THE TRANSITION PERIOD

Before 1994, South Africa had democratic institutions—but they applied only to a small racial minority and were often compromised by the security apparatus. The essence of the transition was extending political democracy to the entire population. This has worked remarkably well. However, black poverty and white privilege were not addressed at Kempton Park and remain largely entrenched into the present.

SOCIOECONOMIC EXCLUSION AND INCLUSION

Class, race, poverty, and wealth continue to be inextricably linked in South African socioeconomic life (see Figure 8). Most blacks and

FIGURE 8. INCOME AND RACE IN SOUTH AFRICA

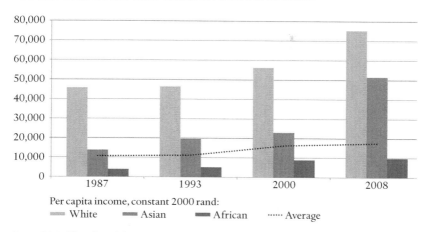

Per capita income, constant 2000 rand:
▬ White   ▬ Asian   ▬ African   ⋯⋯ Average

Source: M. Leibbrandt et al. (2010), "Trends in South African Income Distribution and Poverty since the Fall of Apartheid," OECD Social, Employment and Migration Working Papers, No. 101, OECD Publishing, http://dx.doi.org/10.1787/5kmmsot7p1ms-en. "Average" includes more racial groups than the ones listed.

coloreds are poor. Most whites are middle class, and, increasingly, Indians are as well, now freed of apartheid-era limitations on their economic activity. A significant achievement of the ANC government since 1994 has been to supply water, electricity, trash removal, and toilets to townships and informal settlements. But the location of the major townships, distant from employment centers, remains much the same as under apartheid.

Under apartheid, apprenticeship programs were used to steer non-whites into certain occupations. These programs were associated with racial restrictions on job opportunities. Accordingly, Mandela's government did away with apprenticeship programs, but it did not replace them with an alternative. Despite improvements, only about 30 percent of blacks had completed the equivalent of high school in 2010 (see Figure 9). The result is a shortage of workers in many skilled trades even as the overall unemployment rate remains about 25 percent of the workforce—30 percent if those no longer actively looking for work are included. In some areas, unemployment among black youth exceeds 40 percent. Among whites, unemployment is rare.

BEE, which applies to nonwhite South Africans, has resulted in the transfer of some enterprises to black ownership. At the core of BEE is a process whereby nonwhites can acquire company shares under

FIGURE 9. EDUCATION AND RACE IN SOUTH AFRICA

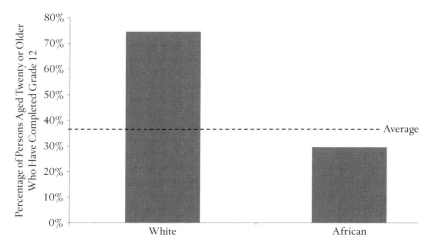

Source: South African Institute of Race Relations, *South Africa Survey 2010/2011*. Data from 2010. "Average" includes more racial groups than those listed.

ostensibly favorable terms. Accordingly, black ownership of companies with stock traded on the Johannesburg Stock Exchange has risen from almost 15 percent in 2000 to 17.4 percent in 2010. However, to meet BEE goals of ownership and leadership (among other categories), too often companies have hived off their weaker sectors, and the new owners find themselves burdened with debt and slow growth. Affirmative action has established black quotas in private enterprises above a certain size threshold. But neither BEE nor affirmative action has had a transformational impact on the economy or the black community.

Most of the growth in the black middle class has been the result of public sector employment, not the private sector or BEE. The public sector employs more than one million people. Up to 75 percent of them are black. Their salaries have been rising more rapidly than in the private sector. Additionally, the government pays about fifteen million South Africans—almost 33 percent of the population—a subsistence allowance that functions much like a guaranteed minimum income. This mitigates the misery of poverty and politically ties the poor to the ANC, but it carries the risk of welfare dependency and strains the tax base of about five million payers.

BEE has enlarged the black elite and tied it to the ANC. Civil service employment has also promoted loyalty to the ANC among its beneficiaries. The subsistence allowance benefits a core ANC constituency, the black poor. However, in the townships, riots break out periodically over the failure of officials to deliver expected services and over corruption. The focus of demonstrator ire tends to be specific officials rather than the ANC as a whole.

The opposition Democratic Alliance is pursuing electoral support from middle-class blacks, especially those in the professions independent of government employment, such as medical doctors, lawyers, and the small class of black entrepreneurs. To that end, the alliance's leadership is seeking a "black face" for the party's leadership. It remains to be seen whether the Democratic Alliance will be successful in wooing significant black support. Its chances are probably best in Gauteng province, which includes the sophisticated economies centered on Johannesburg and Pretoria. In Cape Town, however, tension remains between coloreds and blacks. There, the Democratic Alliance is still thought of as the colored party and thus is unlikely to acquire significant black support.

ECONOMIC STRUCTURE AND POLICIES

According to the World Bank, South Africa has the largest economy in Africa, and the twenty-eighth largest in the world. The World Bank classified South Africa in 2012 as an upper-middle-income country, one of only four in Africa. (The others were Botswana, Gabon, and Mauritius, all small in population.) Thus, South Africa is the only large, diverse African economy in this category.

The post-1994 government inherited an economy riddled with distortions and corruption caused by apartheid-era autarchy encouraged by international sanctions. It depended heavily on extractive industries, which over the past two decades have steadily declined as mines are exhausted and competition from other countries increases. Nevertheless, even while the transition was being implemented, South Africa was being reintegrated into the global economic system and therefore subjected to market discipline. The challenge for the new government was to foster inclusive economic growth to address the country's pervasive poverty and to right the wrongs from the apartheid era. Its fundamental strategy has been to adhere to the so-called Washington Consensus of free-market capitalism.

By conventional measures, official economic policy has generally worked well and has the approval of the international financial institutions. The South African currency, the rand, has remained relatively stable. Post-1994 governments have continued to privatize enterprises and reduce regulation. The Johannesburg Stock Exchange remains the most important in sub-Saharan Africa. Despite some capital flight and some big companies' moving their headquarters out of the country, notably to London, net inflows to South Africa of foreign direct investment grew more than 2,400 percent from 1994 until 2008. The tax base is small because incomes are low, but tax collection is more efficient than in most African countries. (All consumers pay the ubiquitous sales tax.) Given South Africa's competent regulation, rule of law, property rights, and independent judiciary, investors do not face the same level of risk and uncertainty that they do in other parts of Africa. On the other hand, returns can be lower, particularly in the short term.

Economic growth has been restored, albeit at a relatively low level, following a decade of violence, sanctions, and stagnation in the 1980s. According to the World Bank, in 1989, GDP per capita was $3,227 (in constant 2000 prices). By 2010, it was $3,746. The economy is growing, but not quickly enough to meet the rising expectations of a rapidly expanding population.

On the left of the political spectrum, outside the ANC ruling circles, the assumption remains that South Africa is inherently a rich country, and that poverty can be addressed by redistribution of existing wealth. At a basic level, this means taking wealth from whites and giving it to blacks. Hence, Julius Malema, the former head of the ANC Youth League and an African populist, called for the seizure of white-owned farmland without compensation and its distribution to black farmers. He also called for the nationalization of the big mining houses. Although he has been marginalized within the ANC, his views are widely held among the dispossessed. Tellingly, the ANC has removed Malema from the leadership of the youth league, yet he retains substantial support in the townships.

Nelson Mandela and others anticipated that in the aftermath of the transition a flood of foreign direct investment would transform South Africa's economy. That has not happened. Domestic investment in the South African economy also remains low. Hein Marais argues that although the country's labor laws contribute to investor hesitancy, higher and quicker returns elsewhere in Africa are probably a more important factor. Nevertheless, businesses have been investing in equipment, capital improvements, and the like more rapidly over the past ten years than in the years immediately after the end of apartheid.

Some South Africans believe that slow economic growth is the result of maldistribution of wealth; others, that the inflexibility of strong trade unions is a primary cause of the country's high unemployment. The trade unions are certainly powerful, and COSATU is certainly allied with the governing ANC, but COSATU is a confederation of trade unions, not a political organization. Its goals have consistently been to achieve the highest wages and greatest job security for its members rather than maximize employment throughout the economy. Labor inflexibility probably influences the slow economic growth, but a variety of other factors, including gross economic inequality and an educational system that does not meet the needs of a modern economy, are at least as important (see Figure 10).

The labor unrest in the mining sector in 2012 reflected both the poverty of black workers and growing divisions within the labor movement. Protesters initially sought higher wages in a declining industry,

FIGURE 10. UNEMPLOYMENT AND RACE IN SOUTH AFRICA

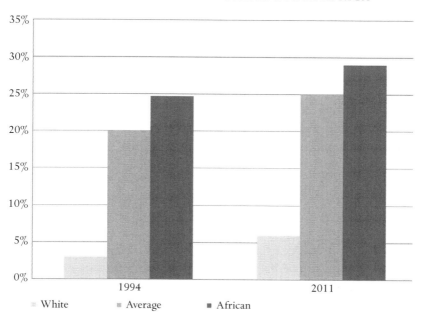

Source: South African Institute of Race Relations, *2009/2010 South Africa Survey.* "Average" includes more racial groups than those listed.

but the unrest was exacerbated by the militancy of a new, radical union that challenged the National Union of Mineworkers (NUM), a pillar of COSATU and a fixture of the ANC. The violence and the subsequent government response highlighted the close relationship between the NUM, the big mining corporations, and the ANC. Nevertheless, the strikes had remarkably little impact on the larger economy, at least in the short term. The value of the rand fell but quickly stabilized. Mining, though a declining dimension of the South African economy, remains important. But it contributes only about 5 percent of gross domestic product. If labor unrest becomes endemic, it could presage more economic bitterness in other parts of the economy. In any event, the widespread perception that Jacob Zuma's government has mishandled the unrest almost certainly undercut his political position within the ANC, exposing him to challenges by more radical figures.

Perhaps a more important drag on employment, however, is the shortage of trained and skilled workers, itself a reflection of the shortcomings of apartheid-era education. According to Statistics South Africa, of those unemployed in 2012, 60 percent have not completed secondary education and 44 percent have never worked. Through BEE and affirmative action, the ANC government has tried to bring more blacks into the upper reaches of the modern economy and to create more job opportunities. But without more expansion of educational and training opportunities, qualified individuals who are black will remain in short supply. On March 25, 2002, *Business Day*, a leading newspaper, calculated that of nineteen thousand chartered accountants, only 246 were black.

Land redistribution, another critical black grievance, was also left out of the transition negotiations. Since then, the ANC government has tried to address apartheid-era confiscation of land from blacks. But wholesale land redistribution is constrained by legal protection of property rights and government budgetary constraints. When it does happen, land redistribution is on the basis of willing seller, willing buyer. Little land has therefore been redistributed.

Finally, the alleged ubiquity of corruption, often referred to as "tenderpreneurship" in the South African press (a reference to government tenders), complicates the issues of inequality and economic growth. It is difficult to know whether corruption is any more common now than it was under apartheid, though the beneficiaries are clearly different. However, the widespread belief that it is out of

control certainly undercuts the moral authority of the former liberation movements that now constitute the government. South Africans
often credibly assume that the small class of black millionaires owe
their fortunes more to ANC connections and to government contracts than to productive economic activity.

CIVIL SOCIETY AND MEDIA

Civil society organizations and the media were at the forefront of the
antiapartheid struggle. Both publicized security service abuses, and
civil society groups often used the judiciary effectively to combat apartheid. Together they convinced many South Africans (including whites)
of the fundamentally unjust nature of apartheid—and of its unsustain-
ability. De Klerk could negotiate with the liberation movements for a
transition to nonracial democracy at Kempton Park only because he
had the support or acquiescence of his white constituency.

The South African press is vibrant, and its freedom has strong constitutional guarantees, which was not the case during the apartheid era,
when the security services often tried to censor it, though with only limited success. For example, as a journalist, Helen Zille, the current leader
of the parliamentary opposition Democratic Alliance, uncovered and
reported the security services' murder of Steve Biko.

Since 1994, both the media and civil society have continued to play
a major role in national life. Civic organizations such as the Treatment
Action Campaign and the newly constituted Corruption Watch have
adhered to civil society's legacy as leaders of the antiapartheid struggle,
working to bring accountability to governance and address South Africa's triple threat of poverty, unemployment, and inequality. Traditionally, they have been strongest within the white population. However,
over the past decade, civic organizations based in the townships have
become vibrant. They often organize demonstrations protesting the
nondelivery of basic urban services, such as water and electricity.

The press in many ways functions as an opposition to the ANC
majority in parliament. Often in conjunction with civil society whistle-
blowers, it regularly ferrets out scandal and corruption. Such misbe-
havior mostly involves blacks because the ANC-led government is
predominately black. Media ownership, however, is highly concentrated
and 86 percent of print media is white-owned. The drumbeat of criticism
by the white-owned media of a black government causes resentment.

Indeed, ANC political figures regularly accuse the press of being biased or seeking to obstruct the transformation of South Africa into a nonracial democracy. Such ANC leaders call for the press to show more balance and to highlight ANC achievements. In turn, critics of the ANC often accuse the press of soft-pedaling criticism of the ANC because of their need for good relations with the government.

This tension has played out most recently in parliamentary debate over the proposed Protection of State Information Act, which would limit the freedom of the press and impede whistle-blowing, mainly because it lacks a defense of the public interest clause. Accordingly, opposition to the draft act is widespread among the opposition parties and even within the ANC. This has already resulted in the government's backing down on some of the more egregious provisions.

LEGAL SYSTEM AND RULE OF LAW

The rule of law has long been deeply entrenched in South Africa. Indeed, apartheid was a legal system. The transition away from it to nonracial democracy was successful because both sides abided by their legal obligations to the negotiated compromise. Negotiators went to great lengths to clearly define the rights South Africans would have in their new constitution. Human rights are defined as essentially individual. Discrimination on the basis of race, ethnicity, religion, language, or sexual orientation is outlawed. Gender equality is affirmed. Capital punishment is abolished.

In addition, the constitution guarantees a range of social and economic rights for South African citizens "to the extent that is practicable." Examples include access to water and housing. Sometimes constitutionally guaranteed rights appear to collide: prominent individuals who appear to defend apartheid and claim freedom of speech may face charges of advocating racial discrimination.

The judiciary, another essential legal institution, is probably more independent now than under apartheid. Then, judges usually reflected the apartheid values of white society. But even under the Nationalists, the government occasionally lost high-profile cases against liberation leaders. Similarly, critics now maintain that some judges reflect the values and policies of the ANC and its labor and Communist allies. According to Jeff Radebe, the judiciary is becoming multiracial in composition and is now less than half white. No person is above the law.

As deputy president, Jacob Zuma was tried for rape and acquitted. As president, he is facing renewed corruption charges, previously thrown out, regarding an arms deal.

Government initiatives are subject to review by the constitutional courts. That has led some court critics to conclude that the independent judiciary is blocking (or could block) government efforts toward more racial economic equality that might, for example, impinge on property rights. Accordingly, calls have been made for restrictions to be imposed on the independence of the courts. Such rhetoric is vociferously opposed by civil society groups and the press.

Under apartheid, some individuals in the security services committed crimes with impunity. It is widely believed that senior National Party political figures were complicit. At the same time, liberation movement "enforcers" were guilty of some of the same practices. Accordingly, the 1994 transition negotiations established the Truth and Reconciliation Commission (TRC), chaired by the Anglican archbishop of Cape Town, Desmond Tutu. In effect, if perpetrators came forward and publicly acknowledged their crimes, they were granted immunity from prosecution. Based on Latin American precedents, the TRC was designed to provide a modicum of justice as it closed the door on the past. Several hundred availed themselves of the TRC. Although some of the "small fry" perpetrators of abuses came forward, none of the leaders of the former apartheid regime or of the liberation movements did so. Public TRC hearings provided an opportunity for many of the victims to tell their story—an important catharsis in individual cases. As such, the TRC contributed to the achievement of political stability in South Africa. But it does not appear to have played a central role in winning white acceptance for the transition, and its influence is probably greater as a model for other countries interested in truth commissions for postconflict resolution.

The police were the first-line enforcers of apartheid. Then, probably half were black, though the leadership was almost entirely white, and police stations in townships were mini-fortresses. Now, township dwellers view the police with ambiguity, if not suspicion. The police in general operate within the bounds of the law. They are, however, often understaffed, undertrained, and underequipped. Their salaries are low, though commensurate with those of other public servants. Anecdotal evidence of police officers accepting bribes exists, but the police force as an institution is not as widely associated with corruption as in other African countries. However, credible concerns have been expressed by civic organizations that the Zuma government is politicizing the police and the intelligence services by using them in support of the targeted prosecution of political enemies. Thus far, the independent judicial system has served as a check on the political use of prosecutorial authority.

Crime rates in South Africa are high. At present, the murder rate is about six times that in the United States, which is one of the highest in the developed world. Most of the violence occurs within the townships, but concern is deep—and borders at times on paranoia—about crime among all racial groups. Potential foreign investors regularly cite crime rates as a reason they are not more active in South Africa. In fact, crime statistics are slowly improving, but not rapidly enough to alter the perception that the country is dangerous.

In wealthy residential areas of major urban centers, especially Cape Town, Johannesburg, and Durban, residents supplement the police by hiring private security forces. It is not uncommon for a private house to be protected by a private security service, another private security service hired by the neighborhood association, and the police. As a result, crime has fallen significantly in areas where, in effect, policing has been privatized.

GOVERNMENT STRUCTURE AND DIVISION OF POWER

The constitution provides for three coequal branches of government: the executive, the legislature, and the judiciary. There are parallel structures in each of the provinces.

However, for some South African observers, the increasingly blurred distinction between the ANC as a political party and the government is troubling. As long as voting continues along racial lines, the ANC's ruling position cannot be challenged, raising concerns that South Africa is evolving into a one-party state. Many citizens question whether South Africa is run from the Union Buildings in Pretoria (the seat of government) or Lithuli House in Johannesburg (the ANC headquarters).

Moreover, the constitution has certain provisions related to proportional representation that limit dissent within political parties. For example, if a member of parliament quits the party on whose list he was elected, he must resign his seat. On the other hand, at times salient signs of democracy within the party are evident. In 2007, Jacob Zuma successfully challenged Thabo Mbeki for the party leadership within the

ANC. The party then recalled a defeated Mbeki from the presidency, and he thereupon resigned. (The deputy president, Kgalema Motlanthe, served as president until national elections.) Zuma, in turn, has faced a significant challenge within the ANC.

Reflecting its roots as a liberation movement, the party (and government) is supposed to be highly disciplined. In fact, both are internally divided and rarely monolithic. The government, specifically, is a formal tripartite alliance of the ANC, the COSATU, and the SACP. Government ministers are drawn from all three.

Hence, the ANC-led government is not as powerful as it appears to be, nor as the old National Party was during the days of apartheid, when parliament had only one opposition member. Speculation about a potential ANC split is ongoing. The 2009 election saw the emergence of one splinter, but it failed to win significant support. Nevertheless, in the face of a slow-growing economy, high unemployment, and the persistence of de facto racial privilege, a split in the party between radicals and conservatives remains plausible. Radicals are particularly at home in the ANC Youth League and the ANC Women's League. The former has been led by Julius Malema, the latter by Winnie Mandela. Thus far, Zuma has been able to curtail the left: he had Malema expelled from the party and Winnie Mandela is marginalized. Yet both retain significant popular support.

Nonetheless, many ANC members are concerned that internal party democracy has been eroding, a process that started under Thabo Mbeki, whose style was to centralize decision-making in the presidency. Critics see a relationship between an increasingly authoritarian ANC and the growth of corruption. That, in turn, results in hostility toward a highly critical press and a judiciary that can challenge party initiatives.

The Democratic Alliance, the ANC's official opposition in parliament, knows and uses all of the parliamentary devices open to a formal opposition, including increasingly cooperating with the other small opposition parties. At the provincial level, it governs the Western Cape, arguably the most developed and best-run province of the country, and Cape Town at the municipal level. Its goal is to capture the city government of Johannesburg in the next elections. Such a goal is plausible because of the Democratic Alliance's reputation for good service delivery.

Despite the strength of the Democratic Alliance, concern is widespread that South Africa could evolve into a one-party state, dominated by an increasingly authoritarian and centralized ANC. But the ANC itself is riddled with factions, and civil society and the press are quick to expose corruption. South Africa's institutions of government and the rule of law provide checks on the growth of an authoritarian ANC. Still, anemic economic growth and the gross inequality of opportunity among the races provide fertile ground for the emergence of a new, authoritarian radical party, either as a spin-off from the ANC or from separate origins.

EDUCATION AND DEMOGRAPHY

South Africa's population is roughly fifty million people. Blacks make up 79.5 percent, whites and coloreds each 9 percent, and Indians 2.5 percent. Illegal immigrants are in the range of three to five million. Overall, whites are steadily declining as a percentage of South Africa's population because of immigration from other parts of Africa and a higher black birth rate: the white population in 1911 was 22 percent; in 1980, it was 16 percent. But Statistics South Africa estimates that the absolute number of whites increased to just under five million over the past decade, including the 212,000 UK citizens immigrating to South Africa since 2000.

The educational burden inherited from apartheid has been especially heavy. Despite blacks' overwhelming majority, access to education remains as racially unequal as income. Thirty percent of blacks have finished high school, compared with 75 percent of whites. Fewer than 3 percent of blacks but more than 22 percent of whites have had some university-level education. Furthermore, black graduation rates from secondary and postsecondary education have changed little over the past ten years.

Multiple reasons explain this failure in education. Rural areas have too few teachers and school buildings, and the quality of those in some townships is low. Many teachers are poorly trained and poorly supervised, and strong teachers' unions make them largely unaccountable. Reasonably high investment in education has still not been enough to make up for the deficits under apartheid. And the growth of the population means there are ever more children and young people to be educated. For whites, the quality of education generally remains high—but even "state" education for whites is often privately subsidized by the payment of special fees by students' families. White schools have been desegregated—most have some black enrollment now—but black students attending formerly white schools are only a small percentage of the black student population.

Higher education under apartheid was divided by race, with separate white, colored, and black institutions. These were further divided between universities and technical institutes. They were also divided into institutions in the so-called self-governing homelands and in white South Africa. Altogether, the country had some nineteen higher education systems. (Nearly all higher education institutions are funded by the government.)

Since the transition, all but the white universities of international standing—Witwatersrand, Cape Town, Stellenbosch, and Pretoria—were placed in groups by the Ministry of Education to foster racial integration. For example, one white and two black institutions around Johannesburg were consolidated into the University of Johannesburg, with the goal of thorough racial integration of students, faculty, and administration. Complaints that consolidation has meant the dumbing down of the historically white universities are inevitable. Yet, overall, access to higher education has improved slightly, the proportion of black students rising from 52.9 percent in 1999 to 61.1 percent in 2009. Most black university enrollment remains in historically black institutions or newly amalgamated universities.

Secondary education was similarly fragmented. Under apartheid, white students in wealthy suburbs had access to high schools as good as those anywhere else in the world. In predominately black areas, whether the townships or rural areas, the quality could be very low.

Efforts have been made to improve access to elite former white high schools across all races. But such schools pose myriad challenges for low-income families, ranging from school fees to uniform requirements. Less elite high schools remain underfunded and understaffed. Primary education has a similar pattern. Notably, public education spending as a proportion of total government spending has declined since the late 1990s, in part because the government has had other priorities, including responding to the HIV/AIDS epidemic.

Nevertheless, among upper-middle-income countries, the proportion of South African public spending on education is relatively high. But apartheid's legacy and a rapidly growing population strain the educational system. In the public debate, awareness is acute that education is important and that the country is falling behind. Even among highly privileged whites, only about 74 percent are high school graduates, far too low for the emerging information economy. Complaints are widespread about the heavy hand of the teachers' unions (an important constituent element of COSATU) in inhibiting improvements in instructional quality and teacher training and oversight.

The debate over education in some ways parallels that over the economy. Should the government follow a redistributive strategy, placing many more poor children in elite schools, or should it "grow" the educational system overall? And, if the latter, how will a massive expansion of education be funded? For the post-1994 ANC government, and an economy growing only slowly, should resources be devoted to housing, electricity, and water, or to education? The ANC opted for the first three; the irony is that some polling data hinted that township dwellers may have preferred transformative spending on education for their children. Nevertheless, it is questionable whether post-1994 South Africa had the human resources—especially trained teachers—necessary for an all-out focus on education.

CONCLUSION

Is the glass half-empty or half-full? South Africa's post-1994 achievements are significant, especially in housing and infrastructure. After years of denial, the government is implementing sound policies to respond to the HIV/AIDS challenge. Well-meaning but less successful efforts have been made at education reform and at economic measures to reduce racial inequality. And, whether true or not, most South Africans believe that corruption has greatly increased, and many believe it is the single greatest threat to a prosperous future. The unanswered question is whether South Africa's liberal democracy can respond soon enough to the demands for economic and social change, which are occurring at only a snail's pace.

Examples of impatience abound. One is the rhetoric calling to reduce the independence of the judiciary. Proposals have been floated for a secrecy act and for restrictions on the freedom of the press. Opposition to gay rights is also growing, reflecting the move of Pentecostalism into the mainstream.

Why do so many black South Africans still lack socioeconomic empowerment? Part of the answer is the shortage of educational facilities for a modern economy: the heritage of apartheid. Part of the answer is demographic: the population is increasing faster than the government can provide better schools that prepare the workforce for a modern economy strangled by the lack of skilled labor. Part of the answer is the heavy disease burden that contributes to the decline in black life expectancy. (More than 25 percent of black males age thirty to thirty-four are living with HIV/AIDS.) And it is easy to overestimate the wealth of the country, given its celebrated mineral resources. In 1994, many liberation leaders found that the treasury was far emptier than they had expected, in part because the country was poorer than they had imagined.

Yet the political opposition continues to function, freedom of speech remains absolute and is ferociously protected, and there are many defenders of judicial independence. Within the ANC, many continue to struggle for the preservation of the party's "democratic space." But others, citing the alleged ubiquity of corruption, see the ANC as having lost its liberation ideals and moving toward the African norm of "big man" politics.

South Africa has an exploding population and its economy is firmly enmeshed in the international system. With respect to poverty alleviation—perhaps the country's greatest challenge—its options are limited. As a practical matter, it cannot simply expropriate white wealth; if it did, foreign direct investment would end. Nevertheless, the durability of the 1994 transition bargain, the enduring strength of the country's political institutions, and the activism of civil society provide credible grounds for optimism that South Africa will continue to evolve in a fundamentally democratic direction. The challenges are huge, but, on balance, the glass is half full.

SOUTH AFRICA TIMELINE

1948: National Party Adopts Apartheid

The Afrikaner-dominated National Party imposes a policy of apartheid, a widespread system of racial segregation meant to preserve white privilege. Black, white, colored, and Indian South Africans are required to live in defined territories, with blacks relegated to poor-quality rural lands and urban townships often lacking basic services. Apartheid also reserves superior jobs, education, and health services for whites. The National Party develops a publicly financed affirmative action program for Afrikaners, largely eliminating white poverty. Indeed, by the 1960s, some observers say that white South Africans have the highest material standard of living in the world, whereas blacks have one of the lowest.

1960: Sharpeville Massacre Occurs, ANC Banned

In the years after the 1948 election, the African National Congress (ANC), a leading liberation movement dominated by blacks, protests apartheid through civil disobedience. The government responds with repression. The Sharpeville Massacre occurs on March 21, when several thousand people gather at a police station in the Sharpeville township to protest pass laws, which restrict the movement of blacks. The police violently repress the insurrection and open fire on the crowd, killing sixty-nine black demonstrators. Later that month, South Africa's government bans the ANC. However, the organization continues to operate underground and outside the country through armed opposition groups.

1964: Mandela Sentenced to Life Imprisonment

Nelson Mandela, a prominent antiapartheid activist and ANC leader, is sentenced to life imprisonment on June 12, after being convicted of sabotage and treason. He spends more than twenty-five years in prison before his release in 1990. During his imprisonment, the ANC continues to contest apartheid through civil disobedience and guerilla tactics. Though it builds the capacity to make the townships ungovernable, it lacks the military strength to defeat the government, requiring a negotiated settlement to eventually end apartheid.

1990: ANC Unbanned, Mandela Released

South African president and National Party leader F. W. de Klerk lifts the ban on the ANC on February 2 and releases Nelson Mandela from prison on February 11. Mandela's release is broadcast live around the world. After leaving prison, he makes a historic speech in Cape Town. Speaking "in the name of peace, democracy, and freedom for all," Mandela urges a continued fight to end apartheid.

1993: Agreement Reached to End Apartheid

South African party leaders meet at Kempton Park outside Johannesburg to negotiate the end of apartheid. They reach a deal for nonracial elections to be held in 1994, followed by a transition period with shared executive authority among the largest parties. Leaders also write a new constitution that takes effect on February 4, 1997, and includes perhaps the most elaborate protection for human rights anywhere in the world.

1994: African National Congress Wins Free Elections

The ANC wins South Africa's first nonracial elections in April and Nelson Mandela becomes the first president of the postapartheid era. A government of national unity is formed, with the participation of the Afrikaner-dominated National Party. Former president F. W. de Klerk serves as deputy president under Mandela until June 1996. The elections cement blacks' full participation in politics and their representation at the highest levels of government. However, the transition to nonracial democracy does little to address the country's wide economic disparities.

1996: Truth and Reconciliation Commission Begins Hearings

The Truth and Reconciliation Commission (TRC), established by the 1994 transition negotiations and chaired by the Anglican archbishop of Cape Town, Desmond Tutu, begins public hearings in April 1996. The TRC addresses human rights crimes committed by the former government and liberation movements during the apartheid era. The process is designed to provide a modicum of justice while offering closure on the past, and it contributes to political stability in the period following the transition.

2002: Unemployment Hits Record High

Unemployment reaches a record high of 30 percent, up from less than 17 percent in 1995. It remains above 22 percent through the present, with rates higher than 40 percent among black youth in some areas. However, with low educational attainment and a lack of apprenticeship programs, there is a shortage of workers in many skilled trades, even as unemployment stays high.

2004: Broad-Based Black Economic Empowerment Act Adopted

The Broad-Based Black Economic Empowerment (BEE) Act of 2003 takes effect on January 9, 2004. BEE aims to redress the inequalities of apartheid by allowing blacks to participate more fully in South Africa's economy. While South Africa develops a sizable black middle class and high-visibility black millionaires, the country fails to alleviate its gross racial inequality in income. In 2008, the aggregate income of blacks is 13 percent that of whites; in 1995, it had been 13.5 percent.

2007: Zuma Wins ANC Party Leadership

In December, Jacob Zuma wrests the ANC leadership from President Thabo Mbeki, who had taken over South Africa's presidency from Nelson Mandela in 1999, when Mandela did not seek reelection. The move sets the stage for parliament to elect Zuma president in May 2009 after the ANC's electoral victory in April. Zuma had long been dogged by corruption charges, with the National Prosecuting Authority dropping a final case against him just before the April 2009 election.

2009: Despite Some Gains, Education Lags

Fifteen years after the end of apartheid, South Africa's education system struggles to remedy the effects of racial inequality and prepare students for the modern economy. Thirty percent of blacks versus 75 percent of whites have finished high school, and fewer than 3 percent of blacks but more than 22 percent of whites have had some university-level education. South Africa devotes a relatively high percentage of its public spending to education, but apartheid's legacy and a rapidly growing population strain its efforts.

2011: Populist Leader Suspended from ANC, Later Expelled

Julius Malema, the populist leader of the ANC's youth league, is suspended from the party for five years in November 2011 and expelled in February 2012. Malema had called for the seizure of white-owned farmland without compensation and its distribution to black farmers. He had also urged the nationalization of the big mining houses and the overthrow of Botswana's democratically elected government. Despite Malema's marginalization within the party, his views are widely held among the dispossessed, and he retains substantial support in the townships.

2012: Labor Unrest Roils Mining Sector

In August, wildcat strikes erupt at the Marikana platinum mine in South Africa's North West province, reflecting both the poverty of black workers and growing divisions within the labor movement. Protesters initially seek higher wages, but the unrest is exacerbated by the militancy of a new, radical union. Forty-six people die during six weeks of violence, including thirty-four miners killed by police on August 16. In September, Marikana miners return to work after accepting a 22 percent pay raise from the mine's operator. However, strikes spread to other platinum, gold, and coal mines throughout the fall, ultimately costing the country an estimated 0.5 percent of GDP.

Indonesia

Joshua Kurlantzick

After its independence from the Netherlands in 1949, Indonesia saw almost two decades of political instability, slow growth, and charismatic if often unstable leadership under Sukarno, its founding father. Sukarno advocated a "guided democracy" that was, in effect, a precarious authoritarianism. He promoted secularism by encouraging use of Indonesian—a language with no class or religious connotations—throughout the archipelago, instead of or in addition to the numerous local languages. Secularism also rested on the concept of *pancasila*, developed in the early Sukarno period. Pancasila was a mix of nationalism, adherence to monotheism, and socialism that Sukarno used to fend off efforts by Islamic parties to make Indonesia—a Muslim-majority country with sizable Christian, animist, Buddhist, and Hindu minorities—an officially Muslim state. But Sukarno also constantly attempted to play left- and right-leaning political groups against one another, which led to years of politically charged and sometimes violent politics and the death of some one million Indonesians in the mid-1960s. During this tumultuous period, Major General Suharto, who had risen in the ranks after independence, seized power from Sukarno in 1967 to become Indonesia's second president. The United States and other Western powers, distracted by the Vietnam War, tacitly or openly backed the takeover.

Under Suharto's one-party developmental state, Indonesia entered a three-decade-long phase of sustained growth but political slumber. Reversing the stagnation that had occurred under Sukarno, Suharto moved quickly to stabilize the economy under his pro-Western "New Order" regime. His was a technocrat-led authoritarian developmental state that invested in physical infrastructure, education, health care, and agriculture; shifted the country from an agrarian base to low-end export-oriented manufacturing; established sufficient rule of law to attract Japanese and other Asian companies for export-oriented manufacturing in

Java; and put in place heavy subsidies and protectionist policies to support local manufacturing, agriculture, and other industries.

For the three decades of Suharto's regime, economic growth was strong, averaging over 7 percent between 1985 and 1997. In the cities, a new consumer class emerged, and across the country, malnutrition, illiteracy, and unemployment declined significantly. As one comprehensive study of the Suharto era noted, the poverty rate fell from almost 60 percent in 1968 to 13 percent before the Asian financial crisis of 1997.

Sukarno and Suharto left the country with three important political legacies: a tradition of highly personalized politics; a commitment to the concept of a secular and inclusive state; and a fragile dictatorship that, under both men, required collaboration with other leading actors and regular—if phony—elections to shore up its legitimacy. Neither Suharto nor Sukarno had the full control over society that a totalitarian ruler like Mao had had in China, so when the country began its transition to democracy, Indonesians already had some experience with voting, opposition politics, and civil society.

Nevertheless, Indonesia's economic miracle came at a significant cost. Suharto's economic policies ran up substantial external debts and did little to strengthen the country's largely unregulated financial sector. To fund projects, Suharto and his allies depended on high-interest foreign loans and those from local banks that did not scrutinize borrowers' ability to repay. In the 1980s and early 1990s, Suharto liberalized the financial system, in large part to create more banks that could lend to his family. He opened banking licenses to a wider range of lenders, reduced the monopoly power of several larger banks, reduced restrictions on loan requirements, and began making it easier for foreign banks to operate in the country. Between 1988 and 1993, the number of banks in the country more than doubled, yet most had inadequate reserves.

Corruption was also endemic. New Indonesian tycoons, having been given monopolies in certain industries, revolved around the Suharto family. As Suharto's children reached adulthood in the 1990s, the family directly controlled a growing share of natural resources, manufacturing, and finance. By the 1990s, the Suharto regime was rated one of the most corrupt in the world: estimates of how much Suharto and his family stole from the state treasury go as high as $35 billion. In the wake of the Asian financial crisis in the late 1990s, Suharto's regime and much of Indonesia's economy collapsed. Indonesia seemed to come unmoored from its political foundations after the dictator resigned.

The rise of several separatist movements threatened to break up the country. Indeed, to those who lived through the chaotic late 1990s in Indonesia, the turnaround to the situation today seems remarkable. The sprawling country, with the fourth-largest population in the world, appears to have achieved stability and largely defused the violence that, a decade ago, threatened to tear the archipelago asunder. It has fostered a broader and more inclusive civil society and politics. A return to strong economic growth has led to a rising middle class. Local areas have gained greater control over their natural resources and their social welfare systems, and have introduced new forms of local elections and other types of voter feedback. Perhaps most impressively, Indonesia has managed to transform its military from the most powerful political actor in the country to one that operates under a reasonable degree of civilian control.

INFLECTION POINTS
OF THE TRANSITION PERIOD

The Asian financial crisis, which began in the summer of 1997, was the critical inflection point in modern Indonesian history. The crisis exposed the weaknesses of Suharto's economic policies—namely, excessive cronyism and corruption, unsustainable foreign debt, weak corporate governance, and too little financial regulation.

The financial crisis began with attacks on the Thai baht in the summer of 1997 and quickly drew in Indonesia. As the crisis intensified, Indonesian companies—many of which were controlled by Suharto and his allies—could not service their debt burden, especially that denominated in foreign currencies. A vicious cycle ensued. Portfolio investors and other creditors, skeptical that Indonesia would improve corporate governance, fled the country en masse, putting further pressure on the rupiah. Meanwhile, scores of Indonesian banks collapsed, wiping out local savings. The effects of the financial crisis were exacerbated by a deterioration of the country's underlying terms of trade. The price of oil, one of the most important Indonesian exports, hit record lows. The rise of China was increasingly challenging Indonesia's advantage in low-end manufacturing, such as apparel, footwear, and basic electronics. The political instability engendered by the crisis only hastened an exodus of foreign manufacturing firms from Indonesia.

As the financial crisis worsened, the Suharto administration appeared paralyzed in its ability to respond. The rupiah plunged more than 50 percent in value in 1997 against the U.S. dollar, and the Jakarta stock market became one of the worst-performing in the world. In 1998, the Indonesian economy shrank by 13.1 percent. Prices for staple goods such as rice and cooking oil rose as the rupiah's value plunged, and an additional 10 percent of the Indonesian population fell below the poverty line between 1998 and 2000.

Given few other options, Suharto was forced to seek a rescue package from the International Monetary Fund (IMF). Even though the IMF had previously praised Suharto's liberalization of the banking sector and paid little attention to his family's graft, it and other creditors now pushed Jakarta to open the economy by breaking up monopolies and allowing more foreign competition in critical areas. In the financial sector, it forced banks to address their nonperforming loans. It also required improvements in corporate governance through increased transparency, the unwinding of links between Suharto cronies and many top companies, and the appointment of genuinely independent directors to corporate boards.

As a result, several of the largest monopolies were broken up and the banking sector was consolidated. Most bad assets, however, were simply written off and many of the largest and most indebted conglomerates survived without serious reforms. Nevertheless, the image of then IMF chief Michel Camdessus towering over Suharto shamed the dictator and made his administration look weak and inept in the eyes of many Indonesians, as well as the army.

With Suharto appearing more and more feeble, protests mounted in the streets of Jakarta and other cities, and average Indonesians increasingly lost their fear of Suharto's security forces. Growing street protests eventually drew in long-time opposition groups like that of Megawati Sukarnoputri, daughter of Sukarno. In 1998, Suharto stepped down and handed power to his vice president, B. J. Habibie, a man who had no constituency of his own.

Habibie's tenure was the second inflection point in Indonesia's transition. A somewhat accidental change agent, the new president turned out to have relatively reformist instincts. He recognized that, faced with multiple crises and little political capital of his own, he needed to compromise. To the surprise of many activists, he was also clearly more open to real political change than Suharto had been. Had Habibie not had such instincts, Indonesia's transition might have stalled indefinitely. Instead, he initiated a process of political and economic decentralization that proved critical to the country's survival. He even allowed East Timor, a territory that Indonesia had forcibly incorporated in 1976 and occupied brutally since then, to hold a referendum on independence, and eventually to separate from Indonesia.

Most important, Habibie proved willing to allow free elections and to tolerate the results. In 1999, he oversaw the first truly open parliamentary elections, which, contrary to many outsiders' predictions, transpired without overwhelming violence. Leaders of the largest religious mass organizations in Indonesia, most of whom accepted the idea of a secular democracy, encouraged people to vote and vote peacefully. Participation in the election was broad. Senior army officers, many of whom had aspirations to run for parliament themselves and to build their own political networks, did not stand in the way. After so many decades of essentially fixed votes under Suharto, the appetite among Indonesians for a true election, something many had never witnessed, was enormous.

Abdurrahman Wahid, a liberal cleric and former leader of the largest religious organization in Indonesia (and indeed the world), became president in November 1999. Wahid was a progressive and thoughtful man, and as president he affirmed the critical idea that Indonesia would remain a secular democracy. Like Habibie, Wahid supported decentralization and took measures to civilianize the military. His presidency, however, was disorganized and often chaotic; he had few trusted advisers; and he had been in poor health since a stroke in 1998 and gave stumbling speeches. Forced to step down in 2001 after threats of indictment, he was succeeded by his vice president, Megawati. In 2004, after a largely ineffective term, she lost the next presidential election to Susilo Bambang Yudhoyono, a former general, but one largely untainted by the army's past human rights abuses.

Yudhoyono's first term marked the third inflection point of Indonesia's transition. Realizing that corruption and insufficient rule of law were depressing investment in the country, Yudhoyono made fighting corruption a centerpiece of his administration, empowering anticorruption bodies and even giving them license to investigate graft within his family. He also appointed a team of reform-minded ministers to run the economy, which accelerated the process of breaking up monopolies, investing in physical infrastructure to improve the efficiency of resource extraction and other industries, cutting red tape for investors, and other reforms started in the late 1990s. Foreign investors returned to Indonesia looking to win over its large, youthful market and to take advantage of freer trade within Southeast Asia. According to the Indonesian Investment Coordinating Board, foreign direct investment more than doubled between 1999 and 2011. Meanwhile, overall growth, which had all but stopped in the late 1990s, accelerated to more than 6 percent annually in the late 2000s. The Organization for Economic Cooperation and Development predicts that growth rates of more than 6 percent will continue at least until 2017.

Yudhoyono was reelected by a large margin in 2009. The next presidential election will be in 2014 but Yudhoyono is term-limited and will not be able to run. In his second term, Yudhoyono has been less reformist. His administration (though not the president himself) has been consumed by corruption scandals. He has become a lame duck, and some of his natural tendency to be a consensus-style, gradualist politician has overwhelmed the desire for change.

LESSONS OF THE TRANSITION PERIOD

SOCIOECONOMIC EXCLUSION AND INCLUSION

Social and economic inequality in Indonesia was one of the sparks of the 1997–98 unrest that presaged the transition period. Public perceptions that Suharto's regime had privileged a small group of mostly ethnic Chinese industrialists, giving them control of critical industries and easy access to credit, led to protests against Suharto that then developed into broader anti-Chinese violence. Although the development policies of the Suharto government vastly improved Indonesians' lives—life expectancy rose from an average of fifty-two years in 1980 to sixty-nine years in 1997—Suharto and his circle of business cronies did not amass their wealth quietly. The flashiness of the oligarchs and the Suharto family and the growing power of the Suharto children in the 1990s eventually alienated the public. In areas outside the main island of Java, public perceptions that non-Javanese were excluded from the senior positions in politics, the army, and business contributed to the atmosphere that almost tore Indonesia apart in the late 1990s.

In the early period of the post-Suharto transition, Indonesia's income inequality, which had been lower than that of some regional competitors, such as Thailand and the Philippines, widened significantly because the economic downturn fell hardest on the poor. To combat inequality, successive Indonesian administrations in the 2000s have expanded antipoverty transfer programs, including subsidies for rice, public health care, and education targeted to the poorest areas. Although the government has not developed as comprehensive a transfer program as Brazil has, its social welfare spending combined with strong economic growth has led to declining poverty rates. Between 2007 to 2011, according to Indonesian statistics, the percentage of the population living in poverty fell from 16.6 to 12.5 percent.

Inequality, however, remains a problem and in some ways has been exacerbated by globalization. The weak primary education system, increasing competition in low-end manufacturing and services from other regional countries, and expanding opportunities in finance, information technology, and other higher-end industries in Java have meant that wealthy urban Indonesians with a strong grasp of English can command extremely high salaries. At the same time, wages in industries like palm oil, rice growing, apparel manufacturing, and other lower-end areas have been stagnant for years.

Decentralization, the separation of East Timor from Indonesia, and the end of the separatist conflict in Aceh have helped reduce public concerns that Java will always be prioritized over all other islands. Still, the Yudhoyono administration remains dominated by Javanese, and most of the contenders for the 2014 presidential election are Javanese.

Indonesian leaders have, however, admirably proved willing to exhume the past—particularly the bloody riots of the mid-1960s—to reintegrate former dissidents, former members of the Communist Party, and ethnic Chinese into Indonesian society. The reintegration of ethnic Chinese in particular has been successful, and many entered politics in the late 2000s, a decision that would have been shocking during Suharto's time. Numerous ethnic Chinese Indonesian business leaders have stated that, compared with even five years ago, they feel much more open to showing their Chinese heritage and culture, and that doing so has minimal or no effect on their place in business and society. Several mentioned that they had become active in politics in Jakarta and nationally in the mid- and late 2000s, and that they took this step only because they felt secure of their place in society.

During the transition, many middle-class and elite Indonesians also lost some faith in the political system. Graft and vote-buying have led to a decline in Indonesian views of democracy as the preferred political system. The failure of Indonesian leaders to effectively manage expectations—so that the public understands that democracy does not immediately bring high growth and lower income inequality—has added to public anger. Some elites worry that if Indonesia democratizes without significantly reducing poverty, populism might take hold and elected leaders might try to reduce elites' social, economic, and political privileges, as happened in neighboring Thailand under the government of Prime Minister Thaksin Shinawatra. Thus, many upper-middle-class and elite Indonesians have not fully bought into the democratic transition. They still often house their capital offshore (principally in Singapore), educate their children outside the public system, and sometimes celebrate potentially antidemocratic solutions to public policy questions.

ECONOMIC STRUCTURE AND POLICIES

Indonesian leaders, acutely aware that the financial crisis helped bring down the Suharto regime, understand that long-term, broad-based economic growth is essential for political stability and continued public support for the democratic transition. To that end, they have worked to address the economic weaknesses of the Suharto period, in particular by tackling corruption, strengthening financial regulation, and improving corporate governance while maintaining the pro-growth macroeconomic policies of the previous regime. Rising investment in the education system, though still not enough to meet needs, and greater cash transfers to the poor have been part of an effort to foster equity, improve human capital, and increase consumer spending.

The country has benefited from a resumption of strong economic growth in recent years (see Figure 11), exceeding 6 percent annually since 2007. Indeed, Indonesia has posted some of the highest growth rates in the world, in part due to the rising price of oil and other export commodities and its large pool of cheap labor.

The country's financial system, once on the verge of bankruptcy, is now stable. Bank consolidation, stemming in part from bank failures during the financial crisis in the late 1990s and from pressure from the IMF and other outside creditors, has resulted in fewer but stronger

FIGURE 11. INCOME AND POVERTY IN INDONESIA

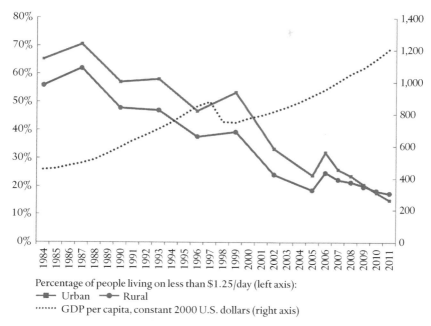

Percentage of people living on less than $1.25/day (left axis):
—■— Urban —●— Rural
······ GDP per capita, constant 2000 U.S. dollars (right axis)

Source: World Bank (poverty data: purchasing power parity, 2005 international dollars, consumption).

financial institutions. The country is now much less vulnerable to external shocks, and Indonesia has joined the Chiang Mai currency swap scheme to protect against another potential run on its currency. Indonesia's total GDP, by far the largest in Southeast Asia, surpassed $1 trillion in 2010 for the first time.

Indonesia has in the past decade begun to diversify away from a heavy reliance on export-oriented agriculture and natural resource extraction, particularly oil, palm oil, gold, timber, and copper. A new McKinsey analysis of the country's economy states that Indonesia's growing consumer market over the next decade will be the largest driver of the economy, not natural resource extraction. As McKinsey noted, "The resource sector's share of the economy has actually fallen since 2000 despite booming resource prices. Mining and oil and gas account for only 11 percent of Indonesia's nominal GDP, similar to more advanced economies such as Australia (8.4 percent) and Russia (11 percent)."

Still, resource extraction remains a heavy part of various local economies, and deep tensions persist over how the costs and benefits of extraction are being shared. In some parts of the country, devolution has helped cool public anger that, during the Suharto era, resource extraction was seen not as benefiting local areas but as contributing significantly to local water, air, and land pollution. Foreign firms such as ExxonMobil in petroleum and Freeport in mining, scarred by their previous experiences dealing with violent movements in Aceh and other regions, have also improved the quality of their interactions with local constituencies.

In Papua, the site of the most lucrative commodity extraction, with the world's largest gold mine and third-largest copper mine, separatist sentiment remains extremely strong. The national government has not put in place an effective devolution plan accepted by most locals, so resource extraction remains highly contentious, and violence is discouraging greater investment by both foreign and local firms in the area. The Yudhoyono government has in its second term passed a series of laws designed to nationalize at least half of many natural resource extraction joint ventures, a move popular with a broad segment of Indonesians but one that could deprive the country of the technology and expertise needed to extract resources safely and with less pollution.

The continuing high level of graft, as well as a lack of coordination between government ministries and national and local leaders, discourage investment—even as Indonesia's large consumer market, demographic dividend, and growing political stability present attractive opportunities. Foreign investment figures are rising sharply, but Indonesia still attracts less U.S. investment than tiny Belgium, and many of Indonesia's largest domestic companies have not made significant investments in the country in the past five years because they have instead shifted their manufacturing operations to Bangladesh and China in search of even cheaper labor. Meanwhile, the persistence of certain protectionist policies from the Suharto era, designed to reduce public anger and meet the basic food needs of the poor, have made it hard for many foreign firms to penetrate Indonesian consumer markets in foodstuffs and other industries.

The Indonesian economy has also made little progress in moving up the value-added scale in manufacturing since Suharto's time. The government has not taken strong measures to capture greater value from the extraction of natural resources such as palm oil and petroleum. In part, this is due to rising nationalist sentiment, among both the public and some policymakers, which has led to increasingly bureaucratic measures designed to hinder greater foreign investment in natural resource industries. As a result, some foreign investors have begun to lose interest in Indonesia. Nor has the government taken enough measures to ensure that resource exploitation is sustainable. Despite some environmental laws put in place over the past decade, the national government has minimal ability to enforce environmental protections, and devolution has made it even more difficult, because local leaders, now able to capture a greater percentage of the income from resource extraction, have shown little interest in environmental protection.

CIVIL SOCIETY AND MEDIA

Indonesia's transition benefited significantly from an engaged, mobilized public. The street protests of 1997 and 1998, as well as the massive popular participation in the 1999 election, made many ordinary Indonesians feel that large-scale popular pressure had been critical to the end of Suharto and the launch of democracy. As a result, Indonesians generally were more willing to live through the economic and political uncertainty of the late 1990s and early 2000s than some of their regional peers, like Thais, who had seen democratization primarily as just a pacted transition among elites.

The early and mid-2000s saw a flourishing of new media. During the 1980s and 1990s, Suharto's soft dictatorship had tolerated several relatively independent media outlets, so when the transition began, Indonesia already had a sizable pool of national journalists with independent media experience. These journalists played a major role in exposing corruption and poking other holes in the fading Suharto regime. They were also instrumental in explaining the transition to a skeptical public and generating buy-in.

In the newly liberalized broadcast environment, community radio stations began providing local news, in local vernaculars, which was critical in such a diverse archipelago. These stations helped foster the process of political and economic devolution of power from Jakarta that began in the late 1990s and accelerated in the 2000s. Local stations, newspapers, and web outlets became the main means for citizens to understand what powers were being transferred to the provinces and cities, and they became the primary vehicles for holding local politicians, who now were being given much larger shares of government revenues, to account.

Indonesia's transition occurred during a period of remarkable growth in intracountry communication—including the introduction of mobile phones, the Internet, and low-cost airlines—that helped foster a greater sense of national identity. Before these advances, most working-class and middle-class Indonesians had never left their own island; the communications revolution of the late 1990s and 2000s helped facilitate the building of national political organizations other than Golkar, Suharto's party, which dominated Indonesian politics during his regime. It also prevented the armed forces and other malignant actors from effectively launching campaigns of disinformation.

In addition, in the late 2000s, Indonesia's middle classes embraced Facebook and other social media, using them to organize rallies and events in a country whose telephone communications infrastructure still remains subpar. In statistics compiled in 2011, Indonesia had 40.8 million Facebook users (third in the world), a penetration rate of nearly 18 percent of the population, remarkably high for a low-income nation.

Of all the elements of civil society that began to emerge in the transition period, the one that appeared most worrying to liberal democrats was the rise of harder-line Islamic organizations. However, at the same time, moderate Islamic organizations, such as Muhamidiyah and Nahdlaltul Ulama (NU), which count tens of millions of members, played a critical role in ensuring that Indonesia's transition proceeded peacefully and led to a secular democracy. The leaders of these organizations, such as Wahid and Muhamidiyah's Amien Rais, had grown up in the era of pancasila and valued political models like Turkey and Malaysia. These leaders helped affirm the power of civil law and uphold the concept of Indonesia as a Muslim-majority but not a Muslim-only nation. Their leadership set a standard for middle- and lower-ranking leaders in NU, Muhamidiyah, and other mass organizations.

Still, radicalism remains a problem in Indonesia. Political decentralization has allowed harder-line Islamic groups and political parties to dominate local politics in some parts of the country. Once in power, their control over local resources helps entrench their position.

Jemaah Islamiah (JI), the most powerful al-Qaeda–linked network, and other militant groups created their own networks of Islamic schools, which usually were cheaper than state schools when parents took into account the sums they needed to pay at state schools to bribe teachers and administrators. These schools became effective recruiting grounds.

The Indonesian government aggressively battled such militant groups, not only through tough security measures but also through media and the court of public opinion. President Yudhoyono in his first term often used his speeches to make the point that militancy is not some bogeyman brought to Indonesia by the West, but a real threat to Indonesians—a point largely ignored by the previous Megawati administration, which appeared fearful of publicly embracing a battle against militancy.

Using former militants on television, the Yudhoyono government also has shown the destructive impact of terrorist attacks on Indonesians and Indonesian society. It has combined this public campaign with an equally high-profile deradicalization campaign. This campaign has been of mixed utility in deradicalizing militants and returning them to society, but according to several researchers who have studied public opinion, it did make Indonesia's battle against militancy appear humane and lawful, which was critical to winning over public opinion. In addition, a decade of stronger economic growth, combined with increased investment in the primary school system and more targeted antipoverty transfer measures, has reduced the appeal of Islamic primary schools to some Indonesian families.

By the late 2000s, the Indonesian government had effectively dismantled JI and, surveys showed, made significant headway in turning public opinion against militant groups. In recent years, however, as the president's power wanes and his potential successors position themselves for the next election, in which they will need the support of some Islamic groups and parties to succeed, the Yudhoyono administration has not taken as strong a stance. Attacks more than doubled on Ahmadiyah, a heterodox Muslim group, and other religious minorities between 2009 and 2010. Sharia has also been imposed for certain family law situations in places like Aceh, where religious police modeled on those of the Persian Gulf countries now watch the beaches to look for unmarried couples who show any displays of open affection.

Yet larger Jakarta-based civil society groups have not pushed back aggressively against these changes because civil society initially supported the process of decentralization, and many civil society groups are more worried about Jakarta's retaking control over people's lives than they are about the imposition of religious law in some parts of the country—particularly if major urban centers in Java do not witness these changes.

LEGAL SYSTEM AND RULE OF LAW

Since the transition, one priority in the rule of law has been to tackle corruption. In 2002, the government created through legislation the Corruption Eradication Commission (KPK), a national anticorruption body. President Yudhoyono, elected in 2004 in part on an anticorruption platform, has personally tried to empower the KPK, backing its independence in several high-profile cases involving the police. He has also said that no one, including his family, should be outside the bounds of the KPK's reach. Over the past decade, Indonesia's global ranking in perceptions of corruption has steadily improved. In 2000, it was among the bottom 10 percent of countries ranked by Transparency International; in 2012, it was among the top half.

Some civil society activists, however, believe that the KPK is far too cautious and brings too few cases. KPK officials counter that they are cautious in order to make strong cases, and that they have delivered a near 100 percent conviction rate on cases they have brought. In addition, though Yudhoyono is regarded as personally clean, a series of graft scandals involving senior officials in his party in 2010, 2011, and 2012 have tarnished his image.

The glaring hole in Indonesia's otherwise improved rule of law has been the failure to address serious human rights abuses, particularly by military leaders. After Suharto, Indonesia created a series of new human rights courts designed to address present and past abuses. Yet in the twelve years since they were created, the courts have never convicted anyone. This whitewashing was perhaps a necessary compromise to get the military to relinquish political power. At the time of transition, civilian leaders made it clear to senior uniformed military leaders that if they went along with political change, no national government was going to prosecute former senior officers for abuses committed in Timor, Aceh, or Papua, or during campaigns against Communists, Islamists, or other political opponents during Suharto's time.

Successive Indonesian governments also offered only minimal cooperation to independent East Timor's truth and reconciliation commission, a sign to the Indonesian military that the civilian government would protect them from international censure as well. However, the lack of accountability for former senior officers did have significant downsides. It has prolonged the climate of impunity that, many human rights activists say, has contributed to continuing abuses by the armed forces in the places where they still hold substantial power, such as Papua. Even when soldiers are put on trial, judges seem reluctant to impose significant sentences, as in the cases of marines who allegedly shot demonstrators in eastern Java in 2007 or the soldiers who allegedly tortured activists in Papua in 2010 and 2011. In addition, the U.S. Congress will not approve a deeper military-military relationship while Indonesian security forces continue to act so brutally in Papua; other established democracies have similar concerns. Moreover, the failure of the human rights courts to effectively address any cases brought against the military has led some in civil society to complain that the military still remains above the law.

GOVERNMENT STRUCTURE AND DIVISION OF POWER

Two major shifts in government structure and division of power have marked Indonesia's transition to democracy. The first has been a significant shift of power away from the central government in Jakarta to provinces and local areas. The second was the civilianization of the military, which for the three decades of Suharto's rule played a dominant role in the country's politics, business life, and security affairs. Through a combination of structural changes and incentives, the post-transition civilian governments have effectively put the armed forces back in the barracks.

Decentralization of power might seem natural for an archipelago of more than fourteen thousand islands and one of the most diverse populations in the world. It was promoted for years by a small group of liberal economists who believed it would deliver stronger economic growth, as well as by many autonomy-seeking leaders in outlying provinces. But Jakarta-based elites resisted. By the late 1990s, however, concern was growing that restive regions such as Timor, Aceh, Papua, and the Malukus would press for independence and that Indonesia would not survive as a country. Devolution came to be seen as the least worst solution to keeping Indonesia unified, preserving secular government, avoiding greater levels of violence, and jump-starting the economy at a time when Indonesia did not have the budget to continue Suharto's developmental state. In return for devolution, national elites would be able to insist on fealty to the primacy of secular law for criminal matters, and on maintaining Indonesia as a secular state.

Relatively soon after the Suharto era, and even before Indonesia's democratization was consolidated, successive governments embarked on programs that devolved significant economic and political power to provinces and cities. The process had several components.

One was allowing provincial, subprovincial, and city governments to keep and use a greater percentage of revenues from local natural resources and from taxation, which ensured greater grassroots participation in economic decision-making. Legislation was passed that both progressively handed over larger portions of local revenues to subprovincial and provincial governments, and declared several regions to have unique historical status, such as the city of Yogyakarta, which was traditionally ruled by a sultan. Those regions declared to have such status were allowed to pass local laws incorporating some of their political traditions into the modern day, such as retaining the Yogyakarta sultan as a kind of local head of state.

A second component was bringing government services closer to the people across the country. This entailed boosting provincial and city-level abilities to handle essential services, and creating a new fiscal system to coordinate hiring and transfer of revenues between the national and provincial governments.

A third component was increasing the scope and frequency of local and provincial elections while maintaining the special status of some regions, such as Yogyakarta and, eventually, Aceh and Papua.

By the early 2010s, the benefits of Indonesia's decentralization process were clear. By devolving power to localities and subprovincial areas, and by bringing government services closer to the ground, the national government had helped cool separatist sentiment in most regions. World Bank surveys across the country showed that a majority of Indonesians believed that decentralization had led to improved public services and infrastructure creation.

Decentralization also naturally improved budget transparency because it was harder for a larger number of officials to keep data secret from the media and from the public. In some ways, it also fostered competition between provinces and cities for domestic and foreign investment. By forcing leaders from different religions and ethnic groups to work together in local councils to obtain and manage greater resources coming from Jakarta, it also helped consolidate democratic political culture.

Of course, decentralization is not without its downsides. Most notably, it has led to a decentralization of graft, perhaps a necessary price to pay. In some ways, decentralized graft might actually have spread funds more evenly throughout the archipelago. Even if it has not led to overall higher levels of corruption, it has led to greater perceptions of graft among the public because corruption has been brought closer to them. The impact on Indonesia's young democracy is particularly notable in that few rules govern how politicians should raise money to campaign. Examples of local officials extorting private firms for campaign funds are increasingly common.

The decentralization of graft is leading to skyrocketing costs in provincial and national campaigns. If this corruption is not curtailed, it could have significant negative effects on democracy by keeping capable candidates out of politics. Because the anticorruption efforts of foreign donors are focused on the national authorities rather than their provincial and subprovincial counterparts, only minimal external funding is available to support local anticorruption efforts.

The other major change in government structure and division of power—the civilianization of the armed forces—had as dramatic an effect on the country's political change as devolution. Under Suharto, the military had control or de facto control over a significant number of Indonesia's preeminent corporations. In outlying regions of the country, such as Timor, Aceh, and Papua, these companies operated with minimal civilian control and engaged in massacres in places such as Timor and Aceh. The public had no mechanism for the accountability of military officers. In addition, a permanent role for them in political life had been written into the constitution, and, by the end of Suharto's rule, they controlled a guaranteed percentage of seats in parliament.

By the late 1990s, Jakarta-based civilian elites clearly recognized that for Indonesia to stay together as a country and proceed toward democracy, the powers of the military had to be reined in. By operating in regional commands with minimal oversight, the armed forces were alienating regions already suffering from separatist tensions. In addition, because the armed forces had been cut off from many exchanges and U.S. and other Western training programs, foreign actors had little influence.

In the transition period, successive civilian governments adopted several strategies to tame the military. First, civilian leaders appealed directly to military leaders to convince them that a divorce from politics was required if the armed forces were to retain a positive national reputation. The military had long been popular, but, swayed by a string of human rights abuses, public sentiment was shifting against it. The government split the armed forces from the police, dividing training programs and cutting off most formal contacts between the two. This emphasized to the public that the police were responsible for domestic matters, including counterterrorism, and allowed the government to create new police divisions, focused on counterterrorism and counter-militancy, that were not tainted by the army's past abuses.

At the same time, civilian leaders essentially offered senior officers financial incentives to leave the political sphere, downsize the armed forces, and accept a narrower role focused on national defense. The Indonesian government slowly replaced some officers on boards of major state companies with civilians, but also simultaneously secured lucrative retirement pensions for many senior officers. In addition, civilian leaders privately reassured the military that, although their business interests would be divested, the government would steadily increase the budget for the military as partial compensation. Indeed, the military budget did increase from roughly $1.18 billion in 2003 to more than $3.6 billion in 2010. The government had the resources for this because, in contrast to the late 1990s, Indonesia's economy was strong again; the overall national budget was growing; the price of oil was once again at record highs; and funds that had been directed to significant fighting on the ground in Aceh and Timor could be redirected to officers' salaries and pensions, as well as to buying new equipment. Although military officers remained individually powerful, and several led presidential tickets, the reduction of the power of rank-and-file officers opened space for all types of civil society across the country to become more active and to fear military reprisals less.

EDUCATION AND DEMOGRAPHY

One of Indonesia's most significant economic advantages today is its young population. Continued robust fertility combined with large decreases in infant mortality during the latter part of the Suharto era and the 2000s has resulted in Indonesia having one of the youngest populations in the world: nearly 60 percent of Indonesians are younger than thirty. The country is enjoying its demographic dividend at a time when many of its Asian competitors have shrinking pools of working-age labor and will soon have to care for expanding pools of elderly without effective national social welfare systems.

Indonesian political and economic leaders are well aware that the next two decades will be critical for the country if it is to fulfill its hope of moving into the ranks of middle-income nations. The World Bank estimates that between 2020 and 2025 Indonesia's demographic dividend will begin to decline.

To take full advantage of this dividend, Indonesia must improve its education system, which has not yet sufficiently benefited from the country's political transition and, though in better shape than it was in the late 1990s, remains weak by regional standards. Few schools have the Internet connections or other technology that is standard in Thailand, Malaysia, Singapore, and even Vietnam. Although education budgets have increased over the past decade, Indonesia's national government devotes a smaller share of the budget to education than regional competitors. Jakarta spends about 18 percent of government expenditures on education, compared with Thailand's nearly 21 percent. This shortfall forces many schools, even though they are technically public schools, to collect school fees from parents.

Decentralization was supposed to help the education system, because local politicians would face greater pressure from parents in their constituencies to allocate their budgets to education, but by and large this has not been the case. The first generation of local leaders empowered with higher budgets has tended to spend the funds on building political parties and on areas that can be quickly and visibly touted to voters and investors: physical infrastructure, projects to attract foreign and local investment, and enhanced local government services. These are reasonable ways to spend the budgets but not to improve the education system. Only in the face of pressure from local voters and civil society, which is beginning to be brought to bear in some outlying regions, will local politicians start increasing the share of their budgets for public education.

As a result of the poor education system, Indonesia's economy depends heavily on lower-skilled resource extraction and agricultural jobs. This has serious long-term environmental consequences, making continued destruction of Indonesia's virgin forests, the largest in the world outside of the Amazon, likely. Given that some twenty million new workers will enter the workforce by 2020, the country could face instability if it does not do a better job preparing its young people for productive employment.

Indonesia's transition from a primarily rural to an increasingly urban country is another important demographic shift with significant political implications. In the 1960s, only about 10 percent of Indonesia's population lived in cities; by the end of the 1990s nearly 50 percent did. Today, more than 50 percent do. Increasing urbanization and use of communications technology played a major role in Suharto's downfall and the country's transition to democracy. In the 1960s, Suharto and his security forces were able to use the isolation of Indonesians from one another to spread rumors and disinformation to spark violence that would, in turn, precipitate the security forces' involvement in politics. In the 1990s, however, these tactics failed, in part because urbanization, the spread of telephone lines and mobile phones, and more widespread use of the Indonesian language made it easier for journalists, opposition groups, and other civil society organizations to counter disinformation and apply pressure on the Suharto regime.

The country's young and increasingly urban demographic profile has caused significant tension during the political transition, particularly in the latter half of the 2000s. In the late 1990s and early 2000s, the transition was a combination of a pacted transition—between Habibie and reformist leaders such as Wahid, Megawati, and others—and one accelerated by large-scale popular protest. Most of the reformist politicians prominent in the late 1990s and early 2000s were in their fifties or older, yet mass movements in the 2000s have been led by younger activists who barely remember the Suharto period, if at all. However, none of the major political parties have absorbed younger activists into their senior-most ranks, and the 2014 presidential election looks to be a contest between older politicians, many with links to the Suharto period. Few of these older politicians have made good use of social media or other modern tools, and the growing disconnect between younger educated Indonesians and political elites runs the risk of fostering severe alienation from national politics.

CONCLUSION

Since the early 2000s, Indonesia's transformation has been touted by many democratization experts and world leaders as the most impressive recent shift to democracy in the developing world. The Indonesian economy has recovered from the shocks of the 1990 and early 2000s. In 2012, the country's bond ratings were upgraded by Moody's, reflecting investors' growing comfort with the stability of its financial system and its prospects for long-term growth, a continuing decline in poverty, and its emerging middle class. Increasingly comfortable about its stability and political transition, Indonesia in the late 2000s returned to its natural role as leader of the Association of Southeast Asian Nations, the major regional organization, mediating regional disputes, leading peacekeeping missions, and helping push forward a regional free trade agreement. As part of the Group of Twenty, Indonesia also began to play a larger international role as an advocate for low-income nations in trade and financial organizations.

Indonesia clearly has much to be proud of today, especially given its perilous state in the late 1990s and early 2000s. On the political side, its transition demonstrates that unity among political elites during the transition period, particularly when it comes with little violence, is an important variable for success—even when that unity is the result not of warm collaboration but of working together for fear of any other alternative. Together, civilian leaders such as Habibie, Wahid, and Megawati launched a process of devolution that has effectively balanced national unity and varying levels of provincial autonomy. In addition, the Indonesian example shows that countries transitioning from a relatively soft dictatorship may have an easier time assimilating the institutions and culture of democracy. Even before Suharto's fall, Indonesians had gained experience with voting, reading and listening to some independent media, and attending popular demonstrations. The spread of new communication technologies across the geographically diverse country has facilitated a process of building national identity. At some point in the near future, the changes that are shrinking Indonesia may also help non-Javanese political and business leaders rise to the apex of Indonesian society. Finally, Indonesia has shown how civilian leaders can use financial incentives and immunity from future prosecutions to civilianize a military long the most important and influential institution in society. This period of immunity may not last indefinitely, however. It is still possible that the next generation of Indonesian leaders, like their peers in countries such as Argentina, will feel comfortable enough that democracy has been consolidated that they can then reopen cases of past military abuses.

Yet these successes may have reached their limit. Although weaker than in the past, security forces have continued to act in outlying regions like Papua much as they did during Suharto's time, using brutal tactics against local separatist movements. Indonesian society may be extremely young and urbanized, and cities on Java no longer totally dominated by Javanese, but politics and the senior military remain controlled by older men. Elite job opportunities remain limited to highly educated Javanese, and the educational system—competent at producing workers for low-value-added manufacturing, agriculture, and resource extraction—is not producing knowledge workers and entrepreneurs. Perhaps most important, the transition in the late 1990s and early 2000s was initially so successful that it created high expectations among the Indonesian population for democracy. Many thought that the political transition would necessarily also include greater economic equality, and already some degree of authoritarian nostalgia, common in other parts of East Asia, has emerged in Indonesia. In a study by the Indonesian research organization Survey Circle, released in late 2011, only 12 percent of respondents believed that politicians in the democratic era are doing a better job than leaders during the Suharto era. The next generation of Indonesian political leaders will have to deliver not only freer politics but also sustained and more inclusive growth to prevent such nostalgia from turning into more concrete demands for a stronger, even autocratic, central government.

INDONESIA TIMELINE

1949: Indonesia Gains Sovereignty, Sukarno Becomes President

After years of struggle for independence from the Netherlands, its longtime colonial master, Indonesia becomes a sovereign country on December 27, and Sukarno becomes its first president. In 1957, he institutes a policy of "guided democracy" that is, in effect, a precarious authoritarianism. Sukarno promotes secularism by encouraging the speaking of Indonesian throughout the archipelago, instead of or in addition to local languages. Secularism also rests on the concept of pancasila, a mix of nationalism, monotheism, and socialism that Sukarno uses to fend off efforts by Islamic parties to make Indonesia an officially Muslim state.

1966: General Suharto Takes Power

After years of politically charged and sometimes violent politics, an anarchic situation leads to the death of some one million Indonesians in the mid-1960s. During this tumultuous period, Major General Suharto seizes power from Sukarno on March 11, 1966.

The transfer marks the beginning of Suharto's pro-Western "New Order" regime, an authoritarian, technocrat-led developmental state that lasts until 1998. It brings Indonesia strong economic growth and socioeconomic gains, with growth averaging over 7 percent per year between 1985 and 1997 and poverty falling from almost 60 percent in 1968 to 13 percent in 1997. However, this economic miracle comes at a significant cost in debt, corruption, and other problems that become apparent in the late 1990s.

1975: Indonesia Battles Separatists in Outlying Regions

Indonesia invades East Timor after the latter declares independence from Portugal. Indonesian forces are accused of gross repression and human rights violations during an occupation of more than two decades as they struggle to counter East Timorese demands for independence. Separatist movements also arise in other outlying regions, including Papua, site of the world's largest gold mine and third-largest copper mine, and Aceh, where an insurgency breaks out in 1976. Eventually, East Timor becomes independent and the conflict in Aceh is resolved, but separatist sentiment remains extremely strong in Papua, and Indonesian security forces continue to commit abuses there.

1997: Asian Financial Crisis Hits Indonesia

The Asian financial crisis, the critical inflection point in Indonesia's modern history, hits Indonesia in the summer. It exposes the weaknesses of Suharto's economic policies, destroying the value of the rupiah and wiping out savings accounts as banks collapse. Indonesia's economy shrinks by 13 percent in 1998 and investors flee. Meanwhile, prices for staple goods rise as the rupiah's value plunges, and an additional 10 percent of the population falls below the poverty line between 1998 and 2000. Suharto is forced to seek a rescue package from the IMF. The economic damage from the crisis and the image of Suharto appearing to cater to the IMF deeply damage the longtime ruler, leading to rising protests in the streets.

1998: Suharto Ends Presidency

After months of violent antigovernment protests and riots, Suharto resigns on May 21, ending his thirty-two-year presidency. Vice President B. J. Habibie takes over as president. Habibie, a somewhat accidental change agent, turns out to have relatively reformist instincts.

He initiates a process of political and economic decentralization that proves critical to the country's survival and oversees the first truly open parliamentary elections in 1999.

1999: Devolution of Power Begins

Relatively soon after the transition from the Suharto era, successive governments begin to devolve significant power to provinces and cities. Subnational governments are allowed to keep and use a greater percentage of revenues captured from local natural resources and taxation, and they are given more responsibility for essential services. Local and provincial elections are also increased. Along these lines, Indonesia's government signs a peace agreement in 2005 to end a long-running separatist conflict in Aceh province. The main rebel group relinquishes its demands for secession, and the government allows rebels to form political parties and contest elections in the province. It also lets Aceh keep 70 percent of local natural resource revenues. By the early 2010s, it is clear that decentralization has helped cool separatist sentiment in most regions, increased satisfaction with public services and infrastructure, and improved budget transparency.

1999: Wahid Becomes President

Following parliamentary elections in June, Abdurrahman Wahid is named president by the parliament in November. Wahid is a progressive and thoughtful leader who supports decentralization and takes measures to civilianize the military. However, his presidency is disorganized and chaotic, in part because of his poor health. Wahid is forced to step down in July 2001 after threats of indictment, and his vice president, Megawati Sukarnoputri, becomes president.

2000: Civilianization of Armed Forces

In August, Indonesia's parliament issues two decrees that begin to reform the role of the long-dominant military and bring it under civilian control. The decrees split the armed forces from the police, and the parliament decides that the military should relinquish its reserved seats in the House of Representatives, the most important entrenched privilege it enjoyed. Along with these measures, civilian leaders essentially offer senior officers financial incentives to leave the political sphere, downsize the armed forces, and take a more narrow role focused on national defense.

2002: Extremist Groups Mount Attacks

On October 12, terrorists from the extremist Islamic group Jemaah Islamiyah bomb a nightclub on the island of Bali, killing 202 people, mainly foreign tourists. The Indonesian government initiates counterradicalism programs to take the militants on and discredit them in society. In addition to security measures, the government uses high-level speeches to make the point that militancy is not a Western import but a real threat to Indonesians, and it uses former militants on television to show the destructive impact of terrorist attacks on the country. A high-profile deradicalization campaign, though of mixed utility in actually deradicalizing militants, makes the battle against militancy appear humane and lawful, which is critical to winning over public opinion. By the late 2000s, Indonesia effectively dismantles Jemaah Islamiyah, but the country continues to face some extremist attacks.

2004: Yudhoyono Wins First Direct Presidential Election

Retired general Susilo Bambang Yudhoyono defeats incumbent president Megawati Sukarnoputri in a runoff election on September 20. Realizing that corruption and insufficient rule of law are depressing investment, Yudhoyono makes fighting corruption a centerpiece of his administration. Growth and foreign investment rise strongly, and Yudhoyono is reelected by a large margin on July 8, 2009. In his second term, he is less reformist, with some of his natural tendency toward consensus overwhelming the desire for change.

2010: GDP Surpasses $1 Trillion

Indonesia's GDP exceeds $1 trillion for the first time in its history. GDP per capita exceeds $3,000, and foreign investment reaches $19 billion the next year. Indonesia has posted some of the highest recent growth rates in the world, though it remains primarily dependent on export-oriented agriculture and natural resource extraction. Between 2007 and 2011, the percentage of Indonesia's population living in poverty falls from 16.6 percent to 12.5 percent. Inequality, however, remains a problem and in some ways is exacerbated by globalization.

Thailand

Joshua Kurlantzick

Following the end of its absolute monarchy in 1932, Thailand was essentially ruled for six decades by the armed forces. Allied with business elites and the king, who still wielded enormous power behind the facade of a constitutional monarchy, Thailand's military rulers maintained tight control over media and politics but generally allowed economic technocrats and the central bank to set the country's economic policies. Valuing Thailand's stability during the Cold War, and the critical role it played in the prosecution of the Vietnam War, successive American administrations supported a series of authoritarian leaders in Bangkok.

Thailand's economic development first took off in the late 1950s and early 1960s, aided by pragmatic macroeconomic policies, abundant resources, and an attractive environment for foreign direct investment. The GDP growth rate between 1960 and 1970 averaged 8.4 percent, among the highest in the world.

Thailand also benefited enormously from American assistance. Between 1950 and 1987, the United States provided Thailand with some $2 billion in military aid and at least twice that in civilian aid. During the Vietnam War, the United States based many of its bombing, planning, and rest and recreation activities in Thailand, and American assistance built new roads, airports, and other major infrastructure projects. The expansion of global airline networks, combined with Thailand's natural attractions, enabled the kingdom to become a major international tourist destination. The number of tourists visiting Thailand annually grew from fewer than one million in 1965 to nearly twelve million by the end of the 2000s.

By the early 1970s, a rising urban middle class began to agitate for a greater say in political affairs. Antimilitary demonstrations in 1973 and 1976 gathered strength and forced a slight political opening. In the 1980s, a technocratic government with some democratic facets (regular, albeit not truly free, elections) ruled the country, in alliance with the military and the palace.

The end of the Cold War at the beginning of the 1990s coincided with a more assertive Bangkok middle class no longer willing to tolerate military rule. Massive popular demonstrations of hundreds of thousands of protestors in Bangkok ousted the military regime in 1992 and ushered in a civilian government.

Following the military's withdrawal in 1992, many Thais and outside observers of the country believed that Thailand was poised for democratic consolidation. The military appeared so shamed by its failed management of the country in 1991 and early 1992 that army commanders throughout the 1990s insisted that the long era of coups had passed.

In 1997, Thailand passed a progressive and groundbreaking constitution guaranteeing many new rights and freedoms. It also created new national institutions to monitor graft and strengthened political parties at the expense of unelected centers of power—the palace, the military, big business, and the elite civil service. It set the stage for elections in 2001 that were probably the freest in Thailand's history and resulted in a political system dominated by two parties, Thai Rak Thai and the Democrat Party. Meanwhile, the Thai media used their new freedoms, along with new technologies, such as the Internet and satellite television, to explore formerly taboo topics, such as political corruption and labor rights.

In 2001, Thaksin Shinawatra, a populist former tycoon, was elected prime minister, primarily by the country's poor, who still make up by far the majority in one of the most unequal countries in Asia. Thailand's nascent judicial and bureaucratic institutions were too weak to control Thaksin's ambitions, and he used his victory, and reelection in 2005, as a pretext to neuter the news media, undermine the independence of the judiciary, and viciously punish political opponents. Frustrated with the polarizing but magnetic Thaksin's "electoral autocracy," but also worried that his populist policies were harming their outsized power, the Bangkok elite and middle class turned against democracy altogether, agitating for a coup, which came in 2006.

Thailand's poor mobilized. Furious that their political will had been thwarted, they took to the streets. Clashes with the government in 2010 resulted in some of the bloodiest violence in Bangkok in decades. Ultimately, another election was held in 2011, and it was won by a pro-Thaksin party led by his sister.

Still, that election has resolved little. The upper and middle classes continue to push for another coup and use lèse-majesté laws (which forbid insulting the monarchy) to imprison hundreds of poor and left-leaning activists. Meanwhile, supporters of Thaksin have organized their own vigilante organizations to fight back, and further unrest and political violence seem likely.

Indeed, today, Thailand looks almost nothing like a model emerging democracy: its political leaders, its royal family, and its upper and middle classes made several major mistakes that halted its democratic transition and ultimately led to a reversal. Namely, they failed to develop the necessary institutions to mediate political conflicts, to include all classes in political life, and to permanently place the armed forces under civilian control. These mistakes, combined with missteps in economic planning, caused the unraveling of the late 2000s and early 2010s.

Thailand's politics are now characterized by a seemingly never-ending cycle of street protest, with the middle class and the poor pitted against each other in a fight for political power; paralyzed policymaking; palpable fear for the future; and declining economic competitiveness compared with neighbors such as Vietnam and China. Overall, the country's future appears bleak.

INFLECTION POINTS
OF THE TRANSITION PERIOD

The military's overreach in the early 1990s marked the first inflection point of Thailand's political transition. Popular pressure for civilian rule had been building for decades, and the government had increasingly moved to make policy separately from the armed forces. When the military brazenly seized power from a civilian government in the early 1990s, large and violent street demonstrations erupted in Bangkok. The army tried to crush the protests, killing at least sixty people, but the demonstrators did not capitulate. The king, who for decades had generally backed the military to guarantee stability, now appeared concerned that the armed forces had become a source of instability. On May 20, 1992, he reprimanded both the junta head and the protest leader on television. Their ceremonial groveling at his feet was interpreted as a sign that the military would no longer be so powerful. Indeed, the military ceded control and the street violence ended.

With this reversion to civilian rule, Thailand seemed poised for democratic consolidation. It held truly free and fair national elections, several of which were won by the Democrat Party, the only national party in the country at that time. Favored primarily by elites, middle classes, and the palace, the Democrat Party generally pursued stable, farsighted macroeconomic policies, and no coherent opposition emerged in the 1990s.

Thai civil society, which had mushroomed in the 1980s and early 1990s, continued to flourish. A diverse group of good government, labor, environmental, and nongovernmental organizations worked together for democratic change. With the end of the Cold War in the early 1990s, the shifting international and regional environment also helped pave the way for civilian democracy. In 1997, Thailand passed a new, reformist constitution with wide-ranging protections for civil liberties and human rights. In retrospect, this was in many ways the high-water mark for Thailand's democratic transition.

The next, and most critical, inflection point was the Asian financial crisis. In July 1997, the Thai government was forced to devalue the baht after months of attacks by speculators who recognized that excessive lending to real estate had left the country financially overextended. The crisis hit Thailand extremely hard: the value of the baht fell against the dollar, from twenty-five to one to more than fifty to one at its lowest point.

Before the crisis, the Democrat Party had done a poor job managing public expectations that democracy would not only improve political and social freedoms but also augment economic growth. Although it pursued moderate, liberal macroeconomic reforms in the wake of the crisis, the Democrat Party was blamed by much of the public for the meltdown. This provided an opportunity for Thaksin Shinawatra, a billionaire telecommunications tycoon, to form his own party, Thai Rak Thai, to challenge the traditionally dominant Democrats.

In the most sophisticated political-advertising campaign in Thai history, Thaksin presented himself during the pivotal 2001 election as a nonpartisan, executive-type leader, a take-charge businessman who would restore the country's economic miracle. Even on the campaign trail, signs were clear enough that he had autocratic tendencies and little respect for institutions, but many voters ignored them, hoping primarily for economic recovery. As the first major Thai politician to appeal directly to the poor with a platform that included universal health care, loans to low-income Thais, and other populist measures, Thaksin gave the rural poor their first real hope in democracy, and proved enormously popular.

By winning the 2001 election, Thaksin provided a coherent alternative to the Democrat Party, pushing Thailand toward a political system dominated by two parties. He also shattered the nexus of economic and political control that had existed for decades among business and military leaders and the palace. In 2005, he was reelected by a wide margin and his party gained a majority in parliament.

The next inflection point came in 2006. Distrustful of Thaksin and his populist measures, middle-class and elite Thais became increasingly distrustful of democracy itself as their Democrat Party proved unable to defeat Thaksin's party. In a notable rejection of democratic forms, they turned to street demonstrations. These mounted throughout 2006, with many protestors calling on the king and the army to intervene. Thaksin had alienated the king by challenging his position as the country's most revered public figure, and the king appeared to be increasingly convinced that the only way to ensure stability was to return power to traditional military, bureaucratic, and palace elites. But the empowerment of the poor through the democratic elections of the 2000s meant that these elites no longer could dominate the country uncontested.

In September 2006, after publicly promising not to get involved in politics, the military staged a coup. Almost immediately, the coup leaders met with the king and he sanctified their putsch. The armed forces replaced the 1997 constitution with a weaker one that served primarily to reinstitute the role of the army in politics. They also badly handled the economy, scaring off investors and leading to runs on the stock exchange. Facing criticism for their ineptness in governance, as well as the need to hold elections to signify a return to democracy, at least in theory, the military allowed elections in 2007. Thaksin himself was in exile (avoiding corruption charges), but a pro-Thaksin party won nevertheless. Thai elites and the middle class then used the judiciary, the palace, and continued army meddling to weaken the elected government and, in 2008, succeeded in reinstalling a Democrat Party government to power.

After 2009, the Thai working class, angry about the new Democrat government, resorted to their own antigovernment protests, mimicking those that had helped oust Thaksin three years earlier. These culminated in two months of bloodshed in the streets in Bangkok in the spring of 2010, during which at least eighty people were killed and hundreds detained. Following the violence, the Democrat government launched a harsh crackdown on civil liberties, abandoning whatever high ground it might have held. In the run-up to the next election, in July 2011, senior military officers appeared on television to warn Thais to vote for the Democrat Party as the government closed down a growing number of websites and jailed hundreds of activists without charges. Still, in the July elections a pro-Thaksin party led by the former prime minister's sister won an absolute majority of parliament again, shocking the Thai middle classes. Some prominent elite intellectuals called for another coup; others suggested the country limit the franchise.

For her part, Thaksin's sister, serving as prime minister, seems to have as little concept of the need for a loyal opposition as her brother, instead taking the view that after an electoral victory the winning party and its leaders should be able to dominate government and enrich their allies.

The result has been paralysis, democratic decline, and a marked deterioration of civil liberties and human rights. Neither the Thai middle class nor the Thai poor truly believe in democracy. Few Thais now trust the integrity of the judiciary, the civil service, or other national institutions. Even the king, once so revered that Thais worshiped him like a god, has had his impartiality questioned. However, harsh lèse-majesté laws, increasingly used to crush political opposition, prevent Thais from openly questioning the value of the monarchy. Still, signs of anger with the monarchy and monarchist elites now abound, including many anonymous postings on social media sites and even loud antimonarch chants during protests in Bangkok. The Thai military once again wields enormous influence behind the scenes, a dramatic reversal from the 1990s, when most Thais believed that the military had returned to the barracks for good.

LESSONS OF THE TRANSITION PERIOD

SOCIOECONOMIC EXCLUSION AND INCLUSION

Of all of the mistakes made by Thailand's leaders during its years of fast growth and democratic opening, the failure to address the country's massive inequalities of wealth, job opportunities, and education proved the most disastrous. More than many other nations in East Asia, Thailand was characterized by severe inequalities. During the absolute monarchy, the country had maintained a rigid and codified caste system called *sakdina*, as well as the concept that nonconfrontation was the central value in Thai life. The monarchy, political leaders, and religious leaders inculcated in the population the idea that the wealthy and successful had earned their privilege through karma, and that the poor, rural masses should defer to urban elites in decision-making about the country's future.

Even during the postwar decades of rapid economic development, Thailand remained an extremely hierarchical society, with the poor, who lived primarily in the rural north and northeast (see Figure 12), deferring to the better-educated and wealthier as well as to local officials. The monarchy, the army, and the monkhood, the three central institutions in the country, encouraged this deference. The hierarchical and patronage-oriented system almost totally excluded from the notion of "Thai-ness" any minority groups, such as Muslims who lived in the deep south, Hmong and other hill tribes who lived primarily in the north, and ethnic Chinese and Indians who migrated to the country in the late nineteenth and early twentieth centuries. Because the state and the armed forces controlled most radio and broadcast television, major media reinforced this idea of deference and spent little time exploring growing grievances among rural Thais. These grievances found outlets in random attacks on local officials, in the growth of a small communist

FIGURE 12. URBAN AND RURAL POVERTY IN THAILAND

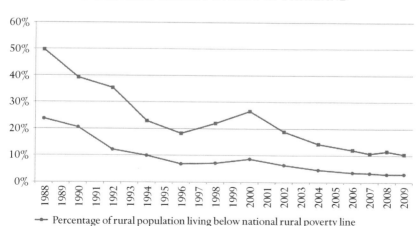

—•— Percentage of rural population living below national rural poverty line
—•— Percentage of urban population living below national urban poverty line

Source: World Bank.

party, and in separatist movements in the 1960s and 1970s in the Muslim-majority south.

The governments that ran Thailand from the early 1960s to the mid-1990s, during the economic boom, had an opportunity to make society more inclusive and to position the country for sustained growth and democratic consolidation while maintaining the pro-growth policies that would have allowed the wealthy and middle classes to preserve their economic holdings. Thailand during this period ran regular budget surpluses that could have been used to broaden growth and make politics more inclusive, but instead were often misallocated to military spending (after the late 1970s Thailand had no serious enemies in the region), politicians' pet projects in their hometowns, and the infrastructure of greater Bangkok as well as tourist destinations. Presumably, the crown's portfolio also benefited, although the palace's holdings are hard to determine because they are managed in such an opaque fashion.

Various governments did address some issues facing the general population, including cutting malnutrition, combating sexually transmitted diseases, improving housing stock, and bolstering primary education. Economic growth led to falling poverty, but the government neglected to invest equitably in all parts of society. Budgets were inordinately directed toward middle-class and elite institutions, and priorities for the majority of the population—such as health care, job retraining, secondary education, and access to broadband Internet or high-speed mobile connections—were ignored. The income tax system was highly regressive, and most high-earning taxpayers simply used their connections to avoid paying any taxes, infuriating the poor. Class disparities, as well as divisions between urban and rural Thais, deepened (see Figure 13).

Exacerbating urban-rural divisions was the fact that economic and political planning remained highly centralized, with nearly all important decisions being made in Bangkok. Thailand during its growth period from the 1960s through the 1990s offered minimal devolution to provinces and provincial officials, even though budget surpluses would have made some degree of devolution relatively painless, and might have helped integrate rural Thais into the nation, increase political consciousness, and pave the way for a real democracy. Offering a high degree of autonomy to some regions also might have prevented an insurgency in Muslim-majority southern Thailand from erupting in the early 2000s.

FIGURE 13. REGIONAL INCOME DISPARITIES IN THAILAND

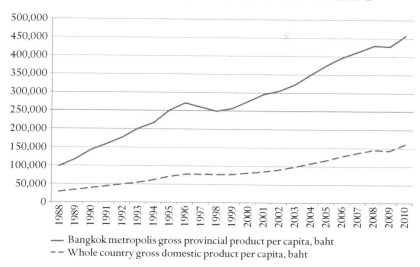

— Bangkok metropolis gross provincial product per capita, baht
-- Whole country gross domestic product per capita, baht

Source: Thailand Office of the National Economic and Social Development Board Statistics, http://bit.ly/
T1Nk7u (GDP/GPP per capita).

Instead, Bangkok elites chose the opposite approach, perhaps fearing that devolution would jeopardize their dominance of society. They tried to create one unified national consciousness centered on religion (Buddhism), nation, and king. But this consciousness left out minorities, tried to bury vast class differences, and put much of the responsibility for maintaining unity on the king, with support from the state-dominated media.

The economic boom that began in the 1960s did benefit all classes, but Bangkok and its suburbs benefited the most. Foreign investors set up manufacturing primarily in Bangkok, its suburbs, and a cluster of eastern coastal towns, and successive governments directed foreign and domestic capital toward Bangkok and its environs. By the 1990s, the Thai capital was more than ten times wealthier than some of the poorer provinces. When the Asian financial crisis hit Thailand in the late 1990s, Bangkok certainly was hurt: real estate prices collapsed and many projects in the capital were left unfinished, their concrete skeletons dotting the skyline. Still, the plummeting cost of land continued to attract foreign investors, who poured into the kingdom in the early 2000s.

The crisis hit the rural poor, still the majority of the population, extremely hard. Income per capita in the poorer provinces fell much further than in the capital. Many rural families had sent at least one family member to the capital in the 1980s and early 1990s, where they could earn a living in manual jobs like construction or restaurant work, but these jobs had no benefits or protections and generally were the first to go when the crisis hit. At the same time, Thailand's deteriorating currency made it harder for farmers to buy critical machinery, and a series of droughts in rural Thailand worsened the crisis. Poverty is overwhelmingly a rural phenomenon today: nearly 90 percent of the country's 5.4 million poor live in rural areas.

With the era of sustained high growth rates ending, competitors emerging for Thailand's low-end export industries, and budget surpluses dwindling, the failure to educate larger portions of the population, to upgrade vocational and secondary schools, and to diversify the economy has made for a hard landing. Thailand's government failed to make the best use of its good times; when the bad times came, much of the country suffered, and formerly placid politics turned violent. As the slowdown hit the rural working class the hardest, some of the older inhibitions against attacking the middle and upper classes began to vanish, and socioeconomic exclusion turned to anger.

ECONOMIC STRUCTURE AND POLICIES

Thailand's economy has been largely managed by civilian bureaucrats and technocrats who provided continuity during the country's numerous coups and short-lived civilian governments. Senior civil servants generally considered themselves the true guardians of Thailand's development, which made sense, given that they rarely had civilian masters for very long. Other unelected institutions, including the army, the palace, and the Bank of Thailand, have also wielded enormous influence.

Beginning in the 1960s, successive governments sought to diversify and modernize the economy by attracting foreign direct investment. Thailand courted manufacturing investment by keeping minimum wages among the lowest in Asia, and adopting tax policies that were among the most favorable in the world for foreign investors. Thailand became a regional manufacturing hub, particularly for Japan, and manufacturing now makes up a third of Thailand's economy.

In terms of employment, however, Thailand is still largely an agricultural country, with more than 40 percent of the population employed in farming. Perhaps its biggest economic challenge today is that the country has not developed a broader economic base and remains primarily dependent on lower-value manufactured exports, agriculture, and tourism.

Thailand's technocrats can be credited with delivering several decades of consistently strong growth, but creating a truly competitive economy was not in fact a priority. Local banking, finance, construction, and many other industries came to be dominated by small groups of tycoons, or by the Crown Property Bureau, a part of the palace's financial empire.

In the 1980s and 1990s, construction and real estate dominated Bangkok's overheated economy. The Bank of Thailand's ultimately unsuccessful attempt to support the baht in the run-up to the 1997 financial crisis was perceived by many rural Thais as a wasteful effort to shield Bangkok banks, finance companies, and crown holdings at the expense of small businesses in other parts of the country.

The Asian financial crisis marked the end of Thailand's so-called economic miracle. Many undercapitalized banks failed; construction dried up, throwing millions into unemployment; and exports ground to halt as the crisis spread to other Asian countries.

By 2001, the economy had begun to slowly recover, with a more consolidated and secure banking sector, a rise in tourism due to a significant devaluation of the baht (which made Thailand relatively inexpensive for foreigners), continued Japanese investment, and a modest shift in the economy from export-oriented growth to domestic consumption.

After its 2001 election in the wake of the crisis, the Thaksin government devoted a higher percentage of the national budget to stimulate the economy, boost domestic consumer spending, and broaden development beyond Bangkok. In the process, it nearly doubled the state's debt with its stimulus programs. Despite his highly populist platforms, however, once in office Thaksin was hardly bad for business, pushing for free trade deals and closer relationships with regional trading partners like China.

The political turmoil of recent years and the global recession have also taken their toll. Growth between 2008 and 2011 averaged only 2 percent, down from 5.6 percent from 2002 to 2006. Still, in 2011, the World Bank upgraded Thailand from a lower-middle-income country to an upper-middle-income country, reflecting the fact that poverty has fallen from a high of 21 percent in the wake of the 1997 financial crisis to under 8 percent today. Thailand's legacy of large foreign investment, attractiveness to tourism, and continued strong low-end manufacturing will for a time sustain its economy, but its inability to upgrade the value of its exports, its political turmoil, and its poor education system are eventually likely to prevent it from escaping the middle-income trap.

CIVIL SOCIETY AND MEDIA

For much of the Cold War, Thailand's civil society and media remained small and highly constrained, akin to many other authoritarian states. The government and the armed forces controlled radio and television broadcasting. Although some independent-minded print publications did challenge state control, their audience was relatively small compared with broadcast media and their penetration outside Bangkok limited. The few civil society organizations that did exist were trade associations, business groups, clan associations, and other relatively apolitical entities. The state exerted control over the *sangha*, the leadership of temples and other Buddhist organizations in the country.

One of the most important factors behind the liberalization of Thai politics in the late 1980s and 1990s was the end of the state monopoly on civil society and media. New television, radio, and eventually Internet publications sprang up, and Thailand was an early adopter of two-way pagers and mobile phones, which allowed a much wider swath of the population to become educated about and participate in politics.

The newly liberalized media covered formerly taboo topics such as high-level corruption cases and army-civilian relations, but their focus was on a set of issues most relevant to urbanites in Bangkok and other cities. With few exceptions, the media had little coverage of the Thai north and northeast, where the majority of the population actually lived, or of the deep south, where an insurgency raged, killing more than four thousand people between 2000 and 2010. When the poor were covered by the media, it was often through spokespeople for the few NGOs that focused on issues related to poverty, rather than by having reporters actually visit the north and northeast.

However, as Thailand's democratization process stalled, the impact of a liberalized media market and mobile telecommunications became more mixed. Technology made it easier to protest, but also fostered extreme partisanship, more vicious political attacks, and greater class conflict. Thaksin and the 2006 coup further divided the media and gave rise to a new crop of even more partisan media outlets, often privately funded by one or two tycoons.

As class division hardened, media abandoned their neutrality. This was a major mistake. With almost all the largest publications taking one side or another, many Thais felt as if they had no neutral voice to turn to anymore. In polls, public trust in the Thai media plummeted to new lows due to the intense polarization of the print and broadcast press. Partly as a result, media outlets found it harder to attract the best university graduates, creating a vicious cycle that only further reduced the quality of publications.

As the mainstream press lost credibility, many Thais turned instead to other, newer types of media outlets: village radio and Internet broadcasts targeted at poorer Thaksin supporters, Bangkok-based websites targeted at middle-class royalists, and social media that tended to aggregate either side of the class divide into groups. By the late 2000s, Thai media had turned into an echo chamber, with each side in the political conflict almost never having any contact with the other. The liberalization of the media has not been a net positive in terms of Thailand's democratic consolidation.

LEGAL SYSTEM AND RULE OF LAW

Thailand suffers from a weak rule of law. For decades, the legal system relied on informal networks presided over by the king. In a few areas, including some types of commercial disputes and family law, Thailand's judiciary was considered relatively professional and apolitical. At the highest levels, however, in cases bearing on the future of the political system or on major corporations (most of which were tied in some ways to the crown, the military, and professional politicians), the rule of law—even in the more democratic 1990s—remained weak and politicized. The judiciary functioned as a tool of the executive branch and deferred to the monarch.

This discouraged innovation, because innovative Thais could not hold onto their intellectual property. It also allowed large, often state-linked companies to dominate markets such as agro-industrial products, cement, and banking. For decades, little copyright protection or effective labor law existed, and there were few legal channels to challenge the political system or the monarchy.

The progressive 1997 constitution was an attempt to strengthen the rule of law and provide some checks and balances. It guaranteed a broad range of freedoms and created new national institutions to monitor corruption. It created a new upper house of parliament designed to scrutinize and potentially check legislation passed in the well-established lower house of parliament. It also intended to strengthen the judiciary by creating a new supreme court to handle disputes passed up from the lower courts. But it did not address the fact that the king and his advisors remained a kind of "deep state" capable of quietly pushing and pulling political parties, shaping budget allocations, or even launching a coup. The continuing, largely unwritten role of the king, and his influence over the levers of power, showed that formal laws still mattered little.

Thaksin's rise further weakened judicial independence and the rule of law. He purposefully undermined the new independent institutions created by the 1997 constitution: he publicly criticized them and told his supporters that they had little value, forced out independent-minded judges, and packed the upper house of parliament with his cronies. He also pressured judges on rulings about himself, his family, and his political and business allies.

Frustrated Bangkok elites and the middle class, including many real reformers, responded by fighting Thaksin through extra-constitutional means, street protests, and informal networks linked to the monarchy. In a time of crisis, the elites and middle class refused to work through the judiciary and other formal institutions. Instead of attempting to try Thaksin's alleged crimes in court or working to change laws in parliament, they blatantly disregarded the rule of law.

The king, too, publicly stepped up his involvement by instructing judges to resolve political disputes, sending a powerful signal that he was taking more control over the judiciary. In the process, he perpetuated the weakness of formal institutions.

The promise of the 1997 constitution was fully swept away by the 2006 coup, which was allegedly instigated by one of the king's closest advisors and backed by elites and the middle class. The government appointed by the generals tore up the 1997 document and replaced it with another constitution, which provided far weaker protections for human rights, a less independent judiciary, and an amnesty for coup-makers.

Thus both Thaksin and the royalist elite undermined the rule of law, and today few Thais have any trust in the judicial system's fairness, especially when it comes to political matters. Many Thais are concerned that if the country does not succeed in developing independent institutions by the time the current king dies (his son has little of his father's moral authority), they will be left with few means other than conflict for resolving political issues.

Thailand's weak rule of law has also resulted in a poor human rights record. Outside pressure, notably from the Clinton administration, did give rise to improvements during the 1990s in the trafficking of people, religious freedoms, and treatment of refugees from neighboring nations. The 1997 reformist constitution provided wide-ranging protections for civil liberties and human rights.

By the 2000s, however, shifts in the international environment made it easier for Thaksin, and later the Thai military, to dominate government and commit significant rights abuses with little punishment or even censure from the United States and other democratic powers. As the country's leaders—first Thaksin and then the coup-makers of 2006—destroyed its democratic institutions and fostered civil conflict, foreign governments and others concerned with democracy largely failed to act.

During Thaksin's tenure as prime minister, Freedom House downgraded Thailand in its political freedom ranking. Thailand also received significant criticism on rights abuses in the State Department's annual country reports on human rights—not least for Thaksin's "war on drugs," which led to the killings of thousands of people. But the Bush administration relied on Thaksin as an important counterterrorism ally. He was given a warm welcome in Washington, with little mention of his government's human rights abuses. This confirmed Thai opinion leaders' belief that Thailand would always be a close friend of the West and not really be punished for anything its government did.

After the coup in 2006, the United States and other established democracies missed another opportunity to apply pressure on Thailand to return to a democratic path and rule of law. The Bush administration worried that if it came down too hard after the coup, it would push Thailand further into the arms of China, which had once again become a major regional player. This, however, was a mistaken assumption and overstated China's attractiveness to Thailand. Despite U.S. disinterest in the region in the 2000s and China's economic emergence, the United States remained by far the preferred partner of Thailand and other emerging democracies in South and Southeast Asia. Instead of protesting that Thaksin, for all his flaws, had been democratically elected, the United States continued joint military exercises with the Thai armed forces and quickly sent the U.S. ambassador in Bangkok to meet with the coup-makers and reassure them of the stability of the U.S.-Thai relationship. The Association of Southeast Asian Nations, too, offered little criticism of Thailand's democratic regression.

GOVERNMENT STRUCTURE AND DIVISION OF POWER

Ostensibly, Thailand is a constitutional monarchy with a civilian government that divides power across the executive (prime minister), legislature, and judiciary. In practice, however, power is manipulated by the military, the king, and—since the dramatic changes to the 1997 constitution—an autocratic prime minister empowered by the rural poor.

Since the end of the absolute monarchy in 1932, the armed forces have been the predominant institution in Thai society, and at times the only national one. After the demise of total military rule in the early 1970s, the army operated in alliance with the king. This alliance is critical to understanding why the Thai military has proved so difficult to place under civilian control.

Thailand seemed on the verge of bringing the military under civilian control by the mid-1990s. Embarrassed by its role in the indiscriminate killing of middle-class protesters and publicly chastised by the king—a deep humiliation—the army's leadership seemed willing to focus on defense and counterinsurgency rather than domestic politics. However, civilian leaders were never willing to assure the senior military of their continued protection from prosecution, and so the army never fully relinquished the reins of power.

When Thaksin rose to power in 2001, he made no effort to assuage the military's concerns, even though some reassurance might have led to its continued withdrawal from political life. Instead, he tried to reduce the military's control over its affairs, cut its budget, and maneuver his allies into the army's senior ranks. The army leadership acquiesced for a time, but many seethed at these actions. Younger officers came to believe that the military should never have stepped out of politics, as it did in the 1990s, and vowed that it never would again.

The king, also seemingly threatened by Thaksin's rise, encouraged the resurgence of the military by lending his enormous popularity to the army. Neither absolute monarch nor ceremonial figurehead, the king is vested with considerable moral authority and exercises significant influence behind the scenes through his network of political allies. Despite his apparent breach with the armed forces in 1992, he continued to maintain close ties with senior royalist officers. In response to Thaksin's overreach, the king supported a narrative that pitted the supposedly nonpartisan, moral, nonpolitical army against venal and corrupt Thai politicians.

The truth, of course, was murkier. Thai politicians did have a long history of graft, but the armed forces were just as corrupt. Although some army regimes could be credited with appointing capable technocrats to run the economy and liberalize the investment environment, incessant military infighting and coups destabilized the country.

Today, few Thai observers see the military voluntarily leaving politics any time soon. Given that the demise of the current king is on the horizon (King Rama IX was born in 1927 and is the world's longest-reigning monarch), many senior military officers believe that the armed forces need to retain a central role in politics to ensure a smooth handover of royal power, especially given that the crown prince is far less popular than his father. Unlike the moderate military leadership of the 1990s, today's military leaders are hawkish. The top commander is known as an archconservative royalist who disdains the elected government, currently led by Thaksin's sister. The military maintains tight control over powerful internal security apparatuses, and enforces a de facto state of martial law in southern Thailand. As recently as 2010, it and its allies in the government used a state of emergency to essentially run the country.

In addition to the army and the palace, Thailand's other power center is the office of the prime minister, which under Thaksin—and now his younger sister, his proxy during his exile—wields considerable influence.

The 1997 constitution unintentionally set the conditions for the rise of an autocratic executive. Aiming to create a more stable two- or three-party system, the constitution both made it harder for small, regional parties to win seats and instituted tough anticorruption electoral laws. As a result, Bangkok politicians could no longer simply buy votes and minimize the influence of rural voters by keeping them splintered. This greatly empowered the rural poor, and opened the possibility that someone could rally the working class to establish a viable opposition to the Democrat Party. This seemed, at the time, like a net positive.

Thaksin quickly exploited the constitutional changes. A savvy politician, he recognized that in a truly open political system, he could triumph primarily by appealing to the poor and some middle-class voters. A billionaire from a wealthy family, Thaksin was an imperfect vehicle for upsetting the old order, but his combination of populist policies and autocratic tendencies, combined with the enabling environment of a liberalized media, was a winning combination. Thailand's weak institutions made it too easy for a cunning politician to scoop up the majority of rural votes and become, essentially, an elected autocrat.

Had Thailand implemented a proportional representation system or a hybrid presidential-parliamentary system, or made its senate strong enough to serve as counterbalance to the lower house, it might have been able to gain the benefits of the 1997 constitution—creating a stable two- or three-party system, bringing more voters into politics, and reducing corruption—without paving the way for an electoral autocracy. It did not make those choices, however.

Thailand had few safeguards to protect the independence of institutions such as the judiciary or the media, and the new watchdogs created in 1997 were just getting their footing when Thaksin was elected. His party became the first in Thai history to win an absolute majority of seats in parliament, setting the stage for dominance. He extended that dominance in the 2005 election and used it to destroy many of the state's nominally independent institutions that had been created in 1997 but that had not had time to establish their utility and independence from electoral politics.

Many Thais looked to the one safeguard that had always existed in the political system, the mediator and problem-solver of last resort: the king. Unfortunately, by bolstering his own power over the years, the king had actually weakened the development of other, independent institutions. Now, in the 2000s, as Thailand's democratization process began to come unhinged, the king was too elderly, unwell, and partisan to play his old role.

EDUCATION AND DEMOGRAPHY

Thailand's leaders in the postwar decades recognized that, to reduce its dependence on agriculture, the country would need broad-based education. The government therefore expanded primary education to cover the entire nation. National primary educational curricula focused on literacy, basic math and science, manual skills, and a nationalist ideology that encouraged obedience and adoration of the king. Rote learning was the norm and questioning teachers was unacceptable. By the end of the 1960s, basic literacy rates had climbed to nearly 98 percent.

This approach proved effective for creating a workforce for the low-end manufacturing flooding into Thailand. With their basic education, Thai students were well prepared to work in the auto parts, electronics, computer, and other manufacturing zones set up in Bangkok and its environs by foreign companies. The focus on primary education also helped maintain a relatively pliable and nonpoliticized population, particularly outside Bangkok—another goal of the military and other leaders. The economic boom of the 1960s and 1970s meant plenty of well-paying work for blue-collar workers and little public pressure for greater access to higher education.

Secondary education was reserved for a sliver of elites. Universal secondary education was not a priority, and neither was upgrading primary education to include higher-value skills such as English, computing, and mobile telecommunications.

Compared with neighbors like Singapore and Malaysia, Thailand had only a few university spaces. The sons and daughters of the Thai military, government, and business elite rarely attended domestic universities, instead going abroad to schools in Britain or the United States. This gave the elite little reason to invest in the country's university system. Thai universities fell behind other regional leaders in research and pedagogy as early as the 1970s, even as Thailand's economic boom continued.

After the financial crisis, and particularly in the 2000s, many senior Thai politicians, officials, and educators recognized that the country's education system was failing and that Thailand was falling behind regional competitors such as Vietnam, China, and Malaysia in critical skills, including information technology, English, and entrepreneurship. Many high-profile Thai foundations, NGOs, and media outlets published reports and articles about Thailand's educational deficit. That Thai students finished behind every other nation in the region in the annual exams in English that help students gain entry to American universities was widely publicized. Both the pro-Thaksin party and the Democrat Party proposed various theoretically laudable education reform initiatives, but political conflict hindered any progress in modernizing the education system during the 2000s.

Thailand's failure to make the necessary investments in quality secondary and higher education to enable a transition to a higher-value economy seriously threatens its continued economic competitiveness. The country has largely gone through its demographic transition: a successful family-planning program brought the country's annual population growth rate down from more than 3 percent in the 1960s to only 0.4 percent today. As a result, less than 20 percent of the population is now under the age of fifteen, which is on par with the United States. To compete with neighbors such as Malaysia and Vietnam, upgrading the skill set of Thailand's labor force is critical.

CONCLUSION

From the early 1990s to the early 2000s, Thailand seemed to be a textbook example of a developing country proceeding cautiously but thoughtfully toward democratization. Visitors from Indonesia, Cambodia, and other countries in the region frequently traveled to Thailand to work with and observe the kingdom's seemingly vibrant NGOs, newspapers, and online news outlets. Before the financial crisis, some predicted that by the turn of the century Thailand would take its place among the ten to fifteen largest economies in the world.

Instead, Thailand experienced almost a perfect storm of factors that ultimately not only derailed its democratization process and slowed growth but also set the stage for prolonged domestic conflict. Some of these factors were relatively outside the control of Thai leaders: the end of the Cold War unleashed the economic potential of regional rivals such as Vietnam, India, and China; the United States became absorbed with the Middle East, Afghanistan, and al-Qaeda; and the king became a less effective mediator as he grew into old age.

Thailand's leaders—civilian, royal, and military—also made a series of shortsighted decisions. When the economy was humming, they failed to invest budget surpluses in educating a workforce more capable of competing in higher-value industries and in reducing social and economic inequality; they maintained a political and social system that privileged Bangkok and its environs over the country's more rural areas; they missed an opportunity while the monarch was still young and highly respected to transition to a truly constitutional monarchy and shift some of the king's mediation powers to independent institutions such as the judiciary; and despite ample time in the mid-1990s to debate the new constitution and imagine its potential flaws, they pushed through a document that, though strong in many ways, unintentionally paved the way for electoral autocracy. In the wake of the financial crisis, the Democrat Party ignored the pain of rural voters and opened the door for a populist like Thaksin. The failure to fully tame the military, however, was perhaps the most critical misstep on the path to democratization.

In today's context of slower economic growth, a fading monarch, splintered and partisan media, a military reentrenched in political meddling, and a profound lack of trust between deeply opposed political camps, Thailand's future appears grim. Indeed, the two most likely scenarios are continued political gridlock that further undermines its competitiveness and, even worse, civil war.

THAILAND TIMELINE

1932: Coup d'État Ends Absolute Monarchy

A group of army officers and civilian officials ends Thailand's absolute monarchy with a coup d'état. King Prajadhipok loses his political powers, though the monarchy remains in place. Thailand is essentially ruled for the next six decades by the armed forces, allied with business elites and the king. The military maintains tight control over media and politics but generally allows technocrats to set economic policy.

1946: Bhumibol Adulyadej Becomes King

The U.S.-born Bhumibol Adulyadej (also known as Rama IX) becomes king of Thailand after the death of his brother, the previous king. Still on the throne in 2013, he is the world's longest-reigning monarch. Neither absolute monarch nor ceremonial figurehead, the king holds considerable moral authority and exercises significant political influence behind the scenes. Many Thais look to him as the mediator and problem-solver of last resort, but in the 2000s, as Thailand's democratization began to come unhinged, he was too elderly, unwell, and partisan to play this role. Although harsh lèse-majesté laws prevent open criticism, signs of anger with the monarchy and monarchist elites now abound.

1950s–1960s: Economic Boom Takes Hold

Thailand's economic development takes off in the late 1950s and early 1960s, aided by pragmatic macroeconomic policies, abundant resources, and an attractive environment for foreign direct investment. The gross domestic product growth rate between 1960 and 1970 averages 8.4 percent, among the highest in the world. Thailand also benefits from billions of dollars in American assistance, as well as Vietnam War–related activities and investment. The economic boom helps all classes, but Bangkok and its suburbs benefit the most.

1991: Military Seizes Power From Civilian Government

A military junta seizes power from Thailand's civilian government in February, committing an overreach that marks the first inflection point of Thailand's political transition. Popular pressure for civilian rule had been building for decades, and after the coup, large and violent street demonstrations erupt in Bangkok. The army tries unsuccessfully to crush the protests, killing at least sixty people. The king, who had long generally backed the military to guarantee stability, now appears concerned that the armed forces have become a source of instability. On May 20, 1992, he reprimands both the junta head and the protest leader on television. The military cedes control and street violence ends.

1992: Elections Usher in Democratic Era

Elections in September begin a period in which Thailand seems poised for democratic consolidation. It holds several free and fair elections, and civil society, which mushroomed in the 1980s and early 1990s, continues to flourish. The Democrat Party, favored primarily by elites, middle classes, and the palace, wins most elections during this period. It generally pursues stable, farsighted macroeconomic policies.

1997: Asian Financial Crisis Hits Thailand

In July, Thailand's government is forced to devalue the baht after months of attacks by speculators. In the ensuing crisis, many banks fail, construction dries up, and exports grind to a halt. Millions of Thais become unemployed. The deteriorating currency also makes it harder for farmers to buy much-needed machinery, and a series of droughts worsens the crisis. Although it pursues moderate macroeconomic reforms, the Democrat Party is largely blamed for the meltdown. This provides an opportunity for Thaksin Shinawatra, a billionaire telecommunications tycoon, to form his own party.

1997: Thailand Adopts New Constitution

In October, Thailand adopts a progressive and groundbreaking constitution guaranteeing many rights and freedoms. It creates new national institutions to monitor graft, establishes an upper house of parliament, creates a new supreme court, and strengthens political parties at the expense of unelected centers of power—the palace, the military, big business, and the elite civil service. The constitution proves in many ways the high-water mark for Thailand's democratic transition.

2001: Thaksin Wins Elections Through Appeal to the Poor

After mounting the most sophisticated political-advertising campaign in Thai history, Thaksin and his Thai Rak Thai Party win the pivotal 2001 election. He presents both a nonpartisan, executive image and a populist platform that includes universal health care and loans to low-income Thais, giving the rural poor their first real hope in democracy. Once in office, Thaksin works to stimulate the economy and broaden development beyond Bangkok. He also pushes for free trade deals and closer relationships with trading partners such as China. Politically, Thaksin weakens judicial independence and the rule of law, forcing out independent-minded judges and packing the upper house of parliament with cronies. Thailand's weak institutions make it easy for him to manipulate rural support to become, essentially, an elected autocrat. He is reelected by a wide margin in 2005.

2006: Military Stages Coup

Thailand's military deposes Thaksin with a coup d'état in September. The coup comes after demonstrations led by middle-class and elite Thais increasingly distrustful of the populist Thaksin. King Bhumibol sanctifies the military's putsch. Thaksin had alienated the king by challenging his position as Thailand's most revered figure, and the king appeared convinced that the only way to ensure stability was to return power to traditional military, bureaucratic, and palace elites. The armed forces replace the 1997 constitution with a weaker version that serves primarily to reinstitute the army's role in politics.

2010: Political Unrest Rocks Bangkok

Anger mounts among working-class Thais after elites use the judiciary, the palace, and army meddling to install a Democrat Party government in late 2008. Antigovernment protests culminate in two months of bloodshed in the streets of Bangkok in the spring of 2010, during which at least eighty people are killed and hundreds detained. Following the violence, the Democrat government launches a harsh crackdown on civil liberties, abandoning whatever high ground it might have held.

2011: Thaksin's Sister Elected Prime Minister

In July, a pro-Thaksin party led by the former prime minister's sister, Yingluck Shinawatra, wins an absolute parliamentary majority, shocking Thailand's middle classes. Senior military officers had appeared on television to warn Thais to vote for the Democrat Party, while the government closed several websites and jailed hundreds of activists without charge. After Yingluck's victory, some prominent intellectuals call for another coup and others suggest limiting the franchise. Yingluck, who serves as prime minister through the present, seems to have as little concept of the need for a loyal opposition as her brother. The result has been paralysis, democratic decline, and a marked deterioration of civil liberties and human rights.

2011: Thailand Reaches Upper-Middle-Income Status

The World Bank upgrades Thailand from a lower-middle-income to an upper-middle-income country, reflecting that poverty has fallen from a high of 21 percent in the wake of the 1997 financial crisis to under 8 percent. Growth, however, averaged only 2 percent per year between 2008 and 2011, down from 5.6 percent from 2002 to 2006. Though Thailand's strengths can sustain its economy for a time, its inability to upgrade the value of its exports, its political turmoil, and its poor education system are likely to prevent it from escaping the middle-income trap.

Ukraine

Andrew Wilson

Ukraine's transition after 1991 involved more than a change of rulers or regime. Ukraine was a completely new entity, both as a state and as a nation. Indeed, Ukrainians had long been divided among rulers with disparate political practices. Although parts of western Ukraine enjoyed some pluralism under Habsburg rule, most Ukrainians, who were subjects of first the Russian Empire and then the Soviet Union, experienced only the briefest flowerings of democracy after 1905 and in 1917. Ukrainians also had competing visions of their ostensible community's borders and disagreed about whether it should be part of some broader whole, and if so, which one—the Russian or the Austro-Hungarian Empire, and later the Soviet Union or Poland. Although decades of Soviet rule eventually blurred many cultural differences, issues of ethnicity, language, and religion remain highly divisive today. The country, though, is committed at least to the discourse of democracy. The idea that *Ukraine Is Not Russia,* the title of a (probably ghostwritten) book by former president Leonid Kuchma, retains considerable power.

As a nascent state after the Soviet Union's collapse, Ukraine had to build institutions, international relations, and an economy more or less from scratch. This new state had, and still has, weak outreach to its regions. In the center, it has been both too strong and too weak: too strong because Ukraine's leaders have sought to re-create the security culture and economic control mechanisms of the Soviet Union, and too weak because most new institutions lack the resources to provide social justice or the organizational strength to resist capture by vested interests. Ukraine is also a new nation. An independent Ukraine never existed within its present borders. Although a smaller version enjoyed precarious independence in various forms between 1917 and 1920, the country's kaleidoscopic historical regions have only just settled into their current configuration. The Ukrainian transition was therefore also one of defining a national identity; battles over that identity have been the central issue in Ukrainian politics since 1991. The region that now constitutes Ukraine used to be multiethnic, but its Jewish, Polish, and German minorities nearly disappeared in the twentieth century. Culture wars are now a bipolar contest between the Ukrainian and Russian language, culture, and history, and the two camps are roughly equal in size.

This internal divide is mirrored regionally in Ukraine's uncertain position between Russia and Europe. Unlike the situation in the central European and Baltic states, which joined the European Union (EU) and North Atlantic Treaty Organization (NATO) between 1999 and 2009, in Ukraine public opinion has always been divided on the economic, military, and cultural merits of alignment with Russia or with Europe. Europe's policy tools for Ukraine have been too ineffective and attenuated to tip the balance, and Russia has tried to maintain in Ukraine the same type of semi-authoritarian system and opaque business practices it has at home. Ukraine's leaders complain publicly that their country is stuck in a diplomatic gray zone between Russia and Europe: prospects of NATO and EU membership remain distant at best, and Ukraine's powerful oligarchs are unenthusiastic about the Russian-led Customs Union and Eurasian Union unless they serve oligarchic interests. But privately, relative isolation suits Ukraine's leaders perfectly well, because it leaves their corruption undisturbed.

INFLECTION POINTS
OF THE TRANSITION PERIOD

Ukraine won independence in 1991 partly through its own efforts but primarily because the Soviet order imploded. There was no social revolution. The old Communist elite remained in charge as the nascent state and nation struggled to emerge. The counter-elite, mainly former dissidents, had been strong enough to win a quarter of the vote during elections held in the late Gorbachev era (1990–91). Unlike their counterparts in the Baltic states, however, the dissidents were not strong enough to win power. Most Ukrainian nationalists were therefore prepared to support the old elite, as long as they backed independence.

Ukraine's first president, Leonid Kravchuk (1991–94), was a typical former Communist Party apparatchik. In his new role he concentrated on state-building, which in practice meant centralizing power rather than building real grassroots democracy. There was little in the way of a civil society to check these autocratic tendencies. Society was atomized by seventy years of Soviet rule; the middle class (technicians and intelligentsia) had been decimated when savings were destroyed by inflation in the early 1990s, and the bureaucracy was the only real available instrument of power.

Nor did Kravchuk's economic policy aim to build a true market economy. Instead, it intended to recreate a smaller version of the Soviet Union, with price, trade, and production controls to cement the new elite's power. Such policies could not build prosperity, however. Gross domestic product (GDP) fell by almost 50 percent as the old Soviet economy was torn apart and disoriented actors resorted to informal or criminal practices to survive. In the 1994 elections, Kravchuk was swept away by the economic crisis. His successor, Leonid Kuchma, forced through a new presidential constitution in 1996, cleverly exploiting both nationalists, who wanted to complete unfinished state-building, and liberals, who thought he would use his powers to enact belated market reforms. Once he had the powers granted by the new constitution, however, he did neither. Another economic mini-collapse in 1998 destroyed Kuchma's hopes of running for a second term with an economic recovery under way, and the 1999 election was crudely fixed to ensure his victory instead.

As the reform process faltered, a new class of oligarchs took over the economy in the late 1990s and early 2000s. They were a mixture of former bureaucrats, commodity traders and speculators from the Soviet youth league, traditional mafia, and Kuchma's family. These new oligarchs exercised their political influence to reshape the economy to serve their interests. A brief period of emergency economic reform, including elementary budget discipline and a new currency, introduced a modicum of stability in the mid-1990s, but an opaque and corrupt privatization process was rigged to serve the oligarchs. Kuchma played a game of balance between the oligarchs, parceling control of Ukraine's heavy industry to rival regional clans in a series of insider deals in the late 1990s and early 2000s: coal and steel in the Donbass, piping and petrochemicals in Dnipropetrovsk, engineering in Kharkiv, and the Soviet vacation industry in Crimea. Substantive economic reform (deregulation of industry and manufacturing, privatization of land ownership, and reduction of trade tariffs and subsidies) was again delayed until this great divvying up was over. Other post-Soviet states that began reform early were recovering by the mid-1990s, but Ukraine's first year of renewed growth came only in 2000. Most of the population struggled to survive and civil society remained weak. Real GDP per capita reached a low of under $650 between 1997 and 1999.

Although Kuchma appeared to have firm control, he overreached in his second term. In 2000, he stage-managed a four-question referendum to further expand his presidential powers. The implausible majorities he claimed, however, all greater than 83 percent, served only to highlight the deterioration of democracy in Ukraine. Economic pressures were also building. Ukraine was almost bankrupt, and in December 1999 Kuchma was forced by an impending balance-of-payments crisis to appoint a reformist prime minister, the former central bank chief Viktor Yushchenko, to negotiate with international lenders. Yushchenko's deputy, a former gas trader named Yulia Tymoshenko, was appointed as poacher-turned-gamekeeper to clean up the energy sector, the most corrupt part of the Ukrainian economy. The duo's reforms kick-started the economy, which ironically made it even harder to dislodge the oligarchs as they began to enjoy the fruits of belated growth.

The final element in this combustible mixture was the Gongadze scandal, named after the journalist Georgiy Gongadze, who founded Ukraine's first website devoted to political exposés and critiques of oligarchic corruption. He disappeared in 2000 and a month later his headless corpse was found in the woods outside Kiev. Sensational secret tapes emerged in which President Kuchma was heard angrily demanding that his subordinates deal with Gongadze in colorful ways.

The protest campaign sparked by the economic collapse and the Gongadze scandal failed to mobilize enough numbers to force substantial change, and it fizzled out by spring 2001. It did succeed, however, in stimulating an upsurge in civic activism, including youth groups, election monitors, and human rights watchdogs.

In the fall of 2004, the Orange Revolution caught the attention of the world. The proximate cause of this uprising was an attempt by the authorities to rig yet another presidential election, this time in favor of Viktor Yanukovych, a favorite of the Donbass clan, who had been appointed prime minister in 2002. Following the vote, hundreds of thousands joined huge demonstrations, which continued in Kiev's main square for two months. The crowds' orange flags and banners (the opposition's campaign color) dominated television coverage, but in fact the protests were possible only because of divisions at the top. The crowd, although large enough to prevent the authorities from declaring Yanukovych the victor, was essentially a passive force. In private, the oligarchs were building bridges with the opposition candidate, former prime minister Viktor Yushchenko, to protect their interests. Some radicals thought the regime should be completely dismantled, but Yushchenko was naturally more cautious. Following negotiations, the election was rerun and Yushchenko emerged victorious.

This turn of events dealt a blow to Moscow, which supported Yanukovych, and appeared to lay the groundwork for real democracy and reform. The parties agreed to change the constitution in time for the next parliamentary elections, in 2006, with amendments to reduce the president's power and to require parliamentary deputies to remain in the parties they were elected to serve. These reforms, however, were also a trap for the election winners: they sabotaged the Orange Revolution by shifting power from the incoming president to the oligarch-dominated parliament. The so-called revolution thus resulted only in a change in elites, and those elites were soon captured and corrupted by the system rather than the other way around. At the same time, a behind-the-scenes amnesty for the perpetrators of the election fraud provided a seeming blanket immunity for the Kuchma-era elite. The new Orange period therefore failed to begin in truth, guaranteeing that controversies would continue to fester.

The revolution was also undermined from the outset by a legitimacy crisis. Pro-Orange voters were nearly all in western and central Ukraine. Thus, the Yanukovych camp, strongly backed by Russia, was able to maintain the fiction in eastern and southern Ukraine that the revolution was only a coup d'état.

In economic terms, the revolution arguably came too early: the economy had been growing for only four years, so the nascent middle class, about 10 percent of the population, and the small and medium enterprise sector, then only 16 percent of GDP, were not yet large enough to sustain robust civil society pressure for accountable democracy.

A lack of real international support also made the road tough for Ukraine's would-be reformers. The Orange Revolution came after the big EU expansion in January 2004. By the time Ukraine's democratic prospects began to seem more promising, the EU was already overextended with new members and not looking to nurture additional transitional economies on the difficult road toward potential EU membership. Orange infighting and Russia's war in Georgia in 2008 destroyed Ukraine's chances of NATO membership. Western support was therefore dissipating precisely when it was needed most, as Russia sought to impede reform and democratization in Ukraine, which it had strong incentives to do. Successful economic and political transformation in a kindred state would have been a mortal threat to the Putinist system and its argument that democracy would bring only chaos to the post-Soviet world. Russia began investing heavily in nongovernmental organizations (NGOs) for Russian speakers to ensure that the anti-Orange half of the population stayed mobilized. The Russian government also helped set up a notorious corruption scheme, the gas import monopoly Rosukrenergo (Russian Ukrainian Energy), which channeled hundreds of millions of dollars to Ukraine's new rulers.

The Orange presidency of Yushchenko was marked by constant political crises. Infighting among political elites, including intraparty power grabs and personal squabbles, made effective governance impossible. Instead of pursuing political and economic reforms, the leaders of Ukraine's ideologically indistinguishable political factions courted the oligarchs, and vice versa, in an effort to consolidate their power.

The global economic crisis hit Ukraine hard in 2009, sending an already weak economy into free fall. GDP fell by 15 percent in 2009; exports fell by 49 percent in the first three quarters, with steel especially hard hit; and the local banking bubble collapsed. Real incomes fell by 8.5 percent in 2009, and official unemployment tripled to more than 9 percent. The government balked at raising domestic gas prices, which ruined relations with the International Monetary Fund (IMF). The brief period when Ukrainian oligarchs had enjoyed access to Western bank loans and initial public offerings was now over as global markets crashed. Most elites, therefore, and many citizens in the southeast, now looked to Russia as the only source of significant funds and swung behind Yanukovych's nominally pro-Russian party. Corruption and constant elite squabbling had also alienated core Orange supporters in west and central Ukraine. Under these conditions, Yanukovych was able to gain the presidency in the second round of the 2010 elections.

The constant infighting of the Orange years had weakened political institutions and created so much voter fatigue that President Yanukovych was able to centralize power with little resistance. Thus, the judiciary was placed under executive control in the summer of 2010, and in October the Constitutional Court was persuaded to reverse the entire 2004 constitutional reform, agreed to during the Orange

Revolution, that had reduced presidential power. The government began to persecute its political opponents, most spectacularly Yulia Tymoshenko, who had served twice as prime minister under Yushchenko and came in a close second to Yanukovych in the 2010 election. In October 2011, she was sentenced to seven years in prison on trumped-up charges. "Orange fatigue," both among Ukrainian voters and internationally, meant that initial protests over the changes were muted. By the time Tymoshenko's case became an international cause célèbre, the damage had been done.

The new authorities raised the gas price and the pension age, which was enough to restart lending from the IMF in the summer of 2010, but relations were ruptured within months as Yanukovych concentrated on repaying his oligarch supporters rather than on structural reforms, as the IMF demanded. Energy distribution companies were sold off in a series of rigged privatizations. The failure to reform left Ukraine economically vulnerable to the persistent global recession, to turmoil in the euro area, and to slowdown in its main export markets.

LESSONS OF THE TRANSITION PERIOD

SOCIOECONOMIC EXCLUSION AND INCLUSION

Ukraine's parasitic economy is stuck in a low-growth trap: there is enough money to make the oligarchs rich, but not the people. The standard of living has never been high, although income and equality have both recovered from disastrous declines in the years after the transition. World Bank figures show that from a starting point of $1,490 in 1991, GDP per capita fell by more than half during the 1990s before recovering over the next decade to $3,615 in 2011. Ukraine's Gini coefficient in 1988 was 23.3, where 0 represents total equality and 100 total inequality. Inequality rose in the catastrophic 1990s recession, and the Gini coefficient peaked at 39.3 in 1995, but more economic growth brought it down to 26.4 in 2009 (see Figure 14). Meanwhile, the proportion of the population living below the national poverty line has fallen from more than 30 percent in the 1990s to less than 10 percent today.

Official figures do not tell the whole story, however. They do not really include the super-rich, who largely escape official taxation and documentation. Ukraine's fifty richest citizens control almost half the

FIGURE 14. INCOME AND INEQUALITY IN UKRAINE

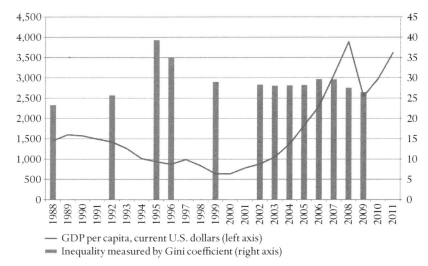

— GDP per capita, current U.S. dollars (left axis)
▬ Inequality measured by Gini coefficient (right axis)

Source: World Bank (GDP per capita). The Gini coefficient is a measure of inequality in which a value of 0 signifies perfect equality and 100 signifies inequality.

FIGURE 15. UKRAINE'S WEALTH CONCENTRATION IN COMPARATIVE PERSPECTIVE

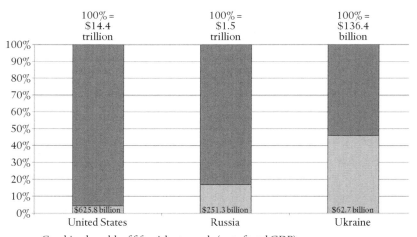

▣ Combined wealth of fifty richest people (out of total GDP)

Source: Wealth of fifty richest people calculated by adding top fifty numbers on the 2010 *Forbes* World's Billionaires list (Russia and the United States) and the top fifty numbers in the *Korrespondent*'s 2010 list of the richest Ukrainians. 2010 GDP in current U.S. dollars from the World Bank.

country's GDP. Even in oligarch-heavy Russia, the fifty richest people control less than 20 percent of GDP (see Figure 15).

Ukraine's cleavage structures make it difficult to challenge oligarchic power. In regional and language terms, the country is evenly split. The Ukrainophone half of the population is disproportionately rural; the Russophone half includes most of the massive pensioner population and big workforces in Soviet-style factories in the east. Ukrainian nationalists ought to be able to mobilize the ethnic Ukrainian majority, who make up 78 percent of the population. Almost 30 percent of the country, however, speaks Russian, primarily in the east and south, and continues to associate Russian language and culture with urbanity and opportunity. The east is indeed still more developed: every region in Ukraine's west, center, and north has a monthly per capita income below the national average. Kiev and the six big cities of the southeast, meanwhile, account for 66 percent of GDP.

Politicians benefit from the stalemate between the Russian- and Ukrainian-speaking camps and play off their complex resentments to stay in power. It has therefore been difficult to form cohesive governments with coherent reform programs. Most Ukrainian elections since 1991 have refought issues of identity, language, and foreign policy orientation. Neither constituency has been able to push strongly for market reform, even in its own half of the country, leaving politics dominated by venal elites and regional patronage networks, which have maintained a dependency culture in both halves of Ukraine. Even if they promise reforms, politicians revert to predatory behavior once in office, so underlying issues are never resolved and simply resurface at the next election.

ECONOMIC STRUCTURE AND POLICIES

Ukraine is afflicted by a classic rentier curse. Oligarchs and politicians, who are often one and the same, can extract rents from Ukraine's role as an energy transit state—80 percent of Russian gas bound for Europe passes through Ukraine—and from leeching the state budget and other scams. Metals and minerals, including iron ore, mercury, titanium, and a quarter of the world's manganese, make up half of Ukraine's total exports. Meanwhile, gas oligarchs depend on joint corruption schemes with their Russian counterparts to secure supply. Other oligarchs, in steel and cars, for example, compete directly with Russians, but this has fed demand for local political protection rather than for market competition and fair rule of law. Given the lack of agreement to open EU markets, export businesses have no incentive to move up the global value chain and tend to sell steel or basic agricultural products.

The oligarchs have also been able to exploit the semi-reformed economy in other ways. Some prices are market based, but others are controlled, which creates huge opportunities for arbitrage. Export licenses, import monopolies, and value-added tax refunds all depend on political favor, creating a dream environment for corrupt lobbying. Although many hoped that oligarchs would eventually seek to "go legit" once most important property was in their hands, oligarch incomes depend on keeping politics corrupt and the economy opaque. Indeed, although many early oligarchs in the 1990s were pure traders and speculators, the new generation that rose in the late 1990s and 2000s has corrupted the policymaking process to ensure a supply of cheap, government-subsidized inputs (mainly gas, coal, and electricity). Ukraine has had two bursts of market reform, in 1994–95 and in 2000–2001, but only the minimum necessary to prevent international lenders from withdrawing completely. On neither occasion was the thicket of monopolies, controls, and subsidies that allow elites to profit truly dismantled.

After the 2004 Orange Revolution, economic policy concentrated on superficial populist measures, such as fuel and meat price freezes, rather than on tackling systemic problems, as had been briefly attempted in 2000–2001. There was no concerted challenge to oligarchic power, as was the case in Georgia after 2003, when the oligarchs and mafia were sidelined one by one. Corruption not only remained endemic, it soon engulfed the new rulers. Most controversial was the energy transit company Rosukrenergo, which was paid billions for overseeing the import of gas from Russia and Central Asia to Ukraine. Controlled by some figures linked to Russia's Gazprom and others linked to former President Kuchma when it was first set up in 2004, Rosukrenergo came to be tied after the Orange Revolution to President Yushchenko's family and the oligarchs around him.

Most of the economy (some 65 percent of GDP) is now private, but privatization was rigged to benefit the oligarchs rather than designed to create a proper, functioning market economy. Ukraine passed relatively liberal privatization laws as early as 1992 and devised a voucher privatization scheme between 1995 and 1997, but neither was implemented. The vouchers, which would have allowed holders to purchase shares in state-owned enterprises, were ravaged by inflation and stockpiled by insiders at steep discounts. Most big enterprises were then sold by closed discount cash sales in the late 1990s and early 2000s. But without an effective legal system, all property remains insecure. Violent corporate raiding is widespread, and oligarchs use mafia muscle to take over each other's firms and scare away all but the hardiest foreign investors. The small and medium enterprise sector accounts for less than 20 percent of GDP and has even shrunk in recent years, hampered by red tape, legal insecurity, and rapacious big business. Overregulation, corruption, and informal employment mean the black economy accounts for 40 to 50 percent of official GDP.

External actors are not strong enough to break these patterns. Ukraine has received significant sums from international financial institutions to support transition and cushion the recessions of 1998 and 2008. However, these funds, totaling $16.6 billion from the IMF and 7.5 billion euros from the European Bank for Reconstruction and Development (EBRD) since 1995, are small relative to the size of Ukraine's economy, which reached $165 billion in 2011. The IMF and EBRD have therefore proved unable to keep Ukraine on the straight and narrow. Indeed, the country's relationship with the IMF has broken down three times when Ukraine failed to stick to a reform agenda, in 2002, 2009, and 2011.

CIVIL SOCIETY AND MEDIA

Although civil society in Ukraine is not as eviscerated as the state and other aspects of democratic governance, it is still quite weak. Civil society did have a moment of prominence at the time of the Orange Revolution. Then, however, cohesion and engagement quickly disintegrated as people grew disillusioned when promises were broken and aspirations of democracy were betrayed by the new political elites. Civil society is not entirely dead—growing numbers of elites are leading civil society organizations instead of pursuing political power, and citizens increasingly believe that civil society is a critical bulwark against a corrupt state—but the average citizen is not mobilized or engaged in any sustained way.

Ukraine's transition, including civil society's mobilization, has been led primarily by elites. Where civil society exists, it concentrates on seeking donors rather than lobbying decision-makers or building real constituencies of support. Only about 5 percent of Ukrainian citizens belong to NGOs. Just 2.6 percent of citizens are confident they can influence government fully; another 15.3 percent say they can influence government to some extent.

Unlike Georgia after its Rose Revolution in 2003, which probably went to the opposite extreme, of absorbing too much NGO capacity into government, the various Orange governments kept Ukrainian NGOs at arm's length after 2004, and vice versa. Civil society thought it had installed good leaders and lapsed into a passive mode. Ukraine failed to develop a proper public space in which NGOs and the authorities could interact, the former providing ideas and advice and the latter drawing on them. Unfortunately, therefore, the new government leaders lacked a supporting structure of ideas and persuasion as they sought to take on the corrupt prerevolution system.

The current Yanukovych administration has been openly hostile to NGOs. In 2010, it dismantled the Civil Society Consultative Groups set up after the Orange Revolution. Freedom of assembly has also been curtailed. In 2011, 90 percent of applications for public meetings or demonstrations were denied by the courts. The security services and tax authorities have likewise been used to harass activists.

Despite, or perhaps because of, this hostile environment, NGO activities are now on the rise. Some elites, exasperated by the void created by a weak and divided political opposition, have begun organizing civil society organizations instead of pursuing power through political means.

Among the wider public, however, the optimism and engagement of 2004 have given way to cynicism after the disappointments of the Orange years. Popular willingness to challenge the authorities and protest has deflated massively: only 24.7 percent say they are willing to take part in lawful meetings and demonstrations, and only 5 percent of young Ukrainians express the desire to become involved in politics. Outside activist circles, popular engagement has so deteriorated that Ukraine now has a rent-a-crowd industry to populate rallies and public protests.

The mass media in Ukraine have tended to function as an instrument of power rather than as an independent fourth estate. Under President Kuchma, a system of *temnyky* (themes for the week) developed whereby the presidential administration instructed the media in private what to cover, what not to cover, and what line to take. Large parts of the media were left in private hands as long as they were under "reliable" oligarchic control. One television channel, however, was owned by an unreliable oligarch, who backed Viktor Yushchenko in 2004. The channel helped expose election fraud and spark the Orange Revolution. When the protests began, many journalists rebelled and demanded the freedom to take a more independent line. Today, however, journalists continue to be bullied by the arbitrary application of the law and are regularly bribed to slant their coverage. Political control of the media is an important tool to disguise state corruption, tarnish opponents with what is locally known as *kompromat* (compromising materials, invented or exaggerated if necessary), and ensure favorable coverage both for loyal parties and the fake parties that are used to take votes from the opposition.

The Orange Revolution allowed a window of freedom from state censorship, and Ukraine became famous for its lively (and lengthy) political talk shows. Subsequent administrations, however, have progressively chipped away at the foundations of media freedom—not by direct censorship, but by ensuring that oligarchic moguls close to the presidency control the leading television channels. This produces a decentralized system of self-censorship.

The Internet remains lively and free, and critical voices increasingly migrate online. Use of social media such as Facebook and *Vkontakte* (In Contact) is growing rapidly. One other bright spot is the emergence of online advocacy sites modeled on anticorruption campaigns in Russia, which publicize abuses by traffic police and the privileged who ignore traffic laws.

LEGAL SYSTEM AND RULE OF LAW

The legal system in Ukraine is not designed to deliver the rule of law. The trial of former prime minister Yulia Tymoshenko in 2011 led to loud international complaints against selective justice. But all justice in Ukraine is selective, and therefore unjust. The law is deliberately capricious and complex, and its application purposely arbitrary. The result is a Kafkaesque system in which the entire population constantly has to break the law. The authorities can therefore decide what laws to enforce and whom to prosecute, and they wield this authority to consolidate their power. The punishment of the law is used to disable anyone who challenges the system; the forgiveness of the law is used as a form of patronage, particularly to bind big business to the state.

The legal system cannot challenge this process; it is in fact designed to implement it. Most judges are holdovers from the Communist era and still practice what is known as telephone justice, named for the practice of Communist officials phoning judges privately with instructions on how to rule. Nowadays this role is played by state prosecutors or the president's office. Conviction rates regularly top 99 percent.

Recent legal "reforms," rushed through in mid-2010 while the rest of the world was looking the other way, have massively increased executive control over a weak and discredited judiciary. Yanukovych's administration created two new courts to bypass those that were still relatively independent, and the Supreme Court, which had delivered a groundbreaking verdict on election fraud in 2004, was purged and weakened. Other executive bodies were given vast new powers over judicial appointments. Members of the Constitutional Court were purged as well. The ease with which the new authorities launched a string of political prosecutions in 2011 and 2012 showed just how supine the new system was, Tymoshenko's case being the most prominent.

Politicians routinely accept bribes from rich and influential oligarchs, or are oligarchs themselves, to make sure businesses stay in the right hands and receive the right favors. All members of parliament have blanket constitutional immunity from prosecution, ensuring that public office remains a gravy train that makes officeholders immensely wealthy. Unsurprisingly, politicians vie for office primarily to enrich themselves by supporting rent-seeking interests. Parliament is an investment: the average price of a seat is estimated to be more than $5 million—not in campaign costs, but in bribes to party leaders to secure a place on an electoral list.

GOVERNMENT STRUCTURE AND DIVISION OF POWER

Whatever elements of democracy exist in Ukraine do so by default, not because of good institutional design. In fact, Ukraine has made almost every wrong move imaginable. In the 1990s, Ukraine built the wrong type of institutions for the new state. Ministries mimicking the Soviet model—based on sectoral divisions of the economy, such as mining and engineering—recreated some of the worst habits of the command economy: the power ministries, such as the former KGB and the state prosecutor, and the administrative bureaucracy, such as the tax police, were given too much power. Tax collection is therefore actually reasonably efficient for such a corrupt state, usually around 20 percent of GDP, because these powerful ministries can coerce payments. The big state companies, on the other hand, had weak corporate structures after independence, leaving them wide open to informal capture by their former Communist bosses and then insider privatization to the new oligarchs, who were often the former Communist bosses themselves.

President Kuchma (1994–2005) expanded presidential power, but used it to act as the oligarchs' patron. Kuchma's idea of balance was to distribute privatization gains among the major clans rather than cultivate a broader base of middle-class support.

The constitutional changes agreed to at the height of the Orange Revolution in December 2004 and introduced after March 2006, which weakened the presidency, were therefore not necessarily bad ideas in themselves. However, they were drafted in haste, badly implemented, and ill-suited to the climate of intense personal political competition between 2005 and 2010. Ultimately, they allowed the oligarchs to deprive Yushchenko of the fruits of victory by building up parliament as an alternative center of power and then using that power to corrupt the presidency. In Georgia, a strong executive began a full-frontal assault on oligarchic power after 2003; however, the Ukrainian oligarchs used the system to play politicians off each other.

However, the reversal of the constitutional changes in 2010 was also a bad decision. It was achieved by dubious means, furthering disrespect for the law and legal process. It restored the status quo ante, rather than keeping the best of the changes made. Worst of all, the aim was not to rebalance the system but to entrench the new authorities (led by President Yanukovych) in power and protect newly unbridled oligarchic corruption. Too many checks and balances were destroyed; power was consolidated in a corrupt rather than reformist executive. Excessive centralization also concentrated rent-seeking among a smaller number of oligarchs, increasingly including the president's family.

EDUCATION AND DEMOGRAPHY

The oligarchs preside over a population that is declining and aging. Ukraine has one of the highest pensioner populations and dependency ratios in Europe, with fourteen million retired people in a population of forty-six million. Pensions absorbed a massive 18 percent of GDP as of 2009. The result is a dependency culture that has fed paternalistic authoritarianism. Most pensioners and most of Ukraine's industrial workers live in the Russian-speaking big cities of southeast Ukraine. The less urbanized Ukrainian-speaking western and central regions are more agricultural and have more migrant workers, so dependency on welfare, state wages, and pensions is also high, which blunts the potential for a true reformist party on the Orange side. Almost 30 percent of Ukrainians still live on the land working for a quasi-feudal collective farm system that has been only partially abolished.

The Orange Revolution may have been fronted by photogenic student activists, but the Ukrainian population is relatively old. The median age in 2010 was 39.3, far higher than 29.0 in Kazakhstan and higher even than Russia's 37.9, according to the 2010 UN World Population Prospects. Only 14.2 percent of the population was fourteen or younger. The Gorbachev era of the late 1980s saw a mini population boom, and these youths are now coming of age, adding temporarily to protest potential and the popularity of new media. But this short-term increase will not prevent a sharp future population decline.

One positive Soviet legacy is mass education: almost 30 percent of the population has completed higher education, which could help build a new middle class in the long term. For the moment, the economy is growing just enough, at 4 to 5 percent per year, to absorb the graduate flow, but a lack of opportunities will be a source of tension later if the economy deteriorates. Corruption in higher education has grown massively since 1991, undermining the value of local qualifications, and the children of the elite increasingly study abroad.

CONCLUSION

Most of Ukraine's problems have been of its own making. The golden opportunity provided by the Orange Revolution was tragically spurned. Individual Orange politicians simply lacked the strength, and in some cases the inclination, to tackle Ukraine's rentier curse, and supporting forces and circumstances simply were not strong enough to help. Ukraine remains the quintessential eastern European land of the oligarchs. After twenty years in the European waiting room, Ukraine has not moved closer to democracy and broad prosperity. Instead it has merely entrenched oligarchic rule, which may now be degenerating into mafia control and the personalized power of President Yanukovych's inner circle.

Yanukovych's attempts to consolidate authority will test the strength of remaining social and political constraints. In some areas, such as disabling the opposition, Yanukovych has been able to move quickly and ruthlessly. In others, such as the resilience of civil society, counter-vailing forces have been surprisingly strong. The main lessons for the outside world should be that change in Ukraine will come about only when a domestic reform lobby is strong enough to take on the country's deeply entrenched oligarchic interests. External voices are much more influential if they make the same demands as empowered local constituencies. Ukraine missed its transition moment in 2004. The optimistic scenario is that the Yanukovych project will implode or provoke popular protests if greedy elites overmonopolize resources and reduce Ukraine's already uneven rate of growth, something that would discourage future Ukrainian autocrats. The realistic scenario is that Ukraine will remain difficult to change.

UKRAINE TIMELINE

1991: Ukraine Becomes Independent

Ukraine emerges from the Soviet Union's collapse as an independent country for the first time in its history. It is a completely new entity, both as a state and as a nation. Leonid Kravchuk, a typical former Communist Party apparatchik, becomes the first president of Ukraine. Kravchuk focuses on centralizing his power rather than building a real grassroots democracy. His economic policy aims to re-create a smaller version of the Soviet Union instead of a true market economy.

1994: Elites Force Early Elections

Members of the business elite, who had taken advantage of the chaotic conditions of the early 1990s to begin enriching themselves, force early elections in summer 1994 by encouraging strikes in eastern Ukrainian cities. These elites back one of their own, former prime minister and missile factory director Leonid Kuchma, for president. Kuchma wins in a runoff on July 11, with especially strong support in the east and south.

1995: Mass Privatization Begins

The government launches a large-scale privatization program, following up on privatization laws passed as early as 1992. Thousands of large and medium enterprises are auctioned off into private hands.

This process increases the private sector's share of GDP, but it is rigged to benefit oligarchs rather than designed to create a proper, functioning market economy. Moreover, an ineffective legal system prevents the emergence of secure property rights. Violent corporate raiding becomes increasingly widespread, with oligarchs taking over each other's firms.

1996: New Constitution Ratified, Expanding Presidential Power

President Leonid Kuchma forces through a new constitution granting him expanded authority, cleverly exploiting both nationalists, who want to complete unfinished state building, and liberals, who think Kuchma will use his powers to force through belated market reforms. Once he has the powers granted by the new constitution, however, he does neither. Kuchma is reelected president in a crudely fixed election on November 14, 1999.

1999: Ukraine's Economy Falters

Ukraine's GDP per capita falls to $636, down from $991 in 1997, and the World Bank temporarily downgrades Ukraine from lower-middle-income to low-income status. More broadly, a new class of oligarchs exercises its political influence to reshape the economy to serve its interests in the late 1990s and early 2000s. While other post-Soviet states began recovering by the mid-1990s, Ukraine's first year of renewed growth comes only in 2000.

1999: Yushchenko Appointed Prime Minister

In December, President Kuchma is forced by an impending balance-of-payments crisis to appoint a reformist prime minister, the former central bank chief Viktor Yushchenko, to negotiate with international lenders. Yulia Tymoshenko, a former gas trader, is appointed deputy prime minister to clean up the energy sector, the most corrupt part of the Ukrainian economy. Though the duo's economic reforms kick-start the economy, Ukraine's oligarchs benefit from growth and become further entrenched in power. Yushchenko and Tymoshenko are ejected from office in the spring of 2001 and go on to found their own political parties.

2000: Gongadze Scandal Erupts

Journalist Georgiy Gongadze, founder of a website devoted to political exposés and critiques of oligarchic corruption, is abducted in September, and his decapitated body is found on November 2.

Sensational secret tapes emerge in which President Kuchma is heard angrily demanding that his subordinates deal with Gongadze in colorful ways. The scandal sparks mass protests against Kuchma's government, with opposition demonstrators demanding his resignation. The European Union calls for an investigation into the murder in 2001. However, Kuchma denies allegations of his involvement.

2004: Orange Revolution Garners Global Attention

The Orange Revolution catches the attention of the world when thousands flood Kiev's central square in a mass demonstration after Russian-backed prime minister Viktor Yanukovych is declared the winner of the November 21 presidential election. Yanukovych's victory over Western-oriented former prime minister Viktor Yushchenko is widely seen as fraudulent. After negotiations, Yushchenko wins a revote on December 26. He is sworn in the next month and appoints Yulia Tymoshenko prime minister. Per the negotiations, the parties also agree to change the constitution and reduce the president's power after the next parliamentary elections in the spring of 2006. The changes prove a trap for the winners of the Orange Revolution, as they shift power from incoming president Yushchenko to the oligarch-dominated parliament.

2005: "Orange" Leadership Plagued by Infighting

The "Orange" presidency of Viktor Yushchenko is marked by constant political crises. Infighting among political elites, including intraparty power grabs and personal squabbles, makes effective governance impossible. The first Orange government led by Prime Minister Tymoshenko collapses in September. Following parliamentary elections in 2006, Yushchenko joins Viktor Yanukovych, his rival from the days of the Orange Revolution, in a coalition that makes Yanukovych prime minister. A constitutional crisis breaks out in 2007 when Yushchenko tries to dissolve the parliament and calls for new elections in response to Yanukovych's attempts to accumulate power and force him from office. Tymoshenko is then reappointed prime minister after elections in September 2007.

2008: Ukraine Enters Economic Crisis

The global economic crisis hits Ukraine hard in 2008–2009, sending an already weak economy into freefall. GDP falls by 15 percent in 2009, while exports (most notably steel) plunge by 49 percent in the first three quarters. Real incomes also drop by 8.5 percent and official unemployment triples to more than 9 percent. The International Monetary Fund extends a loan to help bolster Ukraine's economy, but its relations with the government are ruined when Ukraine balks at raising domestic gas prices.

2010: Yanukovych Wins Presidency, Puts Tymoshenko on Trial

More than five years after failing to capture the presidency in the 2004 election that triggered the Orange Revolution, Viktor Yanukovych wins the presidential election of February 7. The constant infighting of the Orange years had weakened political institutions and created so much voter fatigue that, once in office, Yanukovych is able to centralize power with little resistance. His moves include weakening the courts, reversing the limits on presidential power introduced after the Orange Revolution, and, most brazenly, putting Tymoshenko, his main political rival, on trial. On October 11, 2011, Tymoshenko is sentenced to seven years in prison for abuse of office, a charge stemming from a deal she made with Russia over the price of natural gas in 2009. Ukrainian opposition figures and European leaders criticize Tymoshenko's trial as politically motivated, resulting in the Association and Free Trade Agreements with Brussels being put on ice in December 2011.

2012: Ukraine Holds Parliamentary Elections

The authorities change the rules for the October parliamentary elections, bringing back territorial districts, where fraud and bribery can have a more concentrated effect. Yanukovych's party wins 113 districts out of 225. However, the opposition does surprisingly well in seats allocated by proportional representation, winning 133 out of 225. Opposition parties are helped by some oligarchs rebelling against the growing power of the Yanukovych "family." With the economy faltering again, and Ukraine tempted to turn to Russia for help, the stage is set for yet another bitter contest in the presidential election of 2015.

Nigeria

John Campbell

Nigeria is the giant of Africa. With more than 165 million people divided into three large ethnic and linguistic groups—Fulani, Yoruba, and Igbo—and more than three hundred small ones, it is by the far the most populous country on the continent. Christianity and Islam each claim about half of the population. The nation—its name and its identity—is a British creation. There was no overarching precolonial cultural unity. In the north, the British ruled indirectly through the Islamic emirates they preserved after conquest. To maintain the strength of these traditional institutions, the British discouraged the Christian missionary activity that brought Western education to the southern part of the country. With modern education, trading opportunities, and, later, oil, the south developed more quickly than the north and today enjoys higher levels of economic and social development. One social indicator of north-south differences is the 2010 primary school attendance rate: in the northern state of Zamfara, it was 18 percent; in the southern state of Anambra, it was 86 percent.

Nigeria is the African country of greatest strategic importance to the United States. It is the fifth-largest supplier of oil to the United States, and has reserves exceeding forty billion barrels. It sometimes plays a positive role in African security issues and has aspirations to a permanent seat on the United Nations Security Council.

In 1999, a generation of military rule ended and Nigeria began a transition to civilian democratic governance. Perhaps the three most salient features of the transition were a new constitution that reaffirmed federalism, regular elections, and an understanding within the ruling party that the presidency would alternate between the predominately Christian south and the predominately Muslim north. Nigeria's tragedy since then has been its failure—given its colonial legacy of poor governance and weak institutions, its ethnic and religious divisions, its years of military government, and its oil curse—to fulfill its democratic expectations.

In 1960, the British abruptly brought Nigeria to independence, less because of the strength of local agitation and more because Westminster lost confidence in the colonial system, specifically in the face of liberation movements in Gold Coast (Ghana) and Algeria and concern that such movements could be exploited by the Soviet Union or Egypt's nationalist dictator, Abdul Gamal Nasser. In Nigeria, no cohesive liberation struggle cemented a national identity across ethnic and religious divisions, as it did in India and Ireland.

Ethnicity and personal rivalry dominated postcolonial politics. Starting in 1966, military coups undermined civilian institutions and marginalized or destroyed the late-colonial political elite. In the north, pogroms were carried out against non-indigene ethnic groups and Christians, especially Igbos. These incidents became the pretext for the secession of the Igbo-dominated southeastern part of the country— Biafra—from the federation in 1967. A bloody three-year civil war followed that left at least a million dead, mostly from famine and disease, before the military reincorporated Biafra into the federation.

Brief interregnums aside, military governments ruled Nigeria until 1999. Although some were better than others, they generally failed to address Nigeria's social and economic issues and instead focused on the preservation of national unity. A popular military slogan of the period was "To keep Nigeria one is a task that must be done."

In 1960, observers rated Nigeria's social and economic development as comparable to that of Taiwan or Malaysia. In 1970, civil war hostilities ended at the same time that oil began to produce previously unimaginable riches. Under continuing military government, however, corruption and the focus on oil siphoned off resources, crowded out investment in other sectors, and caused much of the rest of the economy to atrophy. Now, following generations of bad governance and an economy distorted by oil, Nigeria is one of the poorest countries in the world and near the bottom of most human development indices. In some areas, such as per capita power generation and miles of railroad, Nigeria has actually regressed over recent decades.

Competition for control of the state, which distributes oil revenue, came to shape the political culture and fostered the winner-take-all style of governance that characterizes Nigerian public life. For more than thirty years, military governments were largely unaccountable to the population. That behavior, like corruption, persists under civilian politicians, who tend to be closely tied to the same elites who ran Nigeria under military rule.

As a result, development has suffered. Neither the military nor the civilian governments have adequately followed through on plans periodically introduced to expand primary education or medical services. Poverty has increased. From 2004 to 2012, those living on less than $1 a day grew from 55 percent to 69 percent of the population, despite a growing economy.

At present, in the Muslim northern half of the country, an insurrection, often referred to as Boko Haram, is under way against the perceived secular government in Abuja. In the oil-rich Niger Delta, despite an amnesty program for militants, grievances persist over the distribution of oil revenue that suggest the prospect of renewed militia attacks on the oil industry's infrastructure. In the middle of the country, the government has been unable to end an ethnic and religious struggle between Muslim Fulani herdsmen and Christian Berom farmers and other small ethnic groups that has resulted in ethnic cleansing by both sides and the ghettoization of previously integrated communities. The April 2011 presidential elections, Nigeria's fourth since 1999, were seen as legitimate in the southern half of the country but as fraudulent by many in the north. President Goodluck Jonathan, a southerner, has failed to reconcile parts of the north to his government.

Nevertheless, a democratic ideal persists among Nigerian elites, who associate it with modernity and development. The brutality of the last military dictator, Sani Abacha, made Nigeria an international outcast. After his unexpected death, the elites (including the military) adopted a civilian constitution that mimicked the form but not the substance of the American one. The world saw the transition from military to civilian rule as a major step toward democracy. So, too, did many Nigerians. But the reality has been that too little has changed.

Elites walk a fine line—under military and civilian governments alike, they compete with each other for state resources to feed their patronage networks, but they cooperate across ethnic and religious boundaries just enough to not inhibit the flow of oil, on which they all depend for revenue. As under the military, the main purpose of government is to enrich those who control it.

Poor governance and elite competition for oil wealth have created a self-reinforcing feedback loop. Widespread corruption allows Nigerian elites to amass huge personal fortunes while starving the country of investment in the non-oil economy and in human capital. As the economy fails to provide jobs and wealth (except for a few), the state continues to be widely seen as the principal avenue to prosperity, further encouraging corrupt behavior and undermining a democratic transition. Indeed, Transparency International ranks Nigeria 143 of 183 countries in its 2011 Corruption Perceptions Index.

INFLECTION POINTS
OF THE TRANSITION PERIOD

In the aftermath of Sani Abacha's death, the country began its democratic transition in 1999, when a small group of army officers and their civilian allies—motivated by a desire to end Nigeria's international pariah status and to distance themselves from the excesses of the Abacha years—orchestrated a move from military to civilian control of government, framed by democratic rhetoric. Their goal, largely achieved, was to introduce democratic forms but preserve their personal power and wealth. Hence, from the beginning, the scope of the transition was limited. In theory, the adoption of a federalist system was supposed to curtail the significant powers of the presidency, and regular elections were supposed to enhance representative government. In practice, the institutional transition remained separate in many ways from the reality of day-to-day politics, which continued to be shaped by patronage, client relationships, and elite competition. Although the transition to civilian rule did mark the end of the gross human rights violations of the Abacha era, it was halting from the beginning. Despite some progress over the past decade, civil institutions and the rule of law have remained weak, and, despite regular elections, the government remains largely unaccountable to the Nigerian people.

The adoption of the country's aspirational constitution affirmed a federal system with thirty-six states and a division of power across branches of government at the federal and state levels. Although previous constitutions had also contained elements of federalism, military rule had consolidated power at the center. The new constitution aimed to reverse that trajectory by making government more responsive to Nigeria's highly diverse peoples. It has failed, however, to prevent the continued accretion of presidential power, in large part because the nation's revenue is controlled by the chief of state, who has little accountability to other parts of government. The National Assembly should be a check, but the president's virtually unlimited access to oil revenue and his control of the carrots and sticks so central to patronage politics usually ensure that he dominates the legislature.

The judiciary, in theory also a check on the presidency, is in reality beholden to it. The president appoints the members of the Supreme Court, who must be confirmed by the Nigerian senate. The court hears cases on a panel basis, not by the court sitting as a whole. And the chief justice determines the membership of particular panels. In every contested presidential election since 1999, the Supreme Court has ruled in favor of the incumbent, though it has sometimes overturned the election of governors and other officials when the presidency was supportive of or indifferent to that move.

Elections, meant to promote democracy and legitimize government by making it accountable to the people, have not met those goals. "Election-like events" have been manipulated by elites and failed to establish the accountability of many officials to the voters in a meaningful way. Between 1999 and 2007, each election was worse than its predecessor, with widespread, blatant rigging (the 2011 election represented a slight improvement). Not surprisingly, popular participation in elections has steadily declined, from 69 percent of the electorate in 2003, to 58 percent in 2007, to 56 percent in 2011, according to official statistics. Elites, largely united behind a single presidential candidate running on the platform of the ruling party, regularly "over-egg the electoral pudding" to ensure victory. Local- and state-level elections tend to be bloodier than national elections because elite consensus tends to be weaker locally than nationally.

Conscious of the ethnic and religious divisions of the country, the architects of the 1998–99 transition reaffirmed the principle of zoning, or presidential candidate alternation, broadly between north-south and Muslim-Christian, within the ruling party. In accordance with the spirit of power alternation, if the president was Christian, his vice president would be Muslim, and vice versa. Hence, Olusegun Obasanjo, a southern Christian, led the government from 1999 to 2007 with his northern Muslim vice president.

In 2010, Obasanjo's successor, the northern Muslim Umaru Yar'Adua, died in office, making his vice president, the southern Christian Goodluck Jonathan, the chief of state. Initially, Jonathan indicated he would not run for the presidency in 2011 because under the pattern of an eight-year rotation it was still the north's turn. But he changed his mind and, using the powers of incumbency, ended zoning. Some of his supporters justified this move as a step toward democracy because it no longer guaranteed the presidency to a particular region according to a set timeframe. But Jonathan's defeat of a northern Muslim opposition candidate in the 2011 election precipitated the bloodiest postelectoral rioting in the predominantly Muslim northern states since independence. Far from promoting democracy, the end of zoning resulted in an upsurge in violence with religious and ethnic overtones. It has only sharpened ethnic and regional divisions and rivalries and, in some parts of the country, undermined security.

The reality is that Nigerians still do not choose their presidents through the ballot box. The opposition has never come to power by winning the most votes, as it has in Ghana and Zambia. Rigging and voter manipulation remain so pervasive that election results do not necessarily express the popular will. Elections are a matter not of issues but of personality, of patronage, and of regional, religious, and ethnic identities.

But, flawed as the process is, elections are promoting the slow growth of a more democratic culture. Under the military, the chief of state changed in response to a coup or the threat of one. Now, the president is selected by elites and the choice is ratified by an election-like event. Obasanjo, a retired general, ruled Nigeria as a civilian. His successor was also a civilian, as is Jonathan. So the expectation, if not yet the principle, is that the chief of state will be a civilian who comes to office through a process that involves the act of voting. If the transition to democracy is incomplete, that of military to civilian governance is much further along.

LESSONS OF THE TRANSITION PERIOD

The lessons of Nigeria's transition to civilian democracy should be seen in the context of a state with a weak national identity and a population that has always had little confidence in or identification with any government—colonial, military, or civilian. Poverty, poor governance, and pervasive corruption reinforce a widespread sense of alienation from government authority.

SOCIOECONOMIC EXCLUSION AND INCLUSION

In recent decades, the nature of poverty in Nigeria has evolved. The poor were once largely rural—farmers, herdsmen, and fishermen who in some cases could be self-sufficient. In many parts of the country, they were bound to traditional rulers through customary law. However, demographic and other pressures have led to rapid urbanization. More than half of Nigeria's population is now estimated to live in cities, often in sprawling shanty towns, with weakened ties to traditional structures. Since independence, no national government has successfully addressed poverty and the gross inequality of wealth (see Figure 16). Although strategies for economic development have been periodically rolled out, implementation has been limited by weak institutional structures and erratic funding that ultimately depends on the vagaries of petroleum prices.

Since the end of the civil war, a handful of elites has run the government and benefited from oil wealth. Corruption, often involving government contracts, quickly became the road to wealth in Nigeria's oil-based economy. Patronage networks were augmented and new ones established. Often these networks were based on a specific ethnic group, but patrons are usually prepared to cooperate with other networks to ensure continued access to resources. Corruption generates little economic activity, other than the construction of enormous houses, and is

FIGURE 16. POVERTY AND CONSUMPTION IN NIGERIA

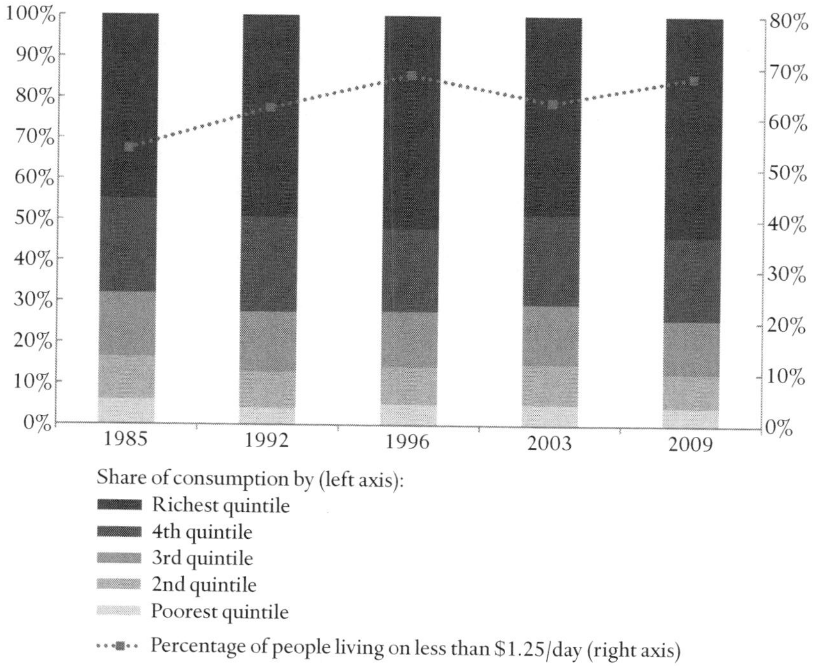
100%
90%
80%
70%
60%
50%
40%
30%
20%
10%
0%
80%
70%
60%
50%
40%
30%
20%
10%
0%
1985
1992
1996
2003
2009
Share of consumption by (left axis):
Richest quintile
4th quintile
3rd quintile
2nd quintile
Poorest quintile
Percentage of people living on less than $1.25/day (right axis)

Source: World Bank (poverty data: purchasing power parity, 2005 international dollars).

characterized by capital flight, which political uncertainty and an over-valued currency encourage. Nigerian elites indulge in conspicuous consumption abroad rather than at home.

Everyone else is largely powerless and poor, aside from a small middle class, mostly in Lagos and Abuja, that exercises only limited political influence or autonomy. The country's Gini coefficient, which measures income inequality on a 0 to 100 scale, rose from an already-high 38.7 in 1985 to 48.8 in 2009. This gulf between the wealthy elites and almost everyone else is probably Nigeria's most significant division. In that sense, Nigerian critics argue that the country has remained fundamentally a state mired in colonialism. From their perspective, a tiny indigenous elite has merely replaced the British colonial masters and has little concern about the vast majority of the population mired in poverty.

The social and economic disparities between the northern and southern parts of the country have not been ameliorated by the ostensibly strong economic growth in the country as a whole. For example, female median age at first marriage in the north remains fifteen years or younger, but in certain southern states it is twenty-one or older. Immunization rates in the north remain much lower than in the south (see Figure 17), and the region remains a reservoir of wild polio virus. Unemployed youth, a problem everywhere, are particularly so in the north and provide the foot soldiers for radical Islamic movements.

Given this intense inequality and many other unaddressed grievances, insurgencies have taken hold. In the Muslim north, Boko Haram is the most visible at present. The similarly marginalized oil-rich Niger Delta in the south has been the scene of recurring insurrections for more than a generation. Kidnapping and attacks on oil facilities were again on the upswing in 2012. The ethnic cleansing in Plateau state, though not directed against Abuja, illustrates government paralysis. There, ethnic, religious, and occupational boundaries coincide: Christian Berom farmers compete against Muslim Fulani herdsmen for land, water, and local political power. Neither the federal nor the state governments have had the capacity to end the violence.

In the late colonial period, a middle class that might demand government accountability did start to emerge, based on small trading, government service, and professional occupations. But it atrophied as non-oil-related trade and manufacturing shrank, in part because successive military governments pursued economic policies favoring the

FIGURE 17. REGIONAL HEALTH DISPARITIES IN NIGERIA

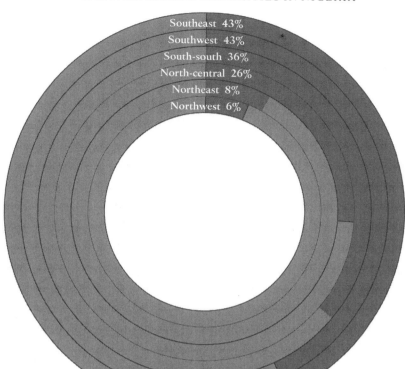

Southeast 43%
Southwest 43%
South-south 36%
North-central 26%
Northeast 8%
Northwest 6%

Eighteen- to twenty-three-month-olds who have had every basic vaccination

Source: 2008 Nigeria Demographic and Health Survey

oil industry and an overvalued currency. Given the military's neglect of primary educational and health facilities, medical doctors and other professionals emigrated whenever they could. The civil service became politicized, bloated, and underpaid. By the turn of the twenty-first century, the middle class had largely disappeared, except in Lagos and among civil servants in Abuja.

In New York, London, and Johannesburg, some observers from the business community see a middle-class revival in the second decade of the twenty-first century. They define middle class as those with some disposable income beyond the basic necessities, including those who have benefited from a reformed banking system and have earned livings in small-scale manufacturing and trade independent of the government. As evidence of the return of the middle class, observers note some ninety million mobile phone subscriptions in Nigeria and shopping centers stocked with a wide range of consumer goods beginning to appear.

That this middle class is thriving has become an article of faith among government spokesmen and foreign investors. But the jury is out on how large this middle class actually is. Many Nigerians own multiple mobile phones yet cannot afford to purchase minutes (most mobile phone services use prepaid cards). And the principal mobile phone service provider is a South African company, as are the developers of the grandest shopping centers, which are located in wealthy neighborhoods in Lagos and Abuja. A middle class is certainly visible in these two cities, but not elsewhere in the country, including Kano, the second-largest city. A "new" middle class may be emerging that is not based on access to the government, but it is not large enough—except possibly in Lagos—to demand more transparency, accountability, and the rule of law.

The elites—not a middle class or the poor—orchestrated the 1998–99 transition from military to civilian rule and were the beneficiaries of the new regime, as they had been of the previous one. Faced with no organized challenge, they have continued to profit from their hold on the levers of power. Thus far, however, they have failed to address Nigeria's basic needs, especially its dire lack of adequate power generation and an educational system to serve the country's exploding population. The end of zoning and the failure to replace it with another form of power alternation has also exacerbated the north's alienation.

ECONOMIC STRUCTURE AND POLICIES

At independence, Nigeria was the breadbasket of West Africa, producing substantial agricultural surpluses. It exported groundnuts (peanuts), cotton, and coal over a regional railroad network. Mining was important (the country is said to have huge coal reserves and gold reserves comparable to South Africa's). Large palm oil plantations were also abundant. Especially in the north, an industrial base was developing around textiles and consumer goods such as furniture. Both internal and external trades were growing, with Kano, the entrepôt of the Sahel and Lagos, by far the largest trade hub on the Anglophone West African coast.

In the aftermath of a generation of military governments and an economy dominated by oil, most of that industry is gone. As the economy has globalized, Nigeria has become less internationally competitive in most major economic areas—except for oil and gas (see Figure 18). For decades, Nigeria has been a net importer of food rather than an exporter. The cotton and groundnut industries deteriorated, in part because of misguided policies of agricultural marketing boards too often driven by special interests in the early years of independence, and in part because of underinvestment in critical infrastructure during later periods. The textile industries in the north have collapsed largely because of inadequate power generation and a dependence on diesel generators that made them uncompetitive on the international market. Coal and other mining is also moribund, thanks to underinvestment and weak infrastructure. The railway network, essential for moving food and mineral exports to markets, is now largely gone, though its restoration, along with power generation, is a priority of the current government.

FIGURE 18. OIL EXPORTS AND POVERTY IN NIGERIA

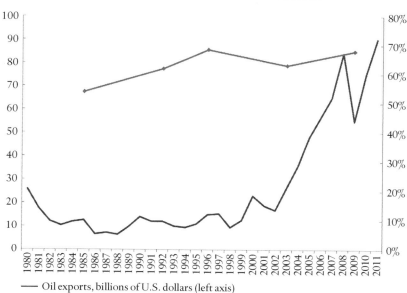

——— Oil exports, billions of U.S. dollars (left axis)
——— Percentage of people living on less than $1.25/day (right axis)

Source: World Bank (poverty data: purchasing power parity, 2005 international dollars).

An overvalued currency—though highly beneficial to those elites sending capital abroad—contributed to making non-oil exports increasingly uncompetitive on world markets and imports cheap. Meanwhile, the oil industry absorbed available capital. For many years, banking and finance were both underdeveloped and weak instruments for capital formation. The availability of capital depended on wildly fluctuating oil prices. Oil sucked up much of the domestic capital that might have been available for agriculture and industry. Outside the oil industry, foreign investors shied away from a country that lurched from one military coup to another and suffered from recurring ethnic and religious conflict. The elites depended on oil revenue for their well-being, giving them little incentive to promote a diversified and developing economy.

In contrast to the diverse economy at independence in 1960, by 2009 oil and gas exports amounted to more than 95 percent of Nigeria's export earnings and more than 80 percent of the federal government's revenue. Oil is the property of the state, and is exploited through joint ventures and other partnership agreements between the government-owned Nigeria National Petroleum Corporation (NNPC) and private oil companies. The profits from oil overwhelmingly accrue to the government. The federal government distributes oil revenues to state and local governments based on a particular formula. Over time, the oil industry has been the creator and mainstay of the elites and has created very few jobs.

Nor have oil riches produced abundant or inexpensive power. Nigeria's refineries, all state owned, have rarely functioned at the same time because of underinvestment and maintenance issues. Efforts to privatize them over the past decade have failed because no private company sees them as potentially profitable as long as the government prices petroleum products for domestic consumption below the world market. As a result, Nigeria exports crude oil and imports refined oil and gasoline. The federal government provides a substantial subsidy for fuel use at home, and the cost amounted to almost a quarter of the budget of the federal government by 2012. Arguing that the revenue used for the oil subsidy could be better spent on economic development, the Jonathan government attempted to abolish it in early 2012. That led to a general strike and widespread unrest. To quell the unrest, Jonathan restored about half the subsidy. International financial and business opinion applauded the subsidy reduction on economic grounds, but it was roundly denounced within Nigeria. For many Nigerians, subsidized oil and gas is the only way they tangibly benefit from the country's petroleum production.

Most of the federal government's share of the oil revenue is consumed by day-to-day operations or simply disappears. Official government salaries are among the highest in the world: a member of the National Assembly receives more than $1 million per year in salary and allowances. That there is so little public outcry is an indicator that most Nigerians regard themselves as powerless. In fact, little federal revenue is left over for economic development, expansion of education and medical services, infrastructure repair, or restoration of the power sector. Presidents Obasanjo, Yar'Adua, and Jonathan have committed millions to the power sector, but much of that money appears to have disappeared through corruption.

CIVIL SOCIETY AND MEDIA

It is often said that civil society is stronger in Nigeria than elsewhere in West Africa. Numerous Christian and Islamic organizations have an important civic dimension. Other nongovernmental organizations have a professional or human rights focus. The Nigeria Bar Association, which has some fifty-five thousand educated members across the country, has been called Nigeria's most successful human rights organization because of the activism of some of its members. It played an important role in the observation of the 2011 elections.

Taken together, civil society and the media have had a positive impact on Nigeria's transition toward democracy by encouraging the growth of a more democratic political culture. However, they have been less important to Nigeria's political evolution than they were, say, in South Africa's struggle against apartheid. Civil society today is probably more fragmented now than under the military, when it was united to restore civilian government. Then, it played a role in convincing the military and civilian establishment to move away from a military structure to democratic forms after Abacha's death. However, since 1999, some of its leaders have been co-opted by the civilian administration, and others have returned to their role as government critics. Civil organizations, more numerous than in the past, played a strong role as election observers in 2011. Most observers believe their presence contributed to the better quality of the polling.

However, the influence and reach of civil society should not be over-estimated. The small size of the middle class, the pervasive poverty of most people, and ethnic and religious divisions limit its strength. Civil society tries to work through the law and the court system. The weak-ness of the rule of law and the shortcomings of the judicial system also reduce the scope for its activity. Nevertheless, the Occupy Nigeria move-ment showed that civil society could—if only briefly—overcome public apathy and the ethnic and religious divisions that have inhibited true reform. It began as a small, generalized protest against Nigeria's political and economic system that mimicked Occupy Wall Street. When Presi-dent Jonathan attempted to eliminate the fuel subsidy that benefits most Nigerians, the movement mushroomed in size. The trade unions nearly sparked a general strike when they joined, and the economy largely closed down for a week. The government responded with a success-ful carrot-and-stick strategy: it restored about half the fuel subsidy and reached a settlement with the trade unions while also arresting some of the demonstrators. It is widely believed that the government made sub-stantial payments to trade union leaders to facilitate a settlement.

Civil society and the media reflect the inequalities between north-ern and southern Nigeria. Both are much stronger and more extensive in the south than in the north. Literacy rates are dramatically lower in the north, and the population is much poorer. For example, in the northern state of Yobe, only 49 percent of those older than fifteen are literate; in the southern state of Abia, 81 percent are. That reality trans-lates into low newspaper readership in the north, which also has less access to television. Nevertheless, the media, especially radio, contrib-ute to the relative openness of Nigerian society; secrets cannot be kept for very long.

During the generation of military rule, the government often sought to suppress news stories it did not like. Its censorship could be subtle. If a newspaper published a story to which the government objected, it would shut the offender down for two or three days, long enough to destroy the enterprise's profitability for the month but not long enough to create martyrs. The result too often was self-censorship.

Since the restoration of civilian government, the media in Nigeria have officially been free. There are a number of television stations, and television is mostly an elite medium. Radio has a major local and regional dimension and reaches nearly everyone; it is especially important in the North as a source of information. International radio stations, including the BBC, Voice of America, Radio France, and Deutsche Welle, have large audiences. Newspapers are expensive and copies are passed hand to hand; their circulation is likely much higher than the number of copies sold. The regional press and radio stations sometimes use indigenous languages. Print media, too, are published without state interference. Especially because of radio, the general population is often well informed about international events.

But Freedom House and the Committee to Protect Journalists, among others, have shown that journalists are regularly subjected to intimidation and even murder. Media intimidation does not appear to be government sponsored or centrally directed, though individual officeholders may be involved. Most often, it appears to be perpetrated by local elites. The state, however, habitually fails to prosecute, convict, and punish the perpetrators. The result is that at various times and places, media freedom is inhibited and the habits of self-censorship inherited from the days of the military persist. Nevertheless, the media are significantly freer now than they were during the days of military government.

Communication technologies and social media are becoming more widespread in Nigeria, especially mobile phones, Twitter, and Facebook. There is a network of Internet cafes throughout the country. Social media was used as part of civil society's monitoring of the April 2011 elections, although evidence of its positive influence remains anecdotal.

LEGAL SYSTEM AND RULE OF LAW

Multiple legal systems, a weak court system, corrupt police, and inhumane prisons and jails all promote the culture of criminal impunity that promotes a feedback loop of popular antipathy to government authority. The move from military to civilian forms of government has changed little. As a result, people occasionally take justice into their own hands, with the "necklacing" of thieves in the markets and extrajudicial killings by the police of notorious criminals who are unlikely to ever be brought to trial. Thousands have died because of ethnic and religious conflict since the restoration of civilian government, but few perpetrators have been arrested and not one had been convicted and punished as of the end of 2011.

A variety of legal systems operate in Nigeria: the legal code inherited from the British and based on English common law; customary law that varies from one ethnic group to another; and Islamic law, or sharia, which applies to criminal and civil matters in the twelve predominately Muslim states. The existence of different legal systems is open to plaintiff shopping, that is, transfer of complaints from one legal system to another—if one can afford legal counsel, which most cannot. As a practical matter, Western law requires a lawyer; sharia and customary law courts do not. Sharia and customary law also have fewer procedural brakes. Thus, civil and criminal matters may take many years to resolve in the civil courts, but they move much more quickly and are far less costly under sharia or customary law, which accounts for these methods' popularity.

The penalties of sharia law, however, are suffered most often by the poor and virtually never by the rich. Nevertheless, there have been no sharia stonings and only a few amputations. Such harsh punishments have usually been overturned by appeal or disallowed by governors. Radical Islamic groups such as Boko Haram decry what they call the political sharia of northern Nigeria, where a thief may be punished for stealing a piece of fruit but a government contractor goes free after defrauding the state of millions of naira.

The police contribute to the country's culture of impunity and are widely hated. The police force is a national institution. Its policy, dating from the colonial period, is to assign personnel in areas different from their own ethnicity, making them less sympathetic to the population they are supposed to protect. Further, training levels are low, and the police are poorly paid. A consequence is that the police regularly extort money from ordinary citizens at traffic checkpoints and other venues.

Multiple legal systems, a weak rule of law, and a culture of impunity not only encourage lawlessness but also inhibit foreign investment—except in oil. Private companies cannot be sure that a court will uphold the sanctity of a contract. Legal and judicial weaknesses also encourage a short investment time frame, for both foreign and domestic investors. The goal is not to promote long-term economic growth but to capture quick profits that can be sent abroad promptly.

GOVERNMENT STRUCTURE AND DIVISION OF POWER

During the years of military rule, the highest federal authority was the Armed Forces Ruling Council (AFRC) and its similar predecessors, a committee of senior officers drawn from all branches of service but dominated by the army. In theory, the AFRC designated one of its members as the military chief of state, who oversaw a cabinet often dominated by civilians. The judiciary, while subject to military meddling, preserved a degree of independence. There was no legislative branch of government.

In reality, successive military generals seized control and had their power grabs legitimized by the AFRC. State governors were also appointed by the AFRC. Local government was largely untouched. Traditional rulers continued to exercise influence, though the military government sometimes intervened to ensure pliable regional leaders.

Each successive military government claimed that it aimed to restore civilian, democratic governance after it had cleaned up the "mess" that had led to its assumption of power. This commitment was central to the legitimacy the military claimed and that Nigerians largely accorded it. For politically aware Nigerians, the aspiration was for a democratic, modern state. Military rule was to be only temporary, but the individual interests of military leaders endured. Hence, the military was directly involved in the formation of political parties—General Ibrahim Babangida, a former military head of state, famously decreed that Nigeria would be a two-party state, "one a little to the left and the other a little to the right." They engaged in constitution writing and organized elections, first at the local, then at the state, and finally at the national level. However, the military annulled the 1992 presidential elections when it was not satisfied with the outcome, setting the stage for Sani Abacha's brutal military dictatorship.

Despite the post-Abacha constitution's federal character, the division of power across central, state, and local governments has been more aspirational than real. Oil revenue is controlled by the president. Indeed, a civilian president's power may in fact be less circumscribed than that of former military chiefs of state, who answered to the Armed Forces Ruling Council. State and local governments depend on the federal government for the disbursement of oil revenue, which is allocated to each state governor according to an established formula. Governors and local leaders, in turn, spend and dole out patronage with no accountability. As a result, politics continues to be dominated by patronage networks at all levels.

Only the state of Lagos funds most of its operations independently of Abuja, from taxes it collects (and one of its political "big men" has a lucrative contract to collect the taxes). In that state, something approaching a civil contract is emerging between the government and the governed. Citizens receive meaningful services from the state in return for their taxes. Lagos is governed by an opposition party, and its residents appear less apathetic and more politically engaged than those elsewhere in the federation. Speculation in the Nigerian press indicates that the Lagos example of better governance has the potential to spread to neighboring states.

In theory, the state assemblies should hold their respective governors accountable. But in practice, the governors usually control the state assemblies through their patron-client networks. Local governments are probably the least accountable of all because of the weakness of grassroots civil institutions. More generally, because they pay few if any taxes and many receive minor monetary benefits from one or another level of government, citizens appear reluctant to hold public officials accountable for how such revenue is used. Even the very poor depend on patron-client networks for alms, if nothing else. Nigeria's constitution, filled with elegant provisions to ensure balance of power, was eviscerated from the start by this reality.

EDUCATION AND DEMOGRAPHY

Demographic figures are imprecise, but Nigeria's current population may be as high as 165 million, and some project that it could reach four hundred million within two generations. Lagos, home to nearly twenty million people, is already one of the largest cities in the world. But population growth has been as explosive in a host of other formerly medium-sized cities. Urbanization is proceeding rapidly, and most of the population now lives in cities. The religious map has also changed dramatically. By 2010, Christians had become half of the population, Muslims half, and traditional religion had all but disappeared or gone underground.

Nigerians are proud of their population size, and both Muslims and Christians have large families. Although condoms are commonly available and either inexpensive or free, no national population policy exists that seeks to reduce the rate of population growth. To the contrary, most Nigerians assume that the bigger the population, the better. Outside investors often cite Nigeria's large and growing population as a plus, and see Nigeria as Africa's largest market. However, absent an expanded education sector, the rapidly growing population is likely to be a drag on development.

Literacy levels remain low, especially in the north, where in some places only 20 percent of women can read. Schools usually charge fees and require uniforms. Both can be impossible barriers for families to surmount. The civilian government has not demonstrated the will to expand primary education nearly quickly enough to keep up with the growing population, in part because elites have devoted too little revenue for such purposes. Hence, Nigeria's literacy rate of 68 percent of the total population is significantly lower than that of Zimbabwe (90 percent) or Kenya (87 percent). A growing population that is unschooled is hardly going to be a force for transformative economic development. Indeed, a huge bulge of unemployed youth is distorting the country's economy and political life.

Many schools are chronically underfunded and severely overcrowded, compromising their quality. At the time of independence, Nigeria had some secondary schools—King's College and Barewa College, among others—that were among the most academically demanding in the world. Some were founded by churches; others were secular. But the post–civil war military government of General Yakubu Gowon, a Christian from the Middle Belt, closed religiously based schools and hospitals or transformed them into secular institutions. Why? Many churchmen, especially Roman Catholics, had supported the Biafra cause during the civil war and there was suspicion that church schools might nurture future separatism. In addition, many in government hoped to replace church schools with a genuinely national system of education that could address the educational gulf between northern Nigeria and the rest of the country. Private universities were also prohibited, and not allowed again until the return to civilian rule in 1999.

The aftermath of the civil war and the first flush of the oil boom saw a huge, popular demand for education. The military government of Obasanjo moved to make primary education universally available in the late 1970s, but before putting necessary infrastructure in place. He and his successors also vastly expanded the university system. Alas, successive governments starved education at all levels of funds, sometimes because of different spending priorities but also because rising and falling oil prices often wreaked havoc with government finances. Because of the lack of decent alternatives, Nigerians are increasingly turning to private education. Although private education is expensive and serves only a small proportion of the population, its example is proving to be salutary in developing higher popular expectations for publicly funded institutions.

CONCLUSION

Given hundreds of ethnic divisions, two major religions, a weak sense of national identity, and elites prepared to exploit these divisions in a quest for state resources, it is no surprise that Nigeria's transition to democracy after 1999 has been incomplete. The causes are domestic. Given the country's enormous size, scope is limited for state and non-state actors to help except at the margins, mostly through limited assistance to civil organizations. Indeed, the largest United States assistance program in Nigeria is focused on HIV/AIDS, although the proportion of the country's population infected with HIV is relatively small—less than 5 percent. The fundamental question might be, given the country's history and demography and the distortions of the economy by oil, how has Nigeria managed to stay together at all?

Ultimately, it has been in the interests of elites that Nigeria remain united. The state provides the mechanism by which the revenue from oil and gas is distributed nationwide. Were Nigeria to split, the oil revenue would likely benefit only the oil patch, making oil, paradoxically, both the glue that holds Nigeria together and what undermines the country's democratic transition.

Therefore, until now, Nigerian elites have shown considerable political skill in reconciling their competing interests but less in fostering democracy. If the elites did little to promote democratic governance, accountability, and the rule of law, they did preserve national unity, as did their military predecessors. This may be changing. The end of presidential power alternation, the overt appeals to religious and ethnic identities in the 2011 election campaign, Boko Haram violence in the north, ethnic and religious conflict in Plateau, and the apparent resumption of an insurrection in the oil patch may have reinforced the feedback loop of poverty and corruption. These trends now seem to be making it more difficult for elites to cooperate and thus weakening the glue that holds the country together.

Twice in recent times Nigeria's elites came close to fragmenting into mutually hostile groups. The first was 2005 through 2007, when President Obasanjo attempted a third presidential term, despite a constitutionally mandated two-term limit; the second was in 2011 and 2012, when President Jonathan's election ended the power alternation agreement between northern and southern elites and established an administration dominated by southern Christians. In the first case, opposition to a third term was so overwhelming that Obasanjo could not overcome it. The second continues to play out.

If the preservation of national unity has directly benefited only elites, the mass of the population at present remains too fragmented to challenge the system effectively. Too often, as in the aftermath of the elections of 2011, political protest degenerates into ethnic and religious conflict, sometimes with a nudge from the elites to advance their particular agendas. The intense poverty of the vast majority of the population also limits the sustainability of protest. This may be changing. Occupy Nigeria could be a sign of a new popular assertiveness toward a government dominated by patron-client networks. Nevertheless, possibilities for sustained protest are limited in such a poor country. The strikes that accompanied Occupy Nigeria lasted for only a few days, in part because people did not have the luxury of being absent from work.

Given these constraints, Nigeria is likely to stay together. Despite the many ethnic and religious fault lines, groups are intermixed throughout the country. It is commonly said that not one of the 774 local government areas is ethnically homogeneous. There have always been significant numbers of Muslims in the south; there are now considerable numbers of Christians in the north. A replay of the secession of Biafra followed by a civil war thus becomes less likely.

Nevertheless, the institutional basis of the state remains weak. Power is concentrated in the presidency. If the president is strong, as Olusegun Obasanjo was, the government can be assertive and Nigeria can play a significant role on the world stage. If the president is weak, as Umaru Yar'Adua was and Goodluck Jonathan is, power ebbs from the center, especially to the governors. Over the past five years, the trend line has been a weakening—if not a withering—of federal institutions and a corresponding increase in power among the states. A weak federal government is less able to control religions and ethnic strife and too often resorts to heavy-handed repression.

In Nigeria's first decade of independence, federal institutions played a major role in keeping the country together. The civil service was a byword for efficiency and largely free of ethnic or sectarian bias. The same was true of the army. The national education and health systems also helped hold the country together. Subsequently, however, during the more than thirty years of military rule, these institutions were largely politicized and starved for funds. Social and economic issues were neglected. This has not changed significantly in the years since 1999.

The decline of central authority provides space for economic and political initiatives at the state level. And that is happening in a few places. Lagos, Cross Rivers, and Rivers states have strong governments and increasingly modern economies that, except for Rivers, do not depend solely on gas and oil.

A democratic state may be defined as one in which the opposition has a reasonable chance of gaining power through credible elections. By that standard, Nigeria is far from democratic and is experiencing only slow movement in that direction. As of now, there has been more continuity than change from the days of military rule, and the early hopes that a democratic Nigeria would emerge after Abacha's death are yet to be realized. The gulf between those with power and those they govern remains vast. Nevertheless, Nigeria's political culture—if not its governance—is more democratic in 2012 than it was in 1999, and its rulers are civilians rather than military officers. That is progress, if not democracy.

NIGERIA TIMELINE

1960: Nigeria Gains Independence

Nigeria achieves independence from the United Kingdom on October 1. The nation—its name and its identity—are British creations. No precolonial cultural unity had held sway in the region. Indeed, Nigeria is divided into three large ethnic and linguistic groups— Fulani, Yoruba, and Igbo—and more than three hundred small ones. In 1960, observers rated Nigeria's social and economic development as comparable to that of Taiwan or Malaysia. Now, following generations of bad governance and an economy distorted by oil, it is one of the poorest countries in the world and near the bottom of most human development indices.

1967: Biafra Secedes, Triggering War

Military coups starting in 1966 undermine civilian institutions and marginalize or destroy the late-colonial political elite. Pogroms in

the north target nonindigenous ethnic groups and Christians, especially Igbos. These incidents become the pretext for the secession of
Biafra, the Igbo-dominated southeastern part of the country, from
Nigeria in May 1967. A civil war ensues in July and lasts until January 1970, with fierce fighting between Biafran rebels and Nigerian
forces. At least one million people die in the conflict, mostly from
famine and disease, before the military reincorporates Biafra into
the Nigerian federation.

1970: Oil Production Begins to Climb

Although oil had been discovered before independence, it is only
after 1970 that production booms, bringing Nigeria unimaginable
riches but also distorting its economy. Over the decades, Nigeria
becomes a major African and global oil producer. Though production varies, it generally rises from about 1.5 million barrels per day in
1971 to more than 2.5 million barrels per day by 2011, making Nigeria
the world's twelfth-largest producer that year.

1993: Abacha Begins Brutal Military Rule

A string of military governments that rule Nigeria for decades—
brief interregnums aside—culminates in the brutal dictatorship of
General Sani Abacha. After seizing power in 1993, Abacha dissolves
state institutions, prosecutes activists and others, and commits gross
human rights violations. The brutality of his regime makes Nigeria
an international outcast.

1999: Military Restores Civilian Authority, New Constitution Adopted

Following General Abacha's death in June 1998, a small group of
army officers and their civilian allies begin a move from military to
civilian control of the government framed by democratic rhetoric.
They are motivated by a desire to end Nigeria's international pariah
status and to distance themselves from the excesses of the Abacha
years. Their goal, largely achieved, is to introduce democratic forms
but preserve their personal power and wealth. The transition culminates in a presidential election on February 27, when elites orches-
trate the victory of the southern Christian and former military
leader Olusegun Obasanjo. The election affirms the principle of
"zoning," which ensures that the presidency will rotate between
the predominately Christian south and the predominately Muslim
north. Meanwhile, a new constitution that mimics the form but not

the substance of the American one is adopted in May. It establishes a federal system, though it fails to prevent the continued accretion of presidential power.

2006: Oil-Related Attacks Spark International Concern

Attacks on foreign oil workers and oil facilities in the Niger Delta increase in 2006, depressing Nigeria's oil output by some 25 percent and garnering international attention. The delta has been the scene of recurring insurrection for over a generation because of grievances about the distribution of oil revenue. An amnesty program for militants in June 2009 attempts to stop the attacks, but the prospect of further violence persists. Kidnapping and attacks on oil facilities are again on the upswing in 2012.

2007: Yar'Adua Wins Presidential Election

Per the zoning principle, the northern Muslim leader Umaru Yar'Adua of the People's Democratic Party (PDP) comes into power in the April 21 presidential election. Opposition figures and international observers condemn the vote as fraudulent, with opposition candidates calling for a new election. However, outgoing president Olusegun Obasanjo urges Nigerians to accept the results, and Yar'Adua takes power.

2008: Nigeria Reaches Lower-Middle-Income Status

The World Bank moves Nigeria from low- to lower-middle-income status as its GDP per capita reaches $1,375. The move comes after years of robust growth, fueled largely by Nigeria's vast supplies of oil. The country earns some $84 billion, or about 40 percent of GDP, from oil exports in 2008 as crude trades above $100 per barrel for the first time ever. However, poverty rates remain high. Some 68 percent of Nigerians live on less than $1.25 per day in 2009, about the same as in 1996 and up from 54 percent in 1985.

2010: Jonathan Becomes President, Ends Zoning

President Yar'Adua dies in office on May 6, making his vice president, the southern Christian Goodluck Jonathan, the chief of state. Initially, Jonathan indicates that he will not run for president in the April 2011 election because, under the zoning pattern of an eight-year rotation, it is still the north's turn. But he changes his mind and, using the powers of incumbency, ends zoning. Some of Jonathan's supporters justify the move as a step toward democracy because it no longer restricts the presidency to a particular region according to a set time frame. But Jonathan's defeat of a northern Muslim opposition candidate precipitates the bloodiest postelectoral rioting in the predominately Muslim northern states since independence.

2011: Militant Attacks Increase

In the Muslim northern half of the country, an insurrection, often referred to as Boko Haram, intensifies against the perceived secular government in Abuja in 2011. In December, President Jonathan announces a state of emergency in four regions of the country because of violence by Boko Haram.

2012: Mass Demonstrations Erupt

Popular demonstrations and union strikes erupt in January after President Jonathan's decision to end fuel subsidies. The Nigerian government argues that removing the subsidies, which cost almost a quarter of the federal budget, will provide increased revenue for economic development. The price of fuel roughly doubles, and many citizens feel that the only benefit they see from the country's oil wealth is gone. Trade unions join other protesters and spark a general strike, largely shutting down Nigeria's economy for a week. President Jonathan reinstates about half the fuel subsidy and reaches a settlement with the trade unions while also arresting some of the demonstrators.

Strategies for Successful Democratization

Isobel Coleman and Terra Lawson-Remer

This volume presents eight case studies of economic and political transitions over the past quarter century, as well as a review of quantitative evidence on the factors that affect such transitions. It is clear from these studies that a complex and unique mix of influences—politics and finance, geography and law, natural resources, and history and culture—shapes every country's trajectory. But there are some common patterns. With appropriate understanding of context, leaders facing the challenges of transitions today and in the future can draw upon the insights of history to identify the circumstances and decisions likely to allow genuine democracy to sustain and endure.

The introductory chapter outlines seven such circumstances and decisions. With those in mind, this concluding chapter offers concrete and practical strategies that domestic reformers and international policymakers can pursue to increase the odds of successful democratization and the realization of freedom and shared opportunity.

New democratic governments should move quickly to adopt policies aimed at materially improving the lives of the poor and dealing with unemployment. New governments often inherit economic circumstances that make delivering on raised expectations for social and economic opportunities extremely difficult. The ability of new democratic leaders to ensure macroeconomic stability while achieving inclusive growth, mitigating social inequality, and reducing unemployment is inevitably constrained. Yet it is critical to identify reforms that can immediately improve people's lives without creating dependency on unsustainable and distortionary economic policies in the longer term.

The specific policy options available in any country are always context specific. Cookie-cutter solutions do not exist. History suggests, however, the general importance of restructuring, and in some cases expanding, social safety nets to more effectively support the poorest while reducing social spending that has been captured by elites and special interest groups.

One important but politically difficult step is the elimination of expensive and inefficient subsidies, such as those for fuel, that impose significant costs on government budgets and distort investment incentives and economic growth. Governments should replace such subsidies with targeted cash transfers to those hurt the most by rising prices in a manner that reassures those affected that the savings from subsidy reform will truly benefit them. Well-placed skepticism on this point prompted protests when Nigerian president Goodluck Jonathan sought to lift fuel subsidies in early 2012.

Conditional cash transfers can also play a vital role in creating equity and shared opportunity by enabling struggling families to invest in health and education—simultaneously cushioning the hardships of the present and laying the foundation for future economic prosperity by developing human capital.

Increasing the availability of capital and reducing arbitrary delays and red tape for small businesses can likewise be critical to creating jobs and opportunities. At the same time, articulating a long-term vision of pro-poor polices that will be pursued as the pie expands can help buy time for the macroeconomic reforms that are essential for stable growth.

International actors can support the economic policies of domestic reformers by providing development grants and loans, sovereign loan guarantees, and debt forgiveness to backstop external financing gaps and create important fiscal space for governments to deliver on the demands of the new, democratic social contract. The original purpose of the International Monetary Fund and the World Bank—institutions arising from the ashes of a world war that had been triggered in large part by severe economic hardships—was to provide economic lifelines for countries faced with current account and balance-of-payments crises, runaway inflation, and the massive expenditures required for development. These multilateral institutions should continue to play an important role in guarding against macroeconomic instability (the IMF) and in financing development investment (the International Bank for Reconstruction and Development, the International Development Association, and regional development banks) for countries now transitioning to democracy.

Rule of law reforms that establish a fair and level playing field and that prevent elites from bending the rules to serve their interests are critical. This does not mean transplanting "model" best practice laws and regulations from other countries; as experts like Katharina Pistor in *The Standardization of Law and Its Effects on Developing Economies* and Thomas Carothers in *Promoting the Rule of Law Abroad: In Search of Knowledge* have argued, history has shown time and again that formal laws imported from outside are doomed to fail if not grounded in and supported by local practices and expectations. Instead, reformers should approach rule of law reform guided by two principles:

- working with local partners to bolster domestic pressures for reforms
- taking a bottom-up, capacity-building approach that supports the ability of average citizens to exercise their rights and the capability of judges, legislatures, and police to implement laws consistently and fairly

International partners, including foreign governments, multilateral organizations, and NGOs, can support such efforts by targeting issues on which external pressure can reinforce the existing agenda of internal reformers. This support should prioritize measures that can be credibly implemented in the near term and that are hard to unwind. Important measures can include:

- public dissemination of revenues, expenditures, and important social and economic statistics
- establishment of transparent auctions to privatize public assets
- reform of laws constraining civil society organizations and NGOs
- disclosure of the assets and income of public officials
- capacity building of the judiciary, parliaments, and civil society to implement rule of law reforms in practice

Making economic aid conditional on paper legal reforms has long been the default mechanism of influence for countries and multilateral organizations seeking to promote democratization and the rule of law. Though this approach is an important point of leverage and tool of influence, on its own it has often failed, leading to laws that are never implemented or that reflect donor priorities rather than country needs. Technical assistance through collaborative partnerships can allow homegrown priorities to drive agendas and enable domestic reformers to tailor priorities to suit diverse local contexts. In this vein, external actors can play another critical role by financing capacity building of civil society, courts, parliaments, police, and lawyers—enabling aspirational laws on the books to be translated into real laws in practice, increasing transparency and accountability and reducing opportunities for corruption. Taken together, conditional aid, technical assistance, and capacity building can create an ecosystem of self-reinforcing legal reform, driven by domestic rather than donor priorities.

Transitioning countries should decentralize in ways that help deepen and sustain democratization efforts. Large and populous countries can often improve public service delivery and government accountability by bringing services and systems of representation closer to the people. Embedded grassroots democracy at the local level can improve government accountability in the short term while watering the seeds of sustainable democratic practices and civic participation for the long term. Countries with existing federal systems, such as Nigeria, should consider ways to realize the benefits of federalism, as Mexico did; those with a unitary system can devolve power through decentralizing budgetary and bureaucratic control to local levels within the existing system of government. In fractious states, decentralization is a perennially fraught issue and should be approached cautiously, but, as Indonesia's experience shows, decentralization of power, including elements of federalism for certain areas, can also be the least bad alternative to debilitating separatist battles.

Foreign governments, multilateral organizations, NGOs, and others seeking to strengthen democracy can support decentralization by nurturing partnerships and building capacity at local levels through community-driven development initiatives. The World Bank did just this in Indonesia beginning in 1998 through the Kecamatan Development Program, a national program that empowered villagers to engage in a participatory decision-making process to allocate resources for self-defined development needs.

Conducting even flawed elections under authoritarian governments is worthwhile. This does not mean turning a blind eye to electoral abuses. To the contrary, the hypocrisy of promises unfulfilled should be denounced. But because even sham elections often lay the groundwork for genuine and surprising movements toward democracy over time, leaders in the United States and other democratic powers should pressure authoritarian regimes to adhere to an electoral process.

Rather than arming insurgents or sponsoring coups d'état, governments and international organizations interested in nurturing democracy should support civil society and independent media under authoritarian regimes through civic exchanges, capacity building, and bottom-up technology transfers. A vibrant, engaged civil society can highlight authoritarian abuses and build domestic and international momentum for change. Robust civil society organizations can also lead peaceful mass mobilizations critical to keeping the public involved and sustaining a commitment to difficult reforms over the longer term. During transitions, a credible and independent media is vital for exposing injustices, demanding accountability, and explaining social and economic dislocations to a skeptical and suffering public, thereby giving vulnerable, young democratic governments time to deliver positive change. International support for civil society organizations and independent media under authoritarian regimes is generally a low-cost, high-return investment.

Given the importance of good neighbors, foreign governments and international and regional organizations must strive to compensate for bad ones. The multilateral development banks have a strong role to play. Their existing relationships, deep pockets, and strong expertise should be mobilized to give domestic democratic reformers support in economic restructuring and investing for inclusive growth. Regional organizations, such as the Economic Community of West African States and the Association of Southeast Asian Nations, could also play a more robust role in bolstering democratic transitions, as the European Union did for Poland and other countries of Eastern Europe after the Soviet Union crumbled. Preferential trade deals and security relationships are other ways for bilateral partners, such as the United States and the European Union, to encourage democratic deepening during and after transitions.

Economic and political "neighbors" can wield two influential instruments to support domestic reformers in their difficult work of building democracies: conditionality and technical assistance. Most obviously, the IMF, the World Bank, and other bilateral development assistance partners should condition their aid on the implementation of governance and rule of law reforms that establish a level playing field, prevent elites from bending the rules to serve their interests, and support the ability of common citizens to exercise their rights. Likewise, access to preferential trade, investment, and security agreements should be conditioned on the implementation of effective homegrown governance reforms that improve accountability in the long term. In most cases, those conditions should be made public, but in certain instances, private bilateral discussions can be a more effective way to convey conditions without undermining the legitimacy of the transitional government.

Good neighbors can also provide technical assistance and facilitate knowledge sharing to help build the capacity and expertise of government bureaucracies, the judiciary, civil society, and other important actors.

Outside states seeking to promote and reinforce democratization should pursue economic strategies—including trade, foreign aid, and investment policies—that spur the emergence of a middle class, rather than promote economic ties that increase overall growth and wealth but concentrate these gains in the hands of elites. Extractive industries—such as oil, cobalt, diamond, and timber businesses—often generate strong economic growth rates and rising gross national income, but the profits accrue to only a few, further entrenching existing autocratic rulers. Concentrated revenue flows facilitate corruption by making it easy for officials to siphon profits for personal gain.

At the same time, export-oriented manufacturing and industry, alongside small-business entrepreneurship, can create low- and moderate-skill jobs that often serve as the first rung on the ladder out of poverty for a nascent middle class. Critical to growth in these sectors is a reliable energy and transit infrastructure that enables goods to move from remote towns to major metropolitan centers around the world and back again, and that keeps the lights on and machines humming on factory floors.

Policymakers interested in encouraging democratization should reject economic development that relies too heavily on investment in extractives to increase growth, and instead should pursue preferential trade and investment deals that give poor countries access to export markets. At the same time, they should unlock the potential for inclusive growth by prioritizing financing for infrastructure investments, such as ports, railroads, and renewable energy, that can overcome transport bottlenecks and energy blackouts. This approach to economic growth will help nurture the nascent middle class that is so vital to safeguard against backsliding once transitions begin, and will also mitigate against the increasing concentration of wealth and power in the hands of autocratic rulers.

CONCLUSION

These policy recommendations are no panacea for the difficult challenge of transforming oppressive states into free and open societies. Each country has its own specific set of challenges, its own configuration of power brokers and entrenched political interests, its own unique fissures and alliances, and its own social, economic, and demographic legacies. There are no preset solutions, and history has made fools of those who believed that they could determine the fate of nations by following a playbook. Even with the best circumstances and wisest decisions by policymakers and publics, the road to democratic consolidation is long and difficult. But there are no failed aspirations for human freedom: dreams of liberty and opportunity are sometimes long deferred, but they cannot be forever denied.

Further Reading

STATISTICAL EVIDENCE

Acemoglu, Daron, and James Robinson. *Economic Origins of Dictatorship and Democracy.* Cambridge: Cambridge University Press, 2006.
>One of the most influential and oft-cited book treatments of democratization in the past decade, arguing in part that both regime transition and survival should be affected by the level of income inequality.

Boix, Carles. *Democracy and Redistribution.* Cambridge: Cambridge University Press, 2003.
>An influential book contending that democratization and democratic stability are largely a function of the level of income inequality and capital mobility.

Boix, Carles. "Democracy, Development, and the International System." *American Political Science Review* 105, no. 4 (2011): 809–28.
>An article offering the latest and most comprehensive test of the effects of socioeconomic modernization on both democratization (transition) and authoritarian backsliding (democratic survival).

Cheibub, Jose Antonio. *Presidentialism, Parliamentarism, and Democracy.* Cambridge: Cambridge University Press, 2006.
>A book offering the most comprehensive study to date of whether the system of government affects democratic survival and arguing that presidential democracies are not less stable than parliamentary ones.

Freeman, John R., and Dennis P. Quinn. "The Economic Origins of Democracy Reconsidered." *American Political Science Review* 106, no. 1 (2012): 58–80.
>A paper challenging the income inequality theory of democratization.

Haber, Stephen, and Victor Menaldo. "Do Natural Resources Fuel Authoritarianism? A Reappraisal of the Resource Curse." *American Political Science Review* 105, no. 1 (2011): 1–26.

A study that takes issue with the notion that natural resource abundance negatively affects democratization.

Haggard, Stephan, and Robert R. Kaufman. "Inequality and Regime Change: Democratic Transitions and the Stability of Democratic Rule." *American Political Science Review* 106, no. 3 (2012): 495–513.
An article arguing that while many transitions to democracy and instances of democratic breakdown in recent decades were marred by socioeconomic conflict, they do not seem to have been affected by the level of income inequality.

Haggard, Stephan, and Robert R. Kaufman. *The Political Economy of Democratic Transitions*. Princeton, NJ: Princeton University Press, 1995.
A book arguing forcefully that the prospects for democratization hinge critically on the incidence of economic crisis.

Linz, Juan J. "Presidential or Parliamentary Democracy: Does it Make a Difference?" in *The Failure of Presidential Democracy: The Case of Latin America*, edited by Juan J. Linz and Arturo Valenzuela. Baltimore: The Johns Hopkins University Press, 1994.
A chapter making the classical argument for why presidential democracies should be shorter-lived than parliamentary ones.

Przeworski, Adam, and Fernando Limongi. "Modernization: Theories and Facts." *World Politics* 49, no. 2 (1997): 155–83.
The first article to argue that socioeconomic modernization affects democratic survival, not transitions to democracy.

Ross, Michael. "Does oil hinder democracy?" *World Politics* 53, no. 3 (2001): 325–61.
A classic article that introduced the "resource curse" to the study of democratization, arguing that natural resource abundance hurts the prospects for democracy.

Teorell, Jan. *Determinants of Democratization: Explaining Regime Change in the World, 1972–2006*. Cambridge: Cambridge University Press, 2010.
A book arguing among other things that democratization is a likely effect of unarmed popular mobilization and the type of authoritarian regime.

MEXICO

Babb, Sarah. *Managing Mexico: Economists from Nationalism to Neoliberalism*. Princeton, NJ: Princeton University Press, 2001.
A book exploring economics as a profession in twentieth-century Mexico, as internationally trained economists grew to dominate the scene.

Eisenstadt, Todd A. *Courting Democracy in Mexico: Party Strategies and Electoral Institutions*. Cambridge: Cambridge University Press, 2004.
A book on Mexico's transition to democracy, focusing on opposition parties' use of electoral courts and other means to advance democratization.

Greene, Kenneth F. *Why Dominant Parties Lose: Mexico's Democratization in Comparative Perspective*. Cambridge: Cambridge University Press, 2007.
A book that applies a general theory of political party dominance to Mexico and the erosion of PRI control.

Haber, Stephen, Herbert S. Klein, Noel Maurer, and Kevin J. Middlebrook. *Mexico Since 1980*. Cambridge: Cambridge University Press, 2008.
A book exploring Mexico's failure to institute the rule of law and strong economic growth despite its economic and political reforms.

Lustig, Nora. *Mexico: The Remaking of an Economy*. 2nd ed. Washington, DC: Brookings Institution Press, 1998.
A book analyzing Mexico's economic performance in the 1990s, including the peso crisis, the response to the crisis, poverty, and inequality.

Magaloni, Beatriz. *Voting for Autocracy: Hegemonic Party Survival and Its Demise in Mexico*. Cambridge: Cambridge University Press, 2006.
A book on how the PRI maintained power in Mexico, focusing on its electoral facade, and on how it eventually fell.

Moreno-Brid, Juan Carlos, and Jaime Ros. *Development and Growth in the Mexican Economy: A Historical Perspective*. Oxford: Oxford University Press, 2009.
A historical book on Mexico's economic development, including its industrialization process, more recent market-oriented reforms, and current challenges.

Selee, Andrew, and Jacqueline Peschard, eds. *Mexico's Democratic Challenges: Politics, Government, and Society*. Palo Alto, CA: Stanford University Press, 2010.

A collection of essays examining Mexico's political evolution since the 2000 election and its prospects for continuing change.

Shirk, David A. *Mexico's New Politics: The PAN and Democratic Change.* Boulder, CO: Lynne Rienner Publishers, 2004.

A book focusing on the development of the National Action Party (PAN), whose presidential victory in 2000 brought an end to PRI rule.

BRAZIL

Cardoso, Fernando Henrique. *The Accidental President of Brazil: A Memoir*. New York: PublicAffairs, 2007.

A firsthand account and analysis of the transformations put in place during Cardoso's two administrations, as well as his unsuccessful attempts to reform the country's institutions more deeply.

Fausto, Boris. *A Concise History of Brazil.* Cambridge: Cambridge University Press, 1999.

A book describing Brazil's historical path since the arrival of the first Portuguese settlers in the sixteenth century.

Fishlow, Albert. *Starting Over: Brazil Since 1985*. Washington, DC: Brookings Institution Press, 2011.

A book that interprets Brazil's economic and political rise as a global player as the result of deliberate choices made by Presidents Cardoso and Lula.

Hagopian, Frances. *Traditional Politics and Regime Change in Brazil.* Reissue ed. Cambridge: Cambridge University Press, 2007. First published 1996.

A book that dissects the way traditional Brazilian elites, particularly in the critical state of Minas Gerais, accommodated themselves to the rise of the military.

Hunter, Wendy. *The Transformation of the Workers' Party in Brazil, 1989–2009*. Cambridge: Cambridge University Press, 2010.

A book that explains the path toward moderation of the once-radical Brazilian Workers' Party.

Kingstone, Peter, and Timothy J. Power, eds. *Democratic Brazil: Actors, Institutions, and Processes.* Pittsburgh: University of Pittsburgh Press, 1999.

A collection of essays examining the final stages of Brazil's transition to democracy, from the inauguration of President Sarney in 1985 to the end of President Cardoso's first term in 1998.

Kingstone, Peter, and Timothy J. Power, eds. *Democratic Brazil Revisited.* Pittsburgh: University of Pittsburgh Press, 2008.

A collection of essays that explore the mixed record of democratic consolidation during the first term of President Lula.

Love, Joseph L., and Werner Baer, eds. *Brazil under Lula: Economy, Politics, and Society under the Worker-President.* New York: Palgrave Macmillan, 2009.

A collection of essays on the policymaking process and major policy choices of Lula's first administration, as well as its initial results.

Rohter, Larry. *Brazil on the Rise: The Story of a Country Transformed.* New York: Palgrave Macmillan, 2010.

A book offering a journalistic account of Brazil's history and present state by a former *New York Times* correspondent.

Scheper-Hughes, Nancy. *Death Without Weeping: The Violence of Everyday Life in Brazil.* Berkeley: University of California Press, 1993.

A book that makes an anthropological excursion into the poverty, deprivation, and violence of northeastern Brazil's shantytowns before the adoption of innovative social policies in the mid-1990s.

Skidmore, Thomas E. *Black into White: Race and Nationality in Brazilian Thought.* Durham, NC: Duke University Press, 1993. First published 1974 by Oxford University Press.

A book that scrutinizes the way Brazilian intellectuals and state officials dealt with the question of race, from the abolition of slavery until the 1920s.

Skidmore, Thomas E. *Politics in Brazil 1930–1964: An Experiment in Democracy.* Updated ed. Oxford: Oxford University Press, 2007. First published 1967.

A book analyzing Brazilian politics from the ascension of Getúlio Vargas as a dictator in 1930 to the 1964 military coup.

Skidmore, Thomas E. *The Politics of Military Rule in Brazil, 1964–1985.* Oxford: Oxford University Press, 1990.

A book that examines the trajectory of Brazil's military regime, including the evolution of its economic and political policies and institutions.

Stepan, Alfred, ed. *Authoritarian Brazil: Origins, Policies, and Future.* New Haven, CT: Yale University Press, 1976.
An edited volume that explores the causes and early dynamics of the military regime that took power in 1964.

Weyland, Kurt. *Democracy Without Equity: Failures of Reform in Brazil.* Pittsburgh: University of Pittsburgh Press, 1996.
A book analyzing Brazil's failed attempts to reform important social institutions in order to create a more inclusive society.

POLAND

Balcerowicz, Leszek. "Understanding Postcommunist Transitions." *Journal of Democracy* 5, no. 4 (1994): 75–80.
An article examining the democratic transitions in postcommunist Europe and their policy implications.

Davies, Norman. *Heart of Europe: The Past in Poland's Present.* Oxford: Oxford University Press, 2001.
A book on Poland's post–World War II history and contemporary situation, placed in a broad European context.

Ekiert, Grzegorz, Jan Kubik, and Milada Vachudova. "Democracy in the Post-Communist World: An Unending Quest?" *East European Politics and Societies* 21, no. 1 (2007): 7–30.
An article examining the domestic and international factors behind the outcomes of democratic transitions in postcommunist Europe.

Ekiert, Grzegorz, and Jan Kubik. *Rebellious Civil Society: Popular Protest and Democratic Consolidation in Poland, 1989–1993.* Ann Arbor: University of Michigan Press, 2001.
A book analyzing the role and character of organized protest in Poland during the postcommunist period of democratic consolidation.

Garton Ash, Timothy. *The Polish Revolution: Solidarity.* 3rd ed. New Haven, CT: Yale University Press, 2002.
A book on the formation and rise of the Solidarity trade union, founded in the Gdansk shipyard in 1980.

Inglot, Tomasz. *Welfare States in East Central Europe, 1919–2004.* Cambridge: Cambridge University Press, 2008.
A book comparing the history and context of welfare regimes in Poland and other regional states.

Jasiewicz, Krzystof. "The Past is Never Dead: Identity, Class and Voting Behavior in Contemporary Poland." *East European Politics and Societies* 23, no. 4 (2009): 491–508.
An article exploring the role of religious, regional, and socioeconomic factors in voters' decisions in Poland's 2007 elections.

Kaminski, Bartlomiej. *The Collapse of State Socialism: The Case of Poland.* Princeton, NJ: Princeton University Press, 1991.
A book analyzing the fall of the economic and political system that dominated Poland and the region for decades.

Poznanski, Kazimierz Z. *Poland's Protracted Transition: Institutional Change and Economic Growth, 1970–1994.* Cambridge: Cambridge University Press, 1997.
A book on the evolution and political context of Poland's economy during the last two decades of communist rule and after the transition.

Sachs, Jeffrey. *Poland's Jump to the Market Economy.* Cambridge, MA: MIT Press, 1994.
A book on Poland's rapid postcommunist economic reforms, their effects, and outstanding economic challenges in the early years of the transition.

SOUTH AFRICA

Booysen, Susan. *The African National Congress and the Regeneration of Political Power.* Johannesburg: Witwatersrand University Press, 2012.
A book on how the African National Congress has built and maintained power in postapartheid South Africa.

Crocker, Chester A. *High Noon in Southern Africa: Making Peace in a Rough Neighborhood.* New York: W. W. Norton & Co., 1993.
A senior U.S. official's account of the diplomacy surrounding such issues as sanctions against apartheid-era South Africa, civil wars in Angola and Mozambique, and Namibia's struggle for independence.

Francis, S., H. Dugmore, and Rico. *Free at Last: The Second Madam and Eve Collection.* Johannesburg: Penguin Books, 1994.
A collection of cartoons from a humorous series on the lives of a white South African woman and her black housekeeper.

Gevisser, Mark. *A Legacy of Liberation: Thabo Mbeki and the Future of the South African Dream.* New York: Palgrave Macmillan, 2009.
A book telling the story of President Thabo Mbeki's family and of today's South Africa more broadly.

Herbst, Jeffrey. "Mbeki's South Africa." *Foreign Affairs* 84, no. 6 (2005): 93–105.
An article examining South Africa's political, economic, and social challenges eleven years after the end of apartheid.

Malan, Rian. *My Traitor's Heart.* New York: Grove Press, 1990.
A book by an Afrikaner related to one of apartheid's main figures that grapples with the effects of apartheid on both black and white South Africans.

Mandela, Nelson. *Long Walk to Freedom: The Autobiography of Nelson Mandela.* Paperback ed. New York: Back Bay Books, 1995.
An autobiography by South Africa's iconic leader recounting his personal and political journeys, including his long imprisonment and the process that led to apartheid's end.

Marais, Hein. *South Africa Pushed to the Limit: The Political Economy of Change.* London: Zed Books, 2011.
A book analyzing South Africa's policy choices since the end of apartheid and its ongoing racial inequalities.

Plaut, Martin. *The Red Flag Rises: South Africa at the Crossroads.* London: Chatham House, 2009.
A report analyzing debates over economic policy within the African National Congress and in its Tripartite Alliance with the South African Communist Party and the Congress of South African Trade Unions.

Sparks, Allister. *Beyond the Miracle: Inside the New South Africa.* Chicago: University of Chicago Press, 2003.
A book that analyzes the first years of South Africa's postapartheid experience and considers its future.

Sparks, Allister. *The Mind of South Africa: The Story of the Rise and Fall of Apartheid.* Johannesburg: Jonathan Ball Publishers, 2006.

A book chronicling the history of apartheid and the views behind it, starting from the beginning of white settlement in South Africa.

Steinberg, Jonny. *Thin Blue: The Unwritten Rules of Policing South Africa.* Johannesburg: Jonathan Ball Publishers, 2009.
   A book exploring the relationship between citizens and the police in South Africa, especially in Johannesburg's townships.

Welsh, David. *The Rise and Fall of Apartheid.* Charlottesville, VA: University of Virginia Press, 2010.
   A book that explores apartheid, the liberation movement that fought it, and the factors that produced a largely peaceful transition to nonracial democracy.

INDONESIA

Archive of reports on Jemaah Islamiyah. Brussels: International Crisis Group.
   An ongoing series of reports offering background and analysis on Jemaah Islamiyah and other Indonesian security issues.

Barton, Greg. *Gus Dur: The Authorized Biography of Abdurrahman Wahid.* Jakarta: Equinox Publishing, 2002.
   A biography of Abdurrahman Wahid, who was elected president of Indonesia in 1999 and forced from office amid scandal in 2001.

Bresnan, John, ed. *Indonesia: The Great Transition.* Lanham, MD: Rowman & Littlefield Publishers, 2005.
   An edited volume exploring the background and challenges of Indonesia's economic and political transition, which began in the late 1990s.

Dhume, Sadanand. *My Friend the Fanatic: Travels with a Radical Islamist.* New York: Skyhorse Publishing, 2009.
   A book recounting a journey across Indonesia, with a focus on the rise of extreme strains of Islam.

Friend, Theodore. *Indonesian Destinies.* Cambridge, MA: Belknap Press, 2003.
   A book offering a history and personal narrative of Indonesia, spanning from the country's emergence from Dutch rule to the post-9/11 era.

The Indonesian Quarterly. Jakarta: Centre for Strategic and International Studies.
> An English-language journal of policy-oriented work on Indonesia.

Paris, Jonathan, and Adam Schwarz, eds. *The Politics of Post-Suharto Indonesia*. New York: Council on Foreign Relations Press, 1999.
> A collection of essays on the issues facing Indonesia after Suharto's fall, including economic, religious, political, and military-related challenges.

Percival, Bronson. *The Dragon Looks South: China and Southeast Asia in the New Century*. Westport, CT: Praeger Security International, 2007.
> A book analyzing the recent evolution of China's relationship with the countries of Southeast Asia.

Pringle, Robert. *Understanding Islam in Indonesia: Politics and Diversity*. Honolulu: University of Hawaii Press, 2010.
> A book on the history and modern practice of Indonesian Islam and the role of Muslim groups in the country's political scene.

Robinson, Geoffre. *If You Leave Us Here, We Will Die: How Genocide Was Stopped in East Timor*. Princeton, NJ: Princeton University Press, 2009.
> A book recounting the abuses committed in East Timor after Indonesia's 1975 invasion and again after East Timor's referendum on independence in 1999.

Schwarz, Adam. *A Nation in Waiting: Indonesia's Search for Stability*. 2nd ed. Boulder, CO: Westview Press, 1999.
> A book analyzing Indonesia's economic and political development under Suharto, the crisis of the late 1990s, and the consequences of Suharto's fall.

THAILAND

Askew, Marc, ed. *Legitimacy Crisis in Thailand*. Chiang Mai, Thailand: Silkworm Books, 2010.
> A collection of essays on topics surrounding Thailand's recent political polarization.

Baker, Chris, and Pasuk Phongpaichit. *A History of Thailand*. 2nd ed. Cambridge: Cambridge University Press, 2009.
> A book on Thailand's demographic, political, economic, and social history over the centuries.

Bello, Walden, Shea Cunningham, and Kheng Poh Li. *A Siamese Tragedy: Development and Disintegration in Modern Thailand*. Oakland: Food First Books, 1999.
A book that criticizes Thailand's open-market economic model.

Fineman, Daniel. *A Special Relationship: The United States and Military Government in Thailand, 1947–1958*. Honolulu: University of Hawaii Press, 1997.
A book tracing the establishment and early evolution of the U.S.-Thailand alliance.

Handley, Paul M. *The King Never Smiles*. New Haven, CT: Yale University Press, 2006.
A biography of Thailand's King Bhumibol, covering his youth, ascension to power, popularity among Thais, and political dealings from the throne.

McCargo, Duncan. *Tearing Apart the Land: Islam and Legitimacy in Southern Thailand*. Ithaca, NY: Cornell University Press, 2008.
A book on the roots, nature, and impact of the long-running rebellion in Thailand's Muslim-majority south.

McCargo, Duncan, and Ukrist Pathmanand. *The Thaksinization of Thailand*. Copenhagen: Nordic Institute of Asian Studies, 2005.
A book on the rise of former prime minister Thaksin Shiniwatra and the impact and character of his rule.

Montesano, Michael J., Pavin Chachavalpongpun, and Aekapol Chongvilaivan, eds. *Bangkok, May 2010: Perspectives on a Divided Thailand*. Singapore: Institute of Southeast Asian Studies, 2012.
An edited volume on the conflict in recent years between Thailand's Red Shirts (largely supporters of former prime minister Thaksin Shiniwatra) and Yellow Shirts (largely supporters of the traditional elite).

Phongpaichit, Pasuk, and Chris Baker. *Thailand's Boom and Bust*. Rev. ed. Chiang Mai, Thailand: Silkworm Books, 1998.
A book reviewing the economic and social trends that shaped Thailand before and during the Asian financial crisis.

The United States-Thailand Alliance: Reinvigorating the Partnership. Seattle: National Bureau of Asian Research, 2010.
A workshop report exploring aspects of the U.S.-Thailand relationship, taking into account Thailand's domestic and regional position.

UKRAINE

Aslund, Anders. *How Ukraine Became a Market Economy and Democracy.* Washington, DC: Peterson Institute for International Economics, 2009.
A book expressing a relatively optimistic view of developments in Ukraine's business and political life.

Kramer, David J., Robert Nurick, Oleksandr Sushko, Viktoria Syumar, Damon Wilson, and Matthew Schaaf. *Sounding the Alarm Round 2: Protecting Democracy in Ukraine.* Washington, DC: Freedom House, July 2012.
Part of a long-running series looking at the reasons for democratic deterioration since Yanukovych's election in 2010.

Kramer, David J., Robert Nurick, and Damon Wilson, with Evan Alterman. *Sounding the Alarm: Protecting Democracy in Ukraine.* Washington, DC: Freedom House, 2011.
Part of a long-running series looking at the reasons for democratic deterioration since Yanukovych's election in 2010.

Matuszak, Slawomir. *The Oligarchic Democracy: The Influence of Business Groups on Ukrainian Politics.* Warsaw: Center for Eastern Studies, 2012.
A report mapping the persistent influence of big-business oligarchs in Ukraine.

Menon, Rajan, and Alexander J. Motyl. "Counterrevolution in Kiev: Hope Fades for Ukraine." *Foreign Affairs* 90, no. 6 (2011): 137–48.
An article looking at Ukraine under Yanukovych, with a focus on the Tymoshenko trial.

Sutela, Pekka. *The Underachiever: Ukraine's Economy Since 1991.* Washington, DC: Carnegie Endowment for International Peace, 2012.
A paper examining the reasons for Ukraine's economic underperformance since independence.

Wilson, Andrew. "Ukraine at Twenty: What Have We Learnt?" *Russia in Global Affairs* 10, no. 1 (2012): 122–34, March 2012.
An article analyzing how Ukraine changed, or failed to change, between independence in 1991 and 2011.

Wilson, Andrew. *Ukraine's Orange Revolution.* New Haven, CT: Yale University Press, 2005.

A book examining the Orange Revolution of 2004, written in a then-justified spirit of relative optimism.

Wilson, Andrew. *The Ukrainians: Unexpected Nation.* 3rd ed. New Haven, CT: Yale University Press, 2009.
A book-length introduction to Ukrainian history and modern politics, with the third edition focusing on events leading up to the 2010 election.

Yekelchyk, Serhy. *Ukraine: Birth of a Modern Nation.* Oxford: Oxford University Press, 2007.
A book concentrating on the twentieth-century history of Ukraine, up to the Orange Revolution in 2004.

NIGERIA

Campbell, John. *Nigeria: Dancing on the Brink.* Lanham, MD: Rowman & Littlefield, 2011.
A book examining the history of postcolonial Nigeria and the factors, such as oil, corruption, and elite behavior, behind the country's daunting troubles.

Campbell, John. "Nigeria's Battle for Stability." *National Interest,* no. 118 (2012): 31–39.
An article analyzing Nigeria's recent political and security developments and offering guidance for U.S. policy.

Enwerem, Iheanyi M. *Crossing the Rubicon: A Socio-Political Analysis of Political Catholicism in Nigeria.* Ibadan, Nigeria: BookBuilders, 2010.
A book on the structure and role of Nigeria's Catholic Church.

Everyone's in on the Game: Corruption and Human Rights Abuses by the Nigeria Police Force. New York: Human Rights Watch, 2011.
A report analyzing the role and practices of Nigerian security forces, as well as atrocities committed by Boko Haram.

Herskovits, Jean. "Reflections on Fifty Years of Change in Nigeria." Speech delivered at the Coventry University African Studies Center/Chatham House Africa Program Conference, November 2010.
A speech reviewing Nigeria's history since independence, focusing on its political structure and institutions.

Kwaja, Chris. *Nigeria's Pernicious Drivers of Ethno-Religious Conflict.* Washington, DC: African Center for Strategic Studies, 2011.
A report that focuses on the causes of Nigeria's ethnic strife and proposes reforms to address them.

Lewis, Peter M. *Nigeria: Assessing Risks to Stability.* Washington, DC: Center for Strategic and International Studies, 2011.
A report, part of a series commissioned by the U.S. Africa Command, that gauges the prospect of instability in Nigeria and outlines scenarios for its future.

Maier, Karl. *This House Has Fallen: Nigeria in Crisis.* New York: Basic Books, 2002.
A book that explores Nigeria's constellation of political, socioeconomic, and security challenges.

Osaghae, Eghosa E. *The Crippled Giant: Nigeria Since Independence.* Indianapolis: Indiana University Press, 1998.
A book that analyzes Nigeria's political and economic dynamics and advances external causes for the country's difficulties.

Paden, John N. *Muslim Civic Cultures and Conflict Resolution: The Challenge of Democratic Federalism in Nigeria.* Washington, DC: Brookings Institution Press, 2005.
A book on the issues surrounding Nigeria's attempt to build a federal democracy and modern rule of law compatible with its Islamic and other traditions.

Paden, John N. *Postelection Conflict Management in Nigeria: The Challenges of National Unity.* Arlington, VA: George Mason University School for Conflict Analysis and Resolution, 2012.
A monograph with analysis and recommendations on the security challenges facing Nigeria in the aftermath of its 2011 presidential election.

Sayne, Aaron. *Climate Change Adaptation and Conflict in Nigeria.* Washington, DC: United States Institute of Peace, 2011.
A report reviewing the prospects for climate-related conflict in Nigeria and outlining climate adaptation measures.

Spiraling Violence: Boko Haram Attacks and Security Force Abuses in Nigeria. New York: Human Rights Watch, 2012.
A report analyzing the role and practices of Nigerian security forces, as well as atrocities committed by Boko Haram.

Walker, Andrew. *What Is Boko Haram?* Washington, DC: United States Institute of Peace, 2012.

A report with background information and analysis on the militant Islamic group and policy suggestions for countering it.

About the Authors

John Campbell is the Ralph Bunche senior fellow for Africa policy studies at the Council on Foreign Relations. Campbell is the author of *Nigeria: Dancing on the Brink* and writes the CFR blog Africa in Transition. From 1975 to 2007, Campbell served as a U.S. Department of State Foreign Service officer. He served twice in Nigeria, as political counselor from 1988 to 1990 and as ambassador from 2004 to 2007. Campbell's additional overseas postings include Lyon, Paris, Geneva, and Pretoria. He also served as deputy assistant secretary for human resources, dean of the Foreign Service Institute's School of Language Studies, and director of the Office of UN Political Affairs. From 2007 to 2008, Campbell was a visiting professor of international relations at the University of Wisconsin–Madison. He was also a Department of State midcareer fellow at Princeton University's Woodrow Wilson School of Public and International Affairs. Prior to Campbell's career in the Foreign Service, he taught British and French history at Mary Baldwin College in Staunton, Virginia. Campbell received a BA and an MA from the University of Virginia and a PhD in seventeenth-century English history from the University of Wisconsin–Madison.

Isobel Coleman is senior fellow for U.S. foreign policy at the Council on Foreign Relations, where she directs CFR's Civil Society, Markets, and Democracy initiative. Her areas of expertise include democratization, civil society, economic development, regional gender issues, educational reform, and microfinance. Coleman is the author and coauthor of numerous publications, including *Paradise Beneath Her Feet: How Women Are Transforming the Middle East*, *Restoring the Balance: A Middle East Strategy for the Next President*, and *Strategic Foreign Assistance: Civil Society in International Security*. Coleman's writings have also appeared in publications such as *Foreign Affairs*, *Foreign Policy*, the *Washington Post*, *Financial Times*, *International*

Herald Tribune, Christian Science Monitor, USA Today, and *Forbes*, and on online venues such as TheAtlantic.com and CNN.com. She also maintains the CFR blog Democracy in Development. She is a frequent speaker at academic, business, and policy conferences. In 2010, she served as the track leader for the Girls and Women Action Area at the Clinton Global Initiative. In 2011, *Newsweek* named her one of 150 Women Who Shake the World. Prior to CFR, Coleman was CEO of a health-care services company and a partner with McKinsey & Co. in New York. A Marshall scholar, she holds a BA in public policy and East Asian studies from Princeton University and MPhil and DPhil degrees in international relations from Oxford University.

Grzegorz Ekiert is professor of government, director of the Minda de Gunzberg Center for European Studies, and senior scholar at the Harvard Academy for International and Area Studies at Harvard University. He is also faculty associate of Harvard's Davis Center for Russian and Eurasian Studies and Weatherhead Center for International Affairs, as well as a member of the Club of Madrid advisory committee. Ekiert's teaching and research interests focus on comparative politics, regime change and democratization, civil society and social movements, and east European politics and societies. Ekiert is the author of *The State Against Society: Political Crises and Their Aftermath in East Central Europe*, coauthor of *Rebellious Civil Society: Popular Protest and Democratic Consolidation in Poland*, and coeditor of *Capitalism and Democracy in Central and Eastern Europe: Assessing the Legacy of Communist Rule*. He has also edited special issues of *East European Politics and Societies* and the *Taiwan Journal of Democracy*. Beyond these publications, Ekiert's papers have appeared in numerous social science journals and edited volumes. He holds an MA in sociology from Jagiellonian University and an MA and a PhD in sociology from Harvard University.

Joshua Kurlantzick is fellow for Southeast Asia at the Council on Foreign Relations. Kurlantzick was most recently a scholar at the Carnegie Endowment for International Peace, where he studied Southeast Asian politics and economics and China's relations with Southeast Asia, including Chinese investment, aid, and diplomacy. Previously, he was a fellow at the University of Southern California Center on Public Diplomacy and a fellow at the Pacific Council on International Policy. Kurlantzick has also served as a columnist for *Time*, a special correspondent for the *New Republic*, a senior correspondent for the *American Prospect*, and a contributing writer for *Mother Jones*. He also serves on the editorial board of *Current History*. He is the winner of the Luce scholarship for journalism in Asia and was selected as a finalist for the Osborn Elliot Prize for journalism in Asia. His first book, *Charm Offensive: How China's Soft Power Is Transforming the World*, was nominated for CFR's 2008 Arthur Ross Book Award. He is the author of *Democracy in Retreat: The Revolt of the Middle Class and the Worldwide Decline of Representative Government*. Kurlantzick received his BA in political science from Haverford College.

Terra Lawson-Remer is fellow for civil society, markets, and democracy at the Council on Foreign Relations and assistant professor of international affairs at the New School, where she serves as chair of the university's advisory committee on investor responsibility. Previously, she was senior adviser for international affairs at the U.S. Department of the Treasury. Lawson-Remer has worked and conducted field studies in Latin America, North and East Africa, Asia, and the South Pacific. She is the author and coauthor of numerous publications, including the forthcoming book *Fulfilling Economic and Social Rights* and articles in academic journals such as *World Development, Brooklyn Journal of International Law, NYU Environmental Law Journal*, and the *Journal of Human Rights*. Her writing has also appeared in publications such as the *Chronicle of Higher Education* and *Huffington Post* and on CNN.com and Reuters. Lawson-Remer previously worked as an organizer, action coordinator, and strategist for a variety of grassroots social justice organizations, including Amnesty International, the Ethical Globalization Initiative, and the New York Civil Liberties Union. She cofounded and codirected STARC: Students Transforming and Resisting Corporations, a national membership-based organization advocating corporate responsibility in the face of increased globalization and greater public accountability by the World Bank, International Monetary Fund, and World Trade Organization. She earned her BA in ethics, politics, and economics from Yale University; her JD from New York University School of Law, where she was a dean's merit scholar; and her PhD in political economy from NYU Law's Institute for Law and Society.

Shannon K. O'Neil is senior fellow for Latin America studies at the Council on Foreign Relations. Her expertise includes U.S.-Latin

America relations, energy policy, trade, political and economic reforms, and immigration. She directed CFR's Independent Task Force on U.S.-Latin America Relations. She is the author of *Two Nations Indivisible: Mexico, the United States, and the Road Ahead*, which analyzes the political, economic, and social transformations Mexico has undergone over the past three decades and their significance for U.S.-Mexico relations. In addition to her work at CFR, O'Neil has taught in the political science department at Columbia University. She is a frequent commentator on major television and radio programs, and her work has appeared in *Foreign Affairs*, *Foreign Affairs Latinoamérica*, *Americas Quarterly*, *Política Exterior*, *Foreign Policy*, the *Washington Post*, and the *Los Angeles Times*, among others, and she has testified before the U.S. Congress on U.S. policy toward Mexico. She writes the CFR blog Latin America's Moment, which analyzes developments in Latin America and U.S. relations in the region. Prior to joining CFR, O'Neil was a justice, welfare, and economics fellow at the Weatherhead Center for International Affairs at Harvard University. She was also a Fulbright scholar in Mexico and Argentina. Prior to her academic work, O'Neil worked in the private sector as an equity analyst at Indosuez Capital Latin America and Credit Lyonnais Securities. She holds a BA from Yale University, an MA in international relations from Yale University, and a PhD in government from Harvard University.

Carlos Pio is professor of international political economy at the Instituto de Relacoes Internacionais of the Universidade de Brasilia and adjunct professor at the School of Politics and International Relations of Australian National University. His principal interests are in international trade and economic development, market reforms and politics in Latin America, and anti-inflation policies in Brazil. Pio previously taught at the Instituto Rio Branco, the training center for Brazil's diplomatic corps. He has also been a visiting researcher at the Latin American Center of the University of Oxford, a visiting Fulbright scholar at the University of California at Berkeley, and president of the Fulbright Alumni Association of Brazil. Among his published works are a textbook on political economy and globalization and numerous scholarly articles and op-eds in the Brazilian press. Pio holds a BA in political science from the Universidade de Brasilia and an MA and doctorate from the Instituto Universitario de Pesquisas do Rio de Janeiro.

George Soroka is a PhD candidate at Harvard University, where he also serves as the government department's assistant director of undergraduate studies. His dissertation examines the role that contentious historical memories play in structuring foreign policy discourses among postcommunist states, with a particular focus on Poland, Ukraine, and Russia. His broader interests include the politics of identity, the changing role of religion in European political life, and the rise of far-right parties across the continent. Soroka is the author of numerous conference papers and has served as an instructor and a teaching fellow at Harvard University for multiple political science courses. Prior to coming to Harvard, he was the director of graduate admissions at Drew University. Soroka holds a BA in anthropology and religion and an MA in liturgical studies from Drew, as well as an AM in regional studies (Russia, Eastern Europe, and Central Asia) from Harvard.

Jan Teorell is professor of political science and director of the PhD program in political science at Lund University. He previously taught at Gothenburg and Uppsala Universities. His research focuses on political participation, public opinion, corruption, and comparative democratization. During his career, Teorell has been a visiting scholar at the Center for Basic Research in the Social Sciences and the Center for European Studies at Harvard University, as well as the Contemporary Europe Research Center at Melbourne University. From 2004 to 2006, he was also project coordinator at the Quality of Government Institute at Gothenburg University, where he continues to serve as a manager of the quality of government dataset. His current projects include efforts to investigate how established democracies abolished electoral fraud and corruption over time and to measure concepts of democracy around the world from 1900 to today. Teorell is the author of *Determinants of Democratization: Explaining Regime Change in the World, 1972–2006* as well as numerous journal articles, book chapters, and working papers in English and Swedish. He holds a PhD from Uppsala University.

Andrew Wilson is a senior policy fellow at the European Council on Foreign Relations and a reader in Ukrainian studies at the School of Slavonic and East European Studies of University College London. He has also been an honorary fellow of the Royal Institute of International

Affairs in the United Kingdom. He has published widely on the politics and culture of the European neighborhood, particularly Russia, Ukraine, and Belarus. He has also written about the comparative politics of democratization in post-Soviet states. His books include *Belarus: The Last European Dictatorship, Ukraine's Orange Revolution, Virtual Politics: Faking Democracy in the Post-Soviet World*, and *The Ukrainians: Unexpected Nation*, all published by Yale University Press. Wilson holds degrees from the University of Oxford and the London School of Economics and Political Science.

DATE DUE

PRINTED IN U.S.A.

Made in the USA
San Bernardino, CA
05 September 2013